"This book reveals in detail, the mixture of drama, fear, and mundane events which were so typical of the experiences of the average American infantryman in Vietnam. The manner in which Dr. Ordóñez ties in the tragedy, the humor, and the pathos, and his revealing insights about the war's impact on his religious perspective makes it a worthwhile, as well as a most enjoyable read."

—**E. R. (Bud) Zumwalt, Jr., Admiral, U. S. Navy (Ret.)**
Chief of Naval Operations, 1970-1974

"A year in Vietnam was a long time...Doc Ordóñez has captured the atmosphere and feelings of being on patrol in the Vietnam jungle...Even the smell of the jungle comes alive with the descriptive discussion of the patrols, the swamps, and the firefights...For those who wonder what it was like in the bush, Doc has depicted it graphically...he makes you feel as though you were there in living—or dying—detail."

—**Colonel Don McCullough**
West Point, Class of 1958

"The odyssey of Robert Ordóñez is at once both disquieting and reassuring. I am made to feel reproachable for the misguided clarity with which I so readily, some 30 years ago, classified the American participants in the Vietnam conflict. But this book is purposefully not political. It is, among other things, a painful and necessary education for those of us who were not there."

—**P. Kent Harman, M. D., P. A.**
Cardiovascular Surgeon

Dedication

In memory of those who gave their lives.

To my family. In serving God, you will serve your country.

To those who served. Though spurned and treated with disdain, your deeds are not forgotten. You honored yourselves and God in giving your youth.

Most of all, to those families who supported your sons, daughters, husbands, brothers, and sisters. When they returned, your war continued—along with that of the veterans. The intent of this book is to reveal—with the honor and respect that you deserve— some of those times not discussed.

When I Was a Boy: One Year in Vietnam

by Robert L. Ordóñez, M.D.

Editing and page design by Lenda L. Ziegler

Permissions, CIMA Publishing Co.

P. O. Box 6494

Lubbock, Texas 79493-6494

or e-mail:

ordr@hub.ofthe.net

ISBN 0-9656070-0-3

When I Was a Boy:

One Year in Vietnam

Robert L. Ordóñez, M.D.

About the Author

Robert Ordóñez, M.D., is originally from Albuquerque, New Mexico, where he lived, with the exception of the period of his military service, until graduation from medical school. Dr. Ordóñez is a board certified Family Physician, currently practicing in Lubbock, Texas, where he lives with his wife, Gloria. Their three sons attend college; Shawn is finishing at Texas Tech University in Lubbock, Texas. Robert and Chris attend Texas A & M University in College Station, Texas.

Acknowledgments

I am very grateful to many people for the successful completion of this book. First and foremost, I thank my wife, Gloria. Without her patience, encouragement, and support, I would not have seen this work to fulfillment. Gloria's endurance of the temperament of this Vietnam veteran is what prompted me to write this account.

I am also indebted to those who continued to encourage me and my efforts from the very early days of this attempt. Among those was P. Kent Harman, M. D., who for more than three years allowed me to take hold of this vision; and Clint Johnson, a comrade in arms, whose voluntary efforts continue to this day as my agent. Also, a special thanks to Dr. Phu Van Ngo and his wife, Cam Nguyen Ngo for their assistance—and to the many others who have kept up my hopes for the book's final debut.

I cannot say enough of the tremendous assistance I have received from Lenda Ziegler, my editor and page designer, whose painstaking efforts and superb professionalism turned this manuscript from a personal diary to a published accomplishment to share with the public.

Finally, I want to thank my sons, Shawn, Robert, and Christopher, my mother Martha, my sister Christine, and my brother Edward for giving me a goal for writing this manuscript, as I originally intended this account for them as a legacy, so that they might understand a part of history that affected them directly.

Contents

List of Cartoons

Prologue

*Grow old along with me. The best is yet to be: the
last of life, for which the first was made. Our
times are in His hands who saith, 'A whole I
planned; youth shows but half. Trust God; see all,
nor be afraid.'*

Robert Browning (1812-1889)

On my son's twenty-first birthday, he and I took a short
trip. As we drove home, neither of us had much to say. He
finally broke the silence by asking whether the years of my life
seemed to become shorter as I grew older.

I responded that some years seem to pass quicker only
because of the routine or the rut that I happened to have placed
myself in at the time. Basically, all the years of my life had
lapsed equally as fast—except for one.

My son inquired, "Except for one?" Then he quickly
remembered what I was talking about and added, "Oh yes, I
forgot."

Of course he was referring to that year I spent in the
Vietnam War. I realized that some twenty-plus years had
passed since I served in Vietnam—college, marriage, medical
school, three sons. And as this oldest son and I made our way
home, I realized that I had withheld from my whole family the

one time in my life that had changed me forever. However, thoughts and dreams of that small portion of my life still pass through my mind daily.

I had just turned twenty-one when the Navy sent me abroad for a year. Though at that particular time, I was not a Christian in the truest sense of the word, that year I spent in 'Nam caused me to evaluate the purpose of life and the meaning of my existence.

For me, God caused a potentially destructive event to become a tool of salvation. Since I had been a witness of, and a participator in so much death, destruction, and bloodshed in Vietnam, my being faced with the death and shedding of the blood of our Lord Jesus Christ meant something very real to me.

Subsequently, much has transpired in my life. I completed college and graduate school, entered a profession, and was given a wonderful family. I accepted Christ as my Savior within four years of returning from the war. Readers of this book should know that I feel a certain uneasiness about exposing a part of my life that the society of a whole era never allowed me to share.

Ultimately, not being able to impart these things over the years has become in me a source of resentment and bitterness toward a cold and indifferent nation. However, I still love this rugged country. And I love my family. This account is written for them.

My father served in Germany in World War II. I remember Dad's telling only bits and pieces of his war experiences. Even before he died, I had a very difficult time getting the whole story from him. He would ask me about my war, but Dad never really grasped what I went through until he read a certain book written by a then-young lieutenant who was placed in the same area of Vietnam as I during the same time period.

The book graphically described the soldier's ordeal and hardships, causing my dad to weep and to say to me, "I didn't realize, son...I just didn't realize."

America had seen Gary Cooper, John Wayne, and Charleton Heston movies, but no one had portrayed anything about us until Hollywood created a surge of Vietnam movies in the 1980s. However, I'm not sure that I can identify with that interpretation of our war. After all these years, I have decided to relate my personal experiences in the war that America lost.

This book is not a commentary of that war. It is not written for personal gratification nor for purging. Rather, this book is an attempt to portray some of the events that changed my life. It is an attempt to depict for the persons dear to me situations that I hope they never have to endure.

Many men faced harder times and much more horror than I did. I cannot speak for them. I can only write of my experience being a boy transported to a war.

While perusing this book, readers will discover the intense detail that might make one assume that fiction comprises much of its core. Combat veterans who have reviewed this writing agree that the experiences of warfare leave an indelible impression of the finest details. These details are often recollected as though they recently occurred. That is true with this book. It is a true and accurate account in every sense.

The names of the men portrayed in this book have been changed to protect them and their innocent families from unnecessary grief. Also, some of the instances have been altered—mellowed—to accommodate the reader.

Even so, the subject matter and attitudes in this book may strike the reader as crude, harsh, and quite biased, but they reflect the views of a 21-year-old away from home for the first time. That youngster had to become a different human being than the one reared by his parents, taught by his teachers, or befriended by his peers.

Animal instincts, as I soon discovered, are present in every human being. No instructor could tutor this young man in the type of behavior I exhibited during the twenty-first year of my life.

I do not currently embrace each of the opinions presented in this account; but combined, they comprise an important part of the beliefs I hold now. Foremost: man is born a sinner and does need a savior.

Chapter 1
The Baptism

After more than seventeen grueling hours across the Pacific, the plane landed. The door opened, and immediately the windows fogged, which obscured all vision from the air conditioned cabin.

As I stepped out onto the foreign land that had drawn so much attention across the globe, it was as if a bucket of hot water had been thrown on me—126 degrees and 100 percent humidity. I gasped, but the saturated air would not enter my lungs. My glasses clouded with steam. This slender 160-pound, 5-foot 9-inch American would be boiled alive in that Southeast Asian country.

The nightmare unfolded slowly. Chaos ruled at that first stopping point. There seemed to be no order to the stream of people moving in and out of the airport. I would find that lack of order to be the rule rather than the exception. Welcome to Da Nang, July, 1970.

The plane from which I had departed had been filled with a cargo of green soldiers, delivered for consumption by an obscure recipient—the U.S. Armed Forces in Vietnam. Our welcoming committee was a ghastly bunch of hardened men whose only words were shouted cursings that we were supposed to decipher. I could not understand any of it.

A military truck drove up and we piled into it—and were off to an unknown destination. After a long ride in the heat, the truck dropped us off at a building they called a hooch where we were supposed to spend our first day. Inside the hooch I noticed a slow-moving overhead fan and a few canvas cots.

Drenched in sweat, I stepped into the hooch and almost tripped over a smelly heap on the dirt floor—a young soldier taking a nap. He reeked of an odor that I would later recognize as the stench of the jungle.

I felt out of place there, dressed in bright Navy whites carrying the corpsman insignia on my sleeve. Turning to leave, I must have disturbed the sleeping soldier.

"Are you a corpsman?" the soldier queried.

"Yes, I am," I answered with hesitation.

"Look at me. I'm an animal. You'll be just like me in a couple of months. I'm a corpsman too."

I stared at the weathered soldier, making a silent determination that I would never become like that hardened, prematurely-aged boy. Fear entered my heart. Even with my firm resolve, the opposite did indeed come true.

Not wanting to face the truth alone, I looked around for my friend, Art. Art, a fellow corpsman from New Mexico, had joined the Navy with me after we both became disillusioned with college and had received our greetings from the President of the United States. We had been friends since our first day of college in August, 1967. Art's real name was Amarante Lucero, and he was from Tierra Amarilla, New Mexico. Art had married fewer than nine months before we shipped out to 'Nam.

Art and I had been given the choice of being assigned to a recon unit (reconnaissance) or a grunt unit (infantry). The recon unit, according to our recruiters, would spend, on the average, two to three days out in the bush and then return to the rear for four to five days each week.

The recon unit sounded ideal, so naturally Art and I chose the grunt unit. I think we both thought that we were being conned in some fashion, so we thought we would outsmart the recruiters. What a mistake! Later, we discovered that those enlisters really told the truth; they were looking out for us.

We did not sleep much that first evening; the suffocating heat and humidity tormented us the entire night. The next day, Art and I were two exhausted young men. That day would be the last time I would see Art for quite some time, since we had been assigned to different units.

Art spent about a month out in the bush before contracting malaria; he spent the rest of his tour in the rear, working at First Med, a field hospital located somewhere in Da Nang.

I was assigned to the 3rd Battalion, 1st Regiment of the 1st Marine Division. For the most part, the group of people I met in the rear had fought in the bush and treated me like they were eager for me to succeed. My arrival to the unit impressed me only in that everything was sandbagged, made with plywood, enclosed with screens, and covered by tin roofs—all very temporary.

I was greeted by a muscular young corpsman who was astonished that I was still wearing my whites. He said I stood out like a sore thumb. The corpsman checked me in, showed me to my quarters, and then began to acclimatize me by requiring that I play basketball with him in the middle of the hot steamy day.

The introduction to the 3rd Battalion and to the climate lasted about four days and then the real tour began. After being issued all the combat necessities, I discovered that my helmet had a hole in it. The supply corporal just smiled and said nothing as he issued it to me.

The issue also included two brand new jungle boots, two camouflage jungle uniforms, a flak jacket, four canteens, a ruck sack, a .45-caliber pistol, ammo, an M-16 rifle, a poncho, a poncho liner, an air mattress, a portable stretcher, a bayonet, and who knows what else.

Then I was off to Battalion Aid Station where I was supplied with a "unit one," which contained battle dressings, two intravenous bottles, a field surgical kit, lots of pills, and a morphine injection set.

As I looked at all my equipment, I recollected the Boy Scout days of backpacking and all the lightweight equipment we used to carry. It seemed like the Marines had never heard of the Boy Scouts. Maybe I could teach them something.

It seemed like many essentials were missing—for instance, a compass, a map, and—what about a mess kit? They did give us a canteen cup and insect repellent. What kind of an outing was this anyway? I would soon find out.

The night that followed was filled with infinite anxiety and restlessness. I still had not adapted to those terribly hot nights of mosquitoes and humidity. I slept in a hooch that had a fan, electric lights, a wooden floor and canvas cots.

Where was I going and for how long? The next day arrived too soon. They loaded me and all my gear into a jeep and I was taken to an observation post (OP) near Kilo Company, 2nd Platoon. That platoon was sort of on an R & R (rest and relaxation.)

There, "Doc" Joshua Potter of Kerrville, Texas, greeted me. The soldiers received me almost warmly—only because I was a corpsman. As I later learned, receiving a new guy usually didn't even amount to a glance to acknowledge his existence. It was not in anyone's best interest to make friends (or "Ps,") especially with a new guy. The survival rate of these kids was very low, and it was much easier to load up a poncho with someone you didn't know. But a corpsman was a different story.

The mind of the Marine Corps is a very peculiar organism. I know, because later, that mind became my very own. The grunts regarded a corpsman as a doctor, an older brother (even though most were the same age), a father, mother, priest, preacher, rabbi, military advisor, and a fill-in grunt. So most marines placed us corpsmen on a pedestal—but only after we had proved ourselves in a sort of unspoken ritual.

First, the Doc that I would eventually replace evaluated me, and then the platoon sergeant and squad leaders did. Somewhere down the line stood the lieutenant also; although I don't think his opinion really counted. The test would be how I handled the wounded and killed in action (KIAs). In the meantime, the men gave me a temporary place of honor.

The first day and night as the new corpsman in a platoon was probably the most awkward. My place to sleep was in the main bunker which was nothing more than sandbagged walls, a dirt floor, and openings for windows and doors.

The few nights I spent there were to be some of the only nights I spent indoors for a whole year. I was totally sleepless the first night because I had to cover my entire body with my poncho liner to minimize mosquito bites. Even at that, I counted more than thirty-five bites on each hand when I awoke the next morning.

Just as when I had first arrived, I could hardly breathe. The nighttime temperature must have been at least 98 degrees with 100 percent humidity, and we were required to sleep completely clothed, including our boots, in case of attack.

"Doc" Potter and the rest of the platoon moved to another observation post (OP), so I became a lone corpsman for two squads.

The personality of each of the platoons' young men was different, as one might expect, but they shared several common peculiarities. The seasoned soldiers seemed to all speak the same dialect, a mixture of English, military, Vietnamese, and French.

Their concerns, too, were similar; the main one simply

being to get home. Distrust of "lifers," dislike of C-rations, and a definite loyalty to each other were some additional distinctive elements I observed. Also, as one might have expected, six of every ten words spoken were four-letter cursings.

One evening, we were scouting with a starlight scope when I spotted movement. Someone said, "Throw a frag (a hand grenade)." So I did, and everyone hit the dirt.

Shortly thereafter, the frag came right back to me—I too hit the dirt! Several seconds later, after nothing happened, someone discovered that I had failed to release the thumb safety. We all were glad that I was just a new guy. The movement I had seen was a rock ape which would always return what was thrown to them. Did I feel dumb?!

A platoon sergeant and two squad leaders piloted my platoon. Each of them were short timers, having already spent close to a year in-country. Only one of the "leaders" attempted to spend time with me to give me advice. The others expected me to already know everything or maybe they just didn't care.

The kind sergeant came from the ghettos of Chicago. He talked to me about fear and choking under fire. He taught me to develop my senses and trained me in many other tricks of physical and mental survival.

Then I met Mackovich, a strange squad leader. Climbing the rank ladder, he was labeled a pseudo-lifer. Once, one of the married grunts received a letter from his wife saying that she was three months pregnant; he had been in 'Nam five months. That caused a severe surge of rage in which the young soldier started shooting his M-16 at anything that moved. I was up on a hill playing cards when I saw tracer rounds flying everywhere. These tracers were phosphorous bullets that shot out like a beam of light.

Dodging the fire, I ran down the hill to the first bunker and then I reached the main bunker where the distraught boy stood.

Mackovich stood in front of him, with his carbine aimed at the head of the troubled soldier. I grabbed the carbine, threw it down, and walked toward the broken lad. As I walked toward him, I watched his eyes to catch any semblance of sanity. The moment I caught his eye, I reached out and grabbed his rifle. He collapsed into my arms, crying. We took him back to the rear, and there he stayed for the remainder of his tour.

I sure was scared, but something overpowered me to save the poor boy from being shot by "a friendly" (Mackovich). After that occurrence, I began to experience—somewhat—the camaraderie shared by those courageous soldiers. I thought there would be a little recognition for my heroic act, but there was not—perhaps because the act had nothing to do with combat or maybe because it was a private matter that needed to be protected and forgotten.

Mackovich was the kind of guy who never seemed to do anything right, who was easy to laugh at, and who got blamed for everything. Once I asked him why he cut his hair short like a lifer. He responded that he wanted to make an impression when he was up for sergeant. Throughout our time together, I prodded him often and once was tempted to put him out of his misery.

A member of the mortar fire team named Dino Milton, was a Filipino who had been reared in Hawaii. We became good friends and planned to spend R & R together in Hawaii. Another squad leader, Sgt. Grant, got into a fist fight with Dino, and beat him to a pulp one day. No one ever knew why or even seemed to care.

Joe, a young corporal who sported a very boyish face, reminding me of Audie Murphy, had war stories and stories about everyone for every minute of the day. Everyone liked Joe. He could compete with the best when it came to combat capability. Joe told stories about one of our men called Big

Man, saying that he was a Golden Glove boxer who could kill a man with one punch. This never was true but it sounded good.

The legend of Big Man somehow got passed on to (and about) me, of course with some changes. The men were led to believe—even though much later—that I had killed men with karate. (Before joining the military I took about four months of Shotokahn karate and was only a white belt.) I think Joe had something to do with starting the tale, but he would never admit that he did. Joe was also a short timer, and I was glad when he gave me his seal of approval.

Most of the boys I knew in 'Nam were nineteen. Eighteen was the age of an occasional new guy, but nineteen was the average age of most of the grunts. The typical ages of officers, lifers, or college dropouts was twenty and older. Being twenty-one, I helped fill the generation gap because I could relate to both groups.

Being twenty-one, I also felt cheated out of my first year at adulthood back in the "world," which was our word for the United States. Nineteen-year-old Lizzio, our resident pretty boy, charmed all the Vietnamese women and children. Instead of asking "number-one GI" for handouts, they brought the gifts to him. Lizzio had been in Vietnam for only a month, so he also was fairly new.

Sergeant Smith, a black man from California, was our platoon sergeant. He seemed more interested in keeping his clothes clean than in seeing to the needs of his men. Smith was so proper it was sickening, but when it came to combat, he was among the best. Smith always talked about the "world," but he had about eight months left in 'Nam. Being a lifer, he really couldn't relate to any of us or even to his "bros." However, I learned proper radio procedure as well as other responsibilities from Smith.

One thing I did notice about that war-weary bunch was that very few of them spoke of their experiences. I had heard more war stories back in the rear than I did in the bush. I did not ask much, but was all ears when someone offered combat advice.

At night, each of us was assigned a watch period, which usually lasted two hours. The communications radio was always on, and I listened to other marines somewhere out in the jungles. Ever so often, we heard excited discussion about a fire fight or a bunker discovery. It sounded like heavy fighting out there at times.

Someone told me that my night vision would develop after a few weeks. I wondered why I didn't already have it and then realized that nighttime back in the world (the U.S.) was never without light. Out here, one couldn't even light a cigarette because of the brilliant light it sent forth, and it seemed like most of the fighting took place at night. In any event, it took a while before I could see what everyone else saw during those dark, obscure hours.

The R & R for OP (observation post) soon came to an end as we received orders to "saddle up" in preparation for a major operation. We were trucked back to the rear to resupply and to be briefed. Since I was a corpsman, my orientation took place at the Battalion Aid Station (BAS), the medical center for our battalion.

The doctor there told all us corpsmen that he expected many casualties so we should take extra supplies and not much else. That was the last time I went to BAS until some nine or ten months later.

From the Marine unit itself, we each received a five- to seven-day supply of C-rations and Long Range Patrol Rations (LRPRs). I saw Doc Potter there and he told me it would be a piece of cake—rotten, dried up cake.

I had to trim down my pack and leave almost everything except my rain gear, poncho liner, and tooth brush, and then carry an abundance of medical equipment besides my food and ammunition.

This was supposed to be a fast-moving operation, so we were told to leave our flak jackets and helmets behind. Even without that extra twenty pounds, our equipment was still very heavy. My gear weighed about fifty pounds, but that of the radioman weighed nearly one hundred.

The operation still felt like a Boy Scout trip; the reality of the event had not yet sunk in. While jumping off of a truck, I twisted my ankle. Had it been a camping trip I would have joined the rest of the men later; but this was the real thing so I mentioned nothing to the others and strangely enough, the ankle never bothered me again. I passed out Chapstick to the grunts thinking I would protect them from dry, chapped lips, but again, my thinking was that of Boy Scout camping in the arid Rocky Mountains, where water is scarce. No lips became chapped here—ever.

After "saddling up" (loading ourselves with all of our gear,) we marched to the landing zone (LZ). There several other companies of Marines piled into choppers with us. The Marines used double-bladed CH-26s, not Hueys like the Army. Each CH-26 had small, open portholes as windows, a rear ramp for loading, and held about twenty combat soldiers in full gear.

In the chopper, we sat facing each other with our sleeves rolled down and towels around our necks. I'm sure it looked like we were a little "touched" by the heat. But we had a reason for covering our skin even though it was so hot. If one of those choppers had crashed, the magnesium—of which most helicopters were constructed—would have burst into flames. The towels and long sleeves would have yielded some protection crucial to life.

As we became airborne, the choppers made so much noise

that when one of us shouted into the ear of the person next to him, no one heard; lips moved but no sound came forth. It was cool up there, though. I always resented the air crew for being fortunate enough to be clothed in clean uniforms, to be allowed cool flights, and to eat warm food.

From our vantage point, the land looked beautiful. We gazed down on water buffaloes—the main farm implement in Vietnam—and rice paddies dotted with people working in their straw hats. We observed white, blue, and red-trimmed, French-style buildings with thatched roofs scattered here and there and cemeteries also in the French tradition.

The green landscape was lush with tropical trees, elephant grass, bamboo shoots, banana orchards, and jungle. As the distant, ominous mountains approached us, the valley next to them seemed so innocent; however, that disjunction became our landing zone.

The chopper ahead of us landed, and we circled until it was our turn. The descent brought the ground closer. We touched ground, and the ramp opened. We all stood up. Since I was in the middle, I could watch what the others did as they dispatched.

We were trained to create a perimeter to defend each other and the helicopter as soon as we disembarked. As I jumped off—only a foot or so to the ground—my legs wobbled, and I almost lost my balance.

It was over. The choppers ejected all the soldiers and escaped as fast as they had arrived. The peaceful valley was smaller than it had seemed from the air; we were surrounded by four-foot high elephant grass with edges like razors on each of its blades.

The heat began to consume me again. Sweat poured out of me like I was a soaked sponge being wrung out. I discovered the second purpose of the towels that some of us wore around our necks—to wipe the salty sweat from faces and eyes so we could see to walk.

We began our ascent of one of the mountains. This was referred to as "humping," and that it was. As we slowly climbed, I could see only what was directly in front of me and could hear only my own intense panting.

Vegetation was everywhere in the thick jungles; the ground could hardly be seen for the leaves and grass. As we plunged deeper into the jungle, the light became dark, since the triple canopy covered the sunlight.

God covered the jungles of Vietnam with three layers of greenery—underbrush, tall trees, and very tall trees—hence the triple canopy. However, as we marched under that thick ceiling, we could easily see the rays of sunlight as they reflected on all the steam. The shadow of the canopy did not make it any cooler either.

We finally stopped for our first rest. Suddenly Sgt. Smith pointed somewhere down the mountain from where we had come. I asked what was going on, and one of the marines said they saw one of our men trailing in the distance, apparently lost.

We waited until he caught up. Not much more was said. I thought, "In a few more minutes, this poor fellow would have been lost for good and no one said anything to him about it. This doesn't make sense."

We continued up into the mountains. Most of us were totally ignorant of our destination and our objective. After several hours of humping, we were told to eat something. Most of the men had conditioned themselves to eating only one and one-half meals each day which cut down on the weight they had to carry. We found that we could make three meals last two days, thereby lightening our loads.

In looking through my pack for my food, I noticed the

candles I had brought had completely melted, coating the inside of my pack with wax. Bringing candles was dumb, not only because of their melting but also because one could never use them, since our superiors permitted no light at night.

We ate, and then the signal for saddling up, as always, came too quickly. We saw no trails; but even if we had seen any, we wouldn't walk on them for fear of booby traps. We encountered huge rocks, cliffs, streams, and plenty of swamps.

We crossed streams by jumping the rocks, but sometimes our footing was not very secure. Once, as I edged my way across one of those rocks, my foot caught in a crevice and I fell backwards into the stream. I was almost upside down with my foot still stuck between the rocks. Finally, after about fifteen seconds, someone released my foot with a light kick.

I sank to the bottom and was deciding whether or not to remove my gear. Then my pack began to lift me up. Thank God for my wax-coated rucksack!

As I surfaced from the crystal clear water, someone helped me out. It was very hard to help anyone without falling in yourself, but no one else fell in that day. Being soaked with that cool, crystal-clear stream water felt better than bathing. Also, the water tasted very refreshing. We traversed many more streams and log bridges over cliffs and rivers; tramped up rocks, up hills, and down hills; but we still saw no sign of hostility.

We set up for the night in the same established routine that night and every night for the next year. The center of the camp, called the command post or CP, held the officers, radioman, and the platoon sergeants. Encircling them, the squads were either on ambush or perimeter guard.

Occasionally, some of the squads would "pull" night patrol in which they went out to search for an enemy ambush—the enemy set up to ambush us. We constructed our shelters by snapping together two ponchos and tying them down through the grommets, creating a small tent. Sometimes four people could sleep under one poncho hooch.

During my first night in the actual bush, I felt as awkward as I had during the first night "in country." I didn't know anyone well enough to assume that I could share their hooch. I was too uncomfortable to ask, so I tried, by myself, to set up my own single poncho hooch.

That night it rained like I had never seen rain before—quite normal for the tropics. It took some time to get the New Mexico desert out of my system.

The first thing I thought of was to catch water off the poncho runoff to refill my canteens, but it turned out to be a totally useless idea since we were almost always encountering water. As I gradually became drenched, from out of the blue, Mackovich asked me to join him and two others in their hooch. I was not too proud—and Mackovich was not all that bad, either.

I pulled my turn at watch that night, just as I would most every night from that moment on. I was told to keep my eye on everything, just as we had done back at the OP. We slept in two-hour increments—the trick was to try to squeeze in six hours of sleep during a twenty-four hour period.

To me, there seemed to be two days packed into each twenty-four hour period. There was the daytime day and the nighttime day—each just as long as the other but the night, by far, the most feared.

The morning appeared after a quiet night. The mosquitoes disappeared at the birth of each new morning; and as the sun rose, the smell of humid vegetation gradually permeated the air. As the squad leaders were being briefed on the day's objectives, the rest of us sat on the ground eating our limited breakfasts. I noticed Doc Potter aiming his forty-five pistol at me. Then he uttered a classic cliché like, "Don't move!"

Believe me, I didn't!

Then without warning—BANG! A splatter of blood hit my sleeve. Almost in shock, I slowly glanced to the side, afraid of what I might see. I caught a glimpse of something dead on the ground, almost touching me. It was a dead cobra! Doc Potter, an expert marksman, had been a member of the National Rifle Association since he was a boy. Thank God he seldom missed his target!

As we commenced the ritual of saddling up, my bones squeaked with stiffness and I found myself still trembling—I hadn't gotten over the cobra incident. Around my waist, I strapped the webbed belt that held two canteens, a Colt .45 semi-automatic pistol, four magazines, and a bayonet. All of that required suspenders to hold up the belt.

Then I bedecked myself with a pack which contained medical gear, food, rain gear, a poncho, a poncho liner, a canteen cup, a few personal items such as writing material, soap, and a toothbrush, and four more canteens filled with water. Then I strapped my weighty medical bag across my chest and over my shoulder. This vital part of my gear held essential medical supplies that I would need in case of an emergency.

Later, when I returned to "the world," my brother commented on the fact that I carried my left shoulder higher than the right one. That medical bag *was* heavy.

As a finishing touch to my "saddling up" routine, I laid a rancid, sweat-soaked towel over my neck.

A month or so later and for the remainder of my time in Vietnam, I added the following to my payload: a flak jacket (it could protect me from the shrapnel of an exploding device but not from a bullet), two bandoleers full of battle dressings, and a bandoleer of M-16 ammunition for when I carried an M-16 rifle, which was about fifty percent of the time. If it became necessary, and I didn't have a rifle, I would use the M-16 of a wounded marine.

Even though the day was young, the temperature had already climbed to higher than ninety degrees. When given the signal, we "saddled" ones began walking in a staggered formation with plenty of space between us.

We placed ourselves alternately so that if we were attacked in an ambush, with a booby-trap, or by incoming rounds, only a few of us would become casualties. Silence prevailed during the day as well as at night, especially when we were moving on a hot day like that one.

The spacing and positions of the soldiers when walking together was very important. The point man claimed to like his spot because he had control over the squad or the platoon, but of course, that was the position hit first if a tripwire went off. During an ambush, the first man out (point) was usually not hit since the enemy liked to have the middle of the group in their sights before commencing firing.

The middle included the leadership, the corpsman, and the remainder of the fire team. Order-givers reserved the tail position for another experienced man to bring up the rear since back activity sometimes was as deadly as that in the front. None of us ever felt protected in his spot; both sides of the patrol line were the deadliest of all. No one was safe anywhere!

As we walked, we made no unnecessary noise. We chose our steps carefully, as our eyes skillfully combed the surroundings and our thoughts constantly anticipated a surprise attack or a booby-trap.

These first days, however, I thought rebellious thoughts of how I would not become like those American savages and how I would not speak the dialect they spoke. I thought of how I hated the military, especially the lifers who had totally sold out to the system.

The attitude of the sixties and early seventies affected all of us young men and probably influenced our families, friends, wives, and girlfriends back home. The reason for the war was a big issue back in "the world," but in 'Nam, no one ever brought it up.

We were there, and with the war a reality, survival was the only issue. I certainly did not appreciate being there at all. I felt like I must be the only person with that attitude, for most of the others seemed to actually enjoy the scenario. My gut hurt with anxiety as we continued to walk slowly.

My dad used to say that in Europe during World War II, the birds were silent. They seemed to be silent in the jungles of Vietnam, too. One might think that jungle sounds would calm us as we advanced. However, the sounds of the jungle brought us no peace.

The unnaturally large size and loud noise of the insects unsettled us. Occasionally, we played catch with potato bugs as big as baseballs, chased daddy longlegs as big as two hands, or heard crickets that were louder than jamboxes. Numerous bubbling streams and raging rivers added to the continuous noise.

After walking for several hours, my whole body felt fatigued from the stress of needing to remain so alert. My arms burned with a multitude of small cuts from the elephant grass, different thorns, and salty perspiration. Sweat soaked every inch of me; I was thirsty and hungry.

As I heard the order to stop for supper, I thought with great relief, "Again, on this second day, nothing happened."

That evening I learned how to cook marine-style. The C-rations were essentially canned meals that could be heated right in the can. A small can opener, called a P-40, came with each case of C-rations, so if a soldier did not have one, eventually it would be his turn to claim one. The cans varied in height, but the diameter was always the same.

The smaller cans usually contained dry food, like crackers or stale, round candy bars. After we emptied them, these smaller cans served as our stoves.

With a beverage can opener called a "stateside," a hungry soldier would cut the familiar triangular holes into the sides of the smaller can, drop a heat tablet (tab) inside, and light it. Then the can containing the food which needed to be heated was placed on top of the small stove and heated.

Heat tabs were sometimes a luxury; if that was the case, we used instead the explosive element (the C-4) from a grenade or a mine (Claymore). If no C-4 was available, a can of peanut butter with insect repellent mixed with it would be used and could actually cook two dinners instead of the one that the heat tab or the C-4 would.

I will reserve for later my comments about the taste of the "LRPRs" or dehydrated food that we received only on rare occasions. We prepared the Long Range Patrol Rations by heating water, pouring it into the bag of dehydrated rations, and letting it sit for five minutes or so before eating it.

As the sun began to set, the mosquitoes appeared once again. The night passed at half the speed of the daytime. The morning arrived; again, the routine seemed to be establishing itself. At the end of the third day, we joined with another platoon, making it a company operation. By that time, I had started to feel "salty" (as though I was experienced,) which was really just a false feeling of security.

That night, I had the privilege of staying in the CP (command post.) Our hooch was pitched over a bomb crater, which provided plenty of room for several of us.

As I wandered into a deep sleep, I experienced a rare happening—a dream. Dreams were usually an output of only rear echelon personnel. We, on the other hand, usually slept so lightly that there was no time for such luxuries as dreams.

I dreamed that I was out in an open field watching an ant pile. After a while, an increasingly loud sound began piercing the air. As I looked up, fear overtook me as I witnessed the descent of a spacecraft. I hid in the brush and watched through a pair of binoculars.

As the craft landed, the little ants on the ground moved about excitedly. The hatch opened and slowly, to my amazement, out marched an upright uniformed ant! Behind the first creature advanced a whole army of similarly large insects. In orderly fashion, they created a huge formation of an ant brigade.

An obvious leader began speaking to the earth ants in a language they seemed to understand. Apparently, the leader was organizing an earth army, using his own members as advisers, much like the U.S. did in Vietnam.

I watched intently for a long time before I realized that the aliens had come to conquer the planet Earth and would use our own ants as their slave soldiers. I beheld their first attack on a country farm as they methodically destroyed the crops and ultimately the family within. I began to experience extreme anxiety as millions of ants took over and destroyed the earth as we knew it. I ran here and there, trying to warn people of what was happening. I knew that in running to warn, I had revealed my cover.

The ants discovered me! It became both the earth ants' and the alien ants' priority to prevent me from spreading the finding. Few people would listen to my outlandish claims, so I was driven to the open countryside where I was entrapped. Before I knew it, the ants had surrounded me and had begun to devour me. Their stings were so real that I was actually hurting all over.

Just at the moment of near destruction, I awoke. Instead of waking from a nightmare, I awoke to a nightmare. I was still hurting!

As I looked down at my legs and arms, there were real ants all over me. Ants scurried everywhere. I had slept on an ant pile. These ants had already eaten holes in my clothes, my pack, and even into my packages of LRPRs. Needless to say, this young soldier wriggled and writhed that morning, while performing an Indian rain dance.

After the ordeal with the ants, it seemed like another routine day—at least that was what I thought. It did not take long to realize that there was no such thing as a routine day out in the bush. Each day had its own uniqueness in that every locale we traversed was different, each moment had its own particular fears, and every step, its own particular dangers.

We kept as quiet as ever as we wound through the steep mountains, with nature being just as unfriendly as the enemy. Many times we, carrying our heavy packs, had to jump across deep crevices or swing like Tarzan from vines across deep ravines. It seemed as if the streams, rivers, and swamps never ended. It is not easy to become accustomed to stepping into something you cannot see or tripping on unseen rocks and holes, all under water.

We walked through swamps filled with stale water with all sorts of gunk floating on top, seeing snakes and other creeping things in those smelly bodies of murky liquid. It seemed that we were always walking through some sort of water that was at least chest deep. Of course, my pack remained dry thanks to those melted candles.

My observing and learning from my comrades' actions and reactions trained and programmed me on basic survival techniques. I observed how my fellow marines always appeared sure of each and every step; that they were firm believers in the reality of land mines, booby-traps, and ambushes.

It seemed like the rules of the game stated that we should patrol during the day and set up ambushes at night. The Viet

Cong did just the opposite. Of course, every once in awhile we (and they) broke the rules and switched times.

One afternoon, as the sun edged farther westward and I looked forward to what might be called a rest. I was not totally accustomed to humping all day and sleeping on rocks at night. That particular evening, while getting situated for the night, the squad leader barked an order for me to go out on ambush with squad.

"Thump, thump, thump, thump, thump!" My heart pounded so loudly that my ears could hear the sound. My first ambush. Would there be fighting, or not? I awkwardly kept quiet and just copied what everyone else did.

We each took a poncho, a poncho liner, a canteen, a rifle and ammo, and, of course, I took my medical gear as well. We had been told about the different types of ambushes. Straight line and L-shaped were the two most common. L-shaped ambushes allowed a face on and a side attack to occur simultaneously. A straight ambush permitted only a side attack of the approaching enemy.

Being part of a small band of soldiers, I had to pull my own weight—a corpsman in 'Nam was more than a medic; he also was a marine.

We walked out to a pre-planned ambush site at dusk so that the enemy would have a difficult time seeing where we set up. Walking in the near-dark was difficult, as we tried to be ever-so-quiet and space ourselves like we had done during the day.

The squad leader positioned us in an L-shaped formation and there we sat, ready. Just before it got dark, some of the guys talked of "staging" a firefight so that we could go back early. Apparently none of them had actually ever done it, but they had heard that we could remove the flash suppressor from the muzzle of the M-16 and it would sound identical to a Chinese AK-47.

We never staged the firefight that night nor did we ever at any later time. The mosquitoes buzzed and bit all night, while we took our two-hour turns at watch and then a two-hour sleep. We each slept for two hours, watched for two and then repeated the cycle one more time. We averaged nearly four hours of sleep during the night and occasionally, one or two additional hours during the day.

When it finally came our turn to sleep, we had to lay on our sides to minimize snoring. That first night ambush was almost entirely sleepless. Anticipation of the unknown raced through my mind all night long. I nearly panicked with each little sound the night brought to the jungle. I could imagine silhouettes of Viet Cong (VC) and of the North Vietnamese Army (NVA) in the branches and surrounding the huge tropical leaves.

Morning appeared, and we returned to our unit delivering only a report of no contact. Although peaceful in one way, those dark hours had frightened me as much as if we had had contact. At least that was what I thought at the time.

The next few days repeated the last two. I was getting to know the other marines better by now. Jose Gonzales was a transfer from a CAG unit. I don't know exactly what CAG meant. I think it stood for Civil something.

Jose, a Rambo-type person, was used to the jungle and could speak fluent Vietnamese. Jose jumped from rock to rock while the rest of us climbed and stumbled over everything. Jose had been born in Mexico but raised in California. He already had two confirmed enemy kills and was ready for more.

Near the end of a certain day, we came upon a wide stream with steep banks; the stream was supposedly a main NVA route. The numerous boulders made ambushing easy—for us and for them. We set up in a long line along the water, mainly because we had a whole company instead of the usual platoon.

I wondered aloud, "What if we did get into a firefight and our men positioned behind us start shooting downstream where we are?"

The lieutenant tried to assure me that the rocks would protect us, but he too looked worried after that statement of my inspirational notion.

Night came, and the leaders ordered us all on ambush watch. Sometime around "dark-thirty o'clock," radio communication from a forward squad said they had spotted movement.

They mentioned lights approaching them, which was puzzling at the time. These were very dim lights that the enemy used. Most of the time, the lights' short range caused them to be overlooked by us. As the lights approached our squad, someone granted permission to fire. It seemed like everyone was shooting.

"Pop pop pop, rat tat tat tat, ping, ping, zing"—all over the place!

Our squad could not shoot because the squad in front of us sat directly in our line of fire. My hand clenched my .45, and trembled with fear and excitement. I envisioned my position being overrun so I rationed and chose my shots carefully.

After a few minutes of gunfire, silence crept in—no hits or kills were confirmed. We, however, had one wounded man. This soldier from another platoon was situated at the rear of our position. He sustained a flesh wound in his buttocks. I still think a stray round from one of our men hit him. We heard no more gunfire for the remainder of the night.

That night, when it was my turn and I tried to sleep, I noticed some phosphorous leaves glowing in the blackness of the night. That beauty could exist in such a horrible situation amazed me.

The nights in the jungle were always so eerie with all their sounds, humid smells, and ever present danger. Still, at that point, I often thought about home and what my brother might be doing with the friends we shared.

"It's not so bad here," I thought to myself. "It's not so bad." Then I must have fallen asleep.

Early the next morning, I got to watch an air extraction of our wounded soldier using a jungle penetrator. The poor young man was teased by his platoon as he was lifted through the trees and vines, obviously very humbled and embarrassed.

How the helicopter found our exact spot, I never knew, but as it lifted up through the trees, I took the last bite of my tiny breakfast. It took a long time for me to get used to eating one and one-half meals a day. Each morning, I was tempted to eat a whole breakfast of scrumptious spaghetti or some other deliciously bland C-ration.

When I heard the order, "Saddle up, search and destroy," I thought, "Ha! The only things getting destroyed are my feet." Another day had begun.

Several days passed—or ran together—and all I can remember is that we toiled through plenty of twisted vines, tall elephant grass, prickly thorns, thick vegetation and steep slopes. At times, our platoon could not travel faster than seventy-five meters in an hour, macheteeing our way through the jungle.

As we approached the edge of the top of a mountain, our lieutenants—both the new and the outgoing—began discussing being lost. It seemed that our only way out of that position was straight down a cliff. We could not see the bottom for the jungle. Lieutenant Jones, being the senior, decided to go down himself.

We tied two 100-foot nylon ropes together, and down the lieutenant went. The ropes acted like a giant rubber band with a soldier clinging to the end. Some time passe d; and we had not heard from Jones. We all worried, but no one offered to go down. I decided that that was a job for "Super Doc."

I prepared to descend the cliff, just as I had seen dozens of times on television. Rappelling was taught to only the elite Recon units, and I was not Recon; therefore, I knew nothing about rappelling.

As I scooted down the ropes with hands ungloved and all my gear on my back, thoughts were battering my head. How could I have been so dumb? How would I survive that mess? I could not believe that I was doing that. As I reached the first knot, which was the 100-foot marker, I was bouncing like a paddle ball on a rubber band.

My body was hitting the rock cliff like it was a piñata. Finally, trembling, puffing, and sweating from fear and fatigue, I literally reached the end of my rope. Where was the ground? There was no ground! I could see bushes about another ten or more feet below me and realized that I had no choice but to jump, or rather, let go. So I did, with closed eyes.

Crash! Thud! The jungle brush broke my fall. As I worked my way out of the thicket of thorns, leaves and branches, I thanked God for no broken bones. I began calling out for the lieutenant softly so as to not give away my position—as if I hadn't already been seen.

Finally the lieutenant walked out of the jungle towards me. He admitted to being totally lost. We waited for the rest of the platoon to come down the rope, but no one came. Those cowards eventually climbed down the easy way. I felt both foolish and somewhat upset, but realized that that was life.

The officers made the decision to follow the stream downhill until we approached the foothills. As we worked our way down, one of our scouts fell on his back, injuring himself such that he could hardly walk. He was an American who was in charge of the Kit Carson (KC) scouts—Vietcong who had surrendered to our side. These KC scouts were fearless and quite likable.

We often wondered how long would it be before they would go back to the VC and fight us again. The KC scouts helped their American comrade keep up with rest of us. Jose Gonzales also fell and hit his head on a rock. He must have been so tired that he fainted. If Jose was tired, one can imagine how the rest of us felt.

Lieutenant Jones decided to break the trail to get out of the rocky stream that already had caused many to fall. As the platoon headed up the steep embankment, I brought up the rear. Why, I'll never know.

Suddenly, "BOOM," a flash with black smoke and a shock wave struck! Everyone hit the ground. Someone yelled, "Incoming!" With my face in the dirt, I waited for more explosions.

Voices were shouting, "Corpsman, up; corpsman, up!" This meant ME! I was so scared that I actually pretended that I had not heard anything. Then again, "Corpsman, up!"

The fellow in front of me turned around and yelled, "Doc, that's YOU!"

I tried to stand up, but my feet kept slipping on the grass and I fell several times in sheer terror. As I made it up the hill, most of the grunts were still lying low. Some, however, were moving about, groaning with pain and shock.

I smelled burnt flesh, gun powder, and an unusual smell which was actually fresh blood. To my left, some twisted figure of a man lay smashed into the bushes. I thought to myself that Doc Potter should take care of that one, as he was really a mess.

First, just as I had been taught, I triaged (sorted) the wounded, from the most seriously hurt to the least injured. At the top of the hill, Doc Potter tended to a wounded KC scout. The scout had a very small wound in his belly but was totally immobilized. Later reports from the rear revealed that the scout had sustained liver and intestinal injuries.

I asked Potter if he had seen the wounded marine thrown into the bushes, but he had not. I asked if I should see about the unfortunate soul. Doc Potter said, "Yes."

Reluctantly, I made my way back to where I had seen the person thrown into the brush. I really did not want to go. As I stopped and looked down at him, I saw movement. Slowly, I edged down and someone cautioned me to watch for more booby traps. That was all I needed.

What I saw next was my baptism to that insanity. The person was unrecognizable. My memory of what I had been trained for became a total blank.

"What do I do?" I thought. The explosion had twisted, bent, and broken his legs. His left arm was torn with flesh and blood exposed. The right arm had been crushed into the shoulder so that only a thumb protruded from the shoulder socket.

His face did not even resemble a face. The chest was full of holes, with one big one in the center. I could actually see his heart still pumping! Adrenaline was pumping through my veins a hundred miles a minute.

"I must save him!" I yelled, as I began taking apart my .45 to use the barrel for an airway, and began performing a cricothyroidotomy with my bayonet. This was a procedure that would produce an airway in the throat to the windpipe. "Oh man, don't die!" I repeated over and over.

I yelled out for some help. One scared young marine made his way down and asked what he could do. By that time it was too late. The heart stopped and the dreaded gurgle had ended.

"Who was this?" I asked.

"Dino, Dino Milton" the marine said.

"Dino? No, not Dino!" I cried out. First he was beaten to a

pulp by his sergeant and now this! What had he done to deserve such treatment? I didn't understand.

Reality had become something I could touch—it felt hard and cold. At that point, all sound seemed to be drowned out.

I left Dino and in a daze, began treating the other wounded soldiers. Everyone was still extremely cautious, looking out for more booby-traps. Some marines positioned themselves for a possible attack. The radioman called for a Medevac (medical evacuation).

As Doc Potter and I bandaged the last marine, I could not stop shaking. Doc was silent. I asked him if I had done well, and he assured me that I had done quite well. That meant a lot to me at that moment. Then I noticed a piece of burned flesh in my mouth. It was nauseating. From that day forward, I sealed my emotions within me, only to have a callous begin to form on my heart.

The chopper arrived to lift the dead and wounded. As we loaded them on board, I longed to leave with them. After they departed, and we began walking again, I could not figure out how I was supposed to act, speak, think, or feel. So I just followed orders.

Marching in a hum-drum manner, I began watching my feet. Water squirted from the vent holes of one boot as if to shoot the other boot. This reminded me of a story that I had read in a combat comic book when I was a boy. It was about a mailman who had been in the infantry during WW II. After the war as he made his rounds, the mailman recalled a time in battle when he could not take a step without getting shot at.

I walked on, giddy and in a light state of shock, finally arriving at the rear that evening. I found Sergeant Grant, who had gone back a week early, and told him about Dino. He shrugged his shoulders and went about his business. I guess I had wanted to make him feel guilty for beating Dino earlier, but I failed.

That evening, someone cooked steak over charcoal for us,

but I don't remember eating any. The next morning, we were out in the field again, without a chance to shower or shave.

One more squawk outta you 'bout the size of these skeeters an' I'll bash yer head in!

Chapter 2
Hill 124

We arrived at Hill 124, known to have seen a lot of action, but still an acceptable place to be sent. The hill amounted to nothing but sandbagged bunkers on a barren hilltop. The marines we replaced seemed quite relieved to be departing, which was somewhat unnerving to me. I looked at those bunkers and thought to myself, "Indoors!"

Lieutenant Winter diminished my excitement when he announced that we would only dismantle the hill; not live in it. However, we did manage a couple of nights in the bunkers before tearing them down. Winter sent out patrols from the hill, and they occasionally came into contact with small arms fire, resulting in a few wounded now and then, but thankfully, no KIAs.

On Hill 124, I learned the art of writing letters that communicated a few thoughts without actually saying anything. The truth would have frightened my family out of their wits. From that hill, I sent my brother a birthday card that I drew on a piece of C-ration box. He still has it.

After we had been on Hill 124 for a few days, a chaplain and his aide visited us to hold a memorial service for Dino. They stuck a rifle with a bayonet into the ground and placed a helmet on top of the rifle, representing Dino. After the chaplain said a few pious platitudes, the aid played Taps on his bugle. It made me think of a few years earlier when they buried JFK and someone played Taps. My dad cried and said that Taps always

"From Hill 124, I sent my brother a birthday card that I drew on a piece of C-ration box. He still has it."

made him do that. The day of Dino's funeral, I discovered that I had no tears to shed, but in the subsequent years, Taps has always produced the tears I withheld then.

That evening, a metamorphosis began to occur. I sat looking out from the hill and realized that I had been "in country" for about a month. I acknowledged that I might actually spend the rest of my living days right here. I could be killed, captured, or wounded to the point of total disability right here. I realized that in order to survive, I needed to conform and quit being so resistant to the way everyone spoke, thought, and acted. Also, I admitted that my inner feelings had become a cancer that would eat me alive if I permitted. So that night as I manned the radio, my whole being changed— conformed—in a private, unannounced, unceremonious rite of passage; even my radio technique became expert.

The following day brought a short bit of action to our agenda. This operation took us through some of the country-side villes, as they were called, and rice paddies. Any time we patrolled these villes, the local people came out to sell useless things to the good ol' Americans. The most reasonable articles they sold us were ice-cold Coca Colas. Yes, even in the remote jungles of Vietnam, one could buy a Coke that had been carried around in a wooden box with ice chunks.

We always wondered about the origin of the ice, but were glad they had it. The locals in the villes also offered an abundance of marijuana, "OB" which was a French diet elixir (speed), and some beer. To take drugs or drink alcohol out in the bush amounted to suicide. Very few members of my platoon did that out in the bush, although some bought the junk to take to the rear.

The villes, small communities of thatched straw hooches, had no electricity, running water, bathrooms, or even motorized vehicles. The people of the villes showed no fear of us; some showed approval and others resentment. A village chief, usually respected by everyone except the Viet Cong, led each ville. I am sure the VC learned much about our tactical maneuvers by seemingly innocent conversations with the chiefs.

We occasionally encountered children with missing limbs or scarred faces. Some of their wounds had been inflicted by the VC in order to bring a family under submission to the communists.

Very brutal, the VC would stop at nothing to accomplish their ultimate goal of total domination. The Viet Cong supposedly were South Vietnamese who fought for the communists. Actually, they were ordinary people like us who had been indoctrinated by some communist politburo which needed pawns to fulfill its ambitions.

We marines acted as mere pawns as well, quite dispensable and molded in our thinking to believe like the VC, that our side was righteous and just. For that and many other reasons, I had respect for the VC.

We and the VC had sort of an unwritten truce which placed the villes off limits to fighting. I knew of many instances; however, that one side or the other broke that truce. In the immediate region, at least, we both kept it. That implied truce meant that outside of a ville's borders, either entering or leaving, we could expect to engage in a firefight.

Even though we would be as prepared as could be— mentally as well as physically—for an anticipated attack, a firefight always caused a sudden and tremendous rush of adrenaline that knew no limits and had no mercy.

One such firefight occurred on a mini-operation from Hill 124. While passing through a ville, some of the boys had bought tiger uniforms, a type of camouflage fatigues that were a novelty. This striped uniform had been introduced by the Special Forces and worn by the South Vietnamese in the earlier years of the war.

After making the purchases, we were offered and shared a hot meal with the locals—good and spicy, just the way I liked it. I guess we seemed pretty content with our tummies nice and full. As we exited the ville, I noticed a Buddhist temple nearly in ruins—very picturesque. Out of the corner of my eye, I made sure I did not break formation and that no one else did, either. Out of the left flank, from the temple itself, gunfire exploded, "Pop-pop-pop......pop-pop......pop-pop-pop...... rat-a-tat-a-tat-tat!"

Immediately, I found myself out of the road, off to one side, and returning fire. The men of our platoon moved briskly. Either we were quick or the enemy ranks held poor marksmen. Amazingly, none of us received a hit. We returned fire longer than necessary so we would not have to chase the "gooks." After a few minutes, the VC high-tailed-it out of there with us trying to catch them. Although we usually chased them, we seldom caught them.

The only way I can describe the rush I felt in a firefight is to compare it to an automobile accident, except that this accident happened very often in the Vietnam jungles, and it had good chances of reoccurring the very next minute, every minute of the day. When we reported the firefight, our crazy lieutenant told us how he wished that he had been there.

After coming and going around the villes, we headed back to the jungles. I guess we were supposed to make Charlie (the VC) know that we were there and try to scare him. Actually, neither he nor we were really ever scared of each other. We soldiers often joked about those rear echelon warriors who created all the stupid tactics for us out on the front lines.

On the day after the firefight by the temple, before we hit the jungles, we made our way through some rice paddies filled with knee-to thigh-deep water and surrounded by mud dikes. The Vietnamese fertilized their rice crops with water buffalo dung, so when one of us had fallen in the paddies, everyone knew about it by the way we smelled.

Maneuvering through the paddies was tricky. For obvious reasons, we would rather walk on the dikes than in the water, but that made us easy targets. Also, the VC often booby-trapped the dikes. If a round went off or an explosion sounded, we all made a quick dive off to one side into that water. I hated that stench-filled water more than anything. Open wounds soaked in that sewage meant instant infection.

At times, the jungle seemed like an old, familiar, friendly place; while in reality, it was always very hostile. Because of the rice paddies, it was easier than in our last operation to see where Charlie had been. But as always, our senses must stay sharp and keen.

A squad ahead of us had radioed a report of movement. Mackovich got so excited that he wanted to talk to everyone at once, so he called us together. The mistake of clustering us just invited Charlie to a turkey shoot. This made all of us mad at Mackovich, but that was not anything unusual.

I could tell that Mackovich was really starting to get on Doc Potter's nerves, so I volunteered to Joshua (Potter) to go out on patrol with his squad even though I also was having a little trouble taking Mackovich's foolishness.

After completing the patrol, walking back to our hill seemed like such a relief. I imagine we must have covered from seven to ten miles a day. Measuring the distances in metrics, a kilometer was a *click* and a meter was a *mike*.

"Our" hill was named 124 because the topographical map labeled it as such. The number corresponded to the number of feet of altitude above sea level at the top of the hill. Walking up that hill normally seemed like nothing, but after the patrol, all of us were dead dog tired.

At top of the hill, we spied a new toy, a personnel carrier

called a "husky," which was basically an oversized pickup truck whose front was flush with the cab like a Volkswagen. It rolled on tracks instead of tires, made lots of noise, and gave us an invigorating ride.

The next morning, I went on a water run with the husky. At first, I tried sitting down in the back, but was bounced several feet up in the air, nearly being thrown out. The only safe way to travel was standing up, leaning against the cab. These amphibious huskies did not need any roads; however, while bouncing around in the back, I wished the driver could have found a road once in a while.

I rode as an armed guard—like shotgun on a stagecoach—on these runs. Hanging on for dear life, I often thought back to the weathered, smelly, animal-of-a-corpsman I had met on my first day in Vietnam and realized that I had become the marine I never intended to. However, I sure had a lot of fun doing it. Initially, I had resisted being "gungie," or enthusiastic over military duties. My delight in being an armed guard on that Huskie made me realize that I actually enjoyed being gungie.

While the choppers were being readied to recover all the weaponry and equipment on the hill, we decided to have a field day test-firing the weapons. It reminded me of going to the New Mexico State Fair. I got to shoot the M-60 machine gun— the platoon wanted to make sure that, in a pinch, I would be able to pull my own weight. Also, I was permitted to fire mortar rounds, throw hand grenades, shoot the M-79 grenade launcher (the blooper) and the LAAW, the classiest weapon ever.

LAAW stood for Land and Anti-Aircraft Weapon. It comprised a fiberglass tube weighing less than five pounds which telescoped on itself. A marine pulled it out to make it longer, took off the covers, opened the safety, aimed, and fired. With a loud blast, the self-contained rocket usually hit its target almost immediately and sent it to smithereens.

I never had a chance to fire the 106 mm recoilless rifle. This tool of destruction looked like a ten-foot long canon sitting on a tripod. The 106 mm round had a casing with multiple holes in it which allowed a lateral blast out the rear of the "rifle." This, in turn, allowed the same force to come out of both ends at the same time, making it recoilless. This gadget definitely could not be hauled around on the back of the average grunt, as it weighed several hundred pounds.

"Beehive" rounds were the favorite of the 106ers. Instead of an exploding projectile, the head of a beehive round opened up and sent thousands of nail-like darts to pierce the surround- ings of its target—very painful, I'd guess.

Lieutenant Winter was finally left in charge without Lt. Jones, as Jones had completed his duty out in the bush. Lieutenant Jones struck us as a "regular ol' Joe," while Lt. Winter had been a "spit and polish" lifer. Even though we tried not to like the new LT, he actually grew on all of us after a while.

The brass sent us on more patrols and more ambushes, and most of the time, I went with Mackovich because of the clash between him and Doc Potter. On one such ambush, Mackovich decided he was too tired to walk to the planned destination and fraudulently called in false "sit reps" (situation reports).

Mackovich had called in the false report just as we neared the foot of Hill 124 and started following his order to set up an ambush (of sorts.) As we proceeded, our guys at the top of the hill with their starlight scopes spotted movement at the bottom of Hill 124. They began pounding what they thought was enemy movement with 60 mm mortar rounds. In panic, we scrambled for cover.

Mackovich placed himself on my dirt list with indelible ink for making such a stupid decision for the sake of his indolence. There is no feeling comparable to that of mortar rounds landing and exploding next to you—especially when you know the rounds have been fired by your friends. Fortunately for us, the uneven terrain provided easy-to-find protective cover.

That night after the firing subsided, I prepared my bed, which consisted of a flak jacket spread open on the ground. The jacket served as a mattress for my torso, and a canteen became my pillow. I had to cover myself with my poncho liner because of the mosquitoes, not to stay warm. I wore a billed cap in order to keep a small air space for breathing within the poncho liner, since everything else was covered. My hand usually lay on top of my weapon, ready for action. By that time in my overseas adventure, it did not take much to awake me.

Sometimes, a shift in the wind, a breaking twig, or a rustle in some distant bush was enough to cause me to open my eyes and tighten my finger on the trigger. At that point of my year in 'Nam, I dreamed absolutely nothing. My personal thoughts had also vanished—I ceased to philosophize or contemplate anything at any time.

Morning appeared, and the mortar barrage seemed like something that had occurred in the distant past. The hike back up Hill 124 was becoming a game. Some of us actually raced the distance against the grade of the hill at a full run. One-hundred and twenty-four feet above sea level equals about twelve stories. Racing up a twelve-story building would add hair to anyone's chest.

The marines who had not been on patrol had completely torn down the bunkers on the hill by the time we returned. A few scattered poncho hooches were the only source of shade. A huge pile of wooden boxes which contained various types of explosives stood at the center of the hill. These were called "retro gear." (I always wondered but never knew what that meant.) A net covered the pile, making the gear ready to be easily lifted by a helicopter. However, due to the heavy rainfall at the beginning of the monsoon season, we experienced a lack of chopper flights, so the "retro gear" just sat there.

Lieutenant Winter decided to leave about six of us on the hill while the rest of the platoon moved to another hill, Hill 111, about three clicks (more than a mile) away.

Guess which squad he picked to leave. Mackovich was determined to do things right even though by that time, most of us had begun to ignore him. The rest of the platoon departed, leaving our squad and the huskies.

The huskies crew had prepared the vehicles to be returned to the rear but they offered to take a few of us out on another water run. I decided to go, as I had a feeling I would experience some kind of action out there. The vehicle bounced down to a nearby stream.

The rain had caused everything to become one giant mud bath. The husky slid several times, almost capsizing. We had finished filling up water cans at a distant stream when a radio message reported an assault on Kilo 2 alpha squad—our little group from the hilltop! We boarded the huskies and could not move back up the hill fast enough. While hauling it as fast as we could, I envisioned the squad being overrun, and my heart beat like a jack hammer.

On arrival, I jumped out of the husky and saw two men down with the remaining two marines holding about ten alleged VC at gun point. I asked, "What happened?"

"They got Lizzio and Johnson," they replied.

"With what?" I asked.

"Concussion grenades," they answered.

Looking at the ten Vietnamese, I filled with rage and reached for my rifle to mow down the scum who had killed the men I was responsible for. Seeing what I was about to do, one of the two marines keeping guard jumped in front of the Vietnamese and yelled, "No!"

Then I removed my foggy, rain-splattered eyeglasses only to discover that these ten enemy men were just children. With mixed emotion, I just stood there with my trigger finger still preparing to open fire. After approximately twenty to thirty seconds, the full impact of what I had about done hit me like a lead balloon. I had almost committed an atrocity.

The muzzle of the M-16 slowly bent toward the muddy ground. Since I heard only the sounds of my rapidly beating heart, I didn't notice the slowly progressive movements of Lizzio and Johnson. Thankfully, Lizzio and Johnson had not died, as was evidenced by their sitting up, half dazed.

One of our men yelled, "The kids were selling us Cokes, but some VC out in the bushes threw a grenade at us." Cold sweat poured out of my pores, even though it was raining. I became weak and nauseated, quivering. It was as if I had actually opened fire on the innocent children.

The border between duty and criminal action is so thin and at times, ill-defined. Thank God for that brave young soldier who stood in my way. Lizzio and Johnson both sustained minor concussions and nothing else. The huskies departed that evening, carrying the village children in for questioning. We passed a silent, placid evening.

Three days passed and the rains continued. We had to remain on Hill 124 as security until the choppers could make it in. Mackovich remained afraid and anxious to the point of being dangerous. One small grenade on the big pile of retro gear could send half the hill to Hong Kong.

Earlier, Mackovich had bought some OB and had saved it for when he needed to keep himself awake. OB was an amphetamine for weight control but it sold as a street drug in the black market. By the fourth night, after not sleeping for over seventy-two hours, Mackovich collapsed. It was about that time that we received communication about movement toward our area. An American marine patrol on another hill said they saw half a dozen or so VC bee-lining it towards our position.

With Mackovich out, we needed a squad leader, so I decided to play a bluff. Taking the remaining five of our squad, I positioned each in different spots telling them to move about frequently and to talk out loud. If fire broke out, each was to fire his weapon from a different location every few rounds or so. We waited anxiously.

Finally, we spotted what we thought were VC. I gave the signal to start some activity. We shot a few flares up in the air and then we began moving about. Just then, a bullet hit the dirt right in front of me. That was all it took! "Fire!" I yelled.

The Fourth of July commenced. Very little fire returned. Either they did not like the show or we had decommissioned the enemy. Body counts were rare since the VC always tried to take their dead with them so we could not boast of the number of enemy dead. After the short firefight, examination of the troops proved none of us had been hurt.

When the shooting stopped, Mackovich finally woke up, just as I was placing a sit rep to the lieutenant. The LT ordered Mackovich to give the report himself. Of course he could not accurately say anything, so we helped him out by telling him exactly what to say. After the report, Mackovich told us he would tell the lieutenant everything, give up the squad, and accept a demotion.

From that point forward, we all began to like (or at least tolerate) Mackovich. Also, after that incident, Mackovich, the clown, ceased to appear so foolish, and blended in with the rest of his fellow marines—finally.

Chapter 3
Friendship

The following day, the lieutenant and another squad ventured back to our hill to find out what damage we had done. We were out of food, so he was a welcome sight. Also, the choppers came that day to pick up our beloved treasure—good riddance! I think we had grown attached to that hill, but joining the rest of the platoon was consolation. It was like a reuniting with your family—a sort of homecoming. The chopper airlifted the retro gear, and then we ate some food and set out to our new home.

Within sight of Hill 124 and pretty much out in the open, sat our new little hill. It made a terrific target since it was located in a big valley. Oddly enough, no one ever attacked us on that little knoll. But on that new height, something else changed in my life as a grunt. A new experience occurred; a strange animal known as friendship was born.

Well into my second month in Vietnam, I had already learned not to make friends because I did not want a reoccurrence of the experience with my friend, Dino. I did not want to endure that type of loss again. I had hardened my heart, leaving very little room for feelings. Although I did encounter friendship that second time, my heart never did cease to be as cold as steel.

Mike Pulos unwittingly called himself "Mike the Greek." At first I could not stomach the creature. He was short, muscular, and very cocky. He grew a mustache and called it a name he adopted from Agatha Christie's detective character, Hercule Perot. Mike read ardently, with his favorite author being, of course, Agatha Christie. I guess that embarrassed me, since I seldom read anything unless assigned to.

Mike had just been transferred from the 5th Marine Division, who were staging down in preparation to return to the States. The brass had transferred all marines with less than nine months in country.

The 5th Marines had seen substantially more action than we had, since they had been out in the Que Son mountains, also known as Indian Country. Mike really resented being stationed with us, it seemed, and he offered nothing but criticism about everything and everyone in our unit.

Mike gave everyone a hard time, heaping his off-color insults with just enough edge to get their goats. I may have been the only one to call his bluff. I really do not know why, but that newcomer did not get to me at all. Mike, an "older" grunt, being twenty-one and a college drop out like me, was a radioman and probably the best any of us had seen.

After several weeks of heaping insults upon each other, arguing, and just being a pain in the neck to each other, Mike and I began communicating like real human beings. Out in the bush on patrols, ambushes, or more mini-operations, Mike proved himself to be a very capable and reliable soldier with keen senses, lacking fear but not acting foolishly.

Since I did not tolerate any type of mediocrity myself, I eventually gravitated towards friendship with Mike. He resisted the pull as much as I did, but after a while, we both appreciated the luxury of having someone to talk to.

The most difficult part of my corpsman job had become not being granted the privilege of talking with or confiding in anyone because I was considered "the support unit." Most of the platoon depended upon me to be available for their wounds, infections, hurts, and heartaches, but most were too numbed out and emotionally drained to befriend the Doc.

About that same time, Doc Potter received his orders to go back to the rear. At first, I thought that he had put in six months out in the bush, but as it turned out, Potter had only spent a total of about three and one-half months with the grunts in the bush. There never has been any logic to military thinking and there probably never will be.

The brass pulled out Doc Potter without any replacement, which left me as the only corpsman with my platoon. That meant that I would have to participate in all patrols and all ambushes, without any breathing time back at the command post (CP).

As the resupply chopper landed to pick up Potter, I eyed with envy the Texan admired and respected by everyone. As he was about to board, Potter grabbed my hand and gave me a solemn look. "Give 'em hell......stay alive." I raised my hand and gave him the thumbs up sign. My sole support was leaving; I must accept that as a way of life out here.

The choppers played Santa Clause each time they arrived. They brought food, mail, ammo, sometimes medical equipment, and occasionally clothes. The clothes, somehow, were never new, but at least they smelled clean, and we acted like little waifs when the goodies arrived. We each, more or less, dug for our size of clothes and socks in a big pile tossed on the ground. Then we exchanged our dirty, torn uniforms so someone could launder or trash them.

A month or more always passed before our supply of clean, used, or patched battle gear arrived. We marines used camouflage uniforms, but after a week or two in the bush, they appeared earthen brown and void of the camouflage look.

My requests to the rear for medical supplies were seldom

completely filled, but fortunately, I had connections back at Long Beach Naval Hospital. It seemed crazy that I could get supplies quicker from California than from Da Nang. Also, I received CARE packages from other friends almost weekly and from my family once a month. As soon as food arrived in these packages, I always shared it.

We all valued pre-sweetened, ready-to-mix Kool Aid more than any other article received. One could easily sell a one-quart package of Pre-sweetened Kool Aid Mix for five or ten dollars. All we ever had to drink was stale water and the coffee and cocoa that accompanied our C-rations.

No one shared his Kool Aid with anyone—no one except Mike and I. We thought it idiosyncratic of the Vietnam war that the main sign of true friendship was the sharing of Kool Aid.

On the day of resupplying, we enjoyed preparing a huge banquet. Several of the young warriors grouped together and combined foods into a type of Mulligan Stew. Our steel pot helmets served as cooking vats. Each little gathering created its own recipe. Sampling each other's concoction put us in hog heaven. Enjoying eating reminded us that we actually did belong to the human race.

Letters, our main link to sanity, didn't arrive often enough; we indulged and memorized each letter the minute it arrived. Due to the reality of the ever-present war, after we read our letters, we had to burn them. The VC loved to find a letter with a return address on it so they could send messages of harassment home. We had enough trouble keeping the horrors of that madness out of our correspondence without worrying whether Charlie would add to the havoc back home. To this day, I recall many of those letters that I memorized.

Out in the bush, time had its own peculiar way of manifesting itself. We hardly ever counted days as days, for we did not think of time in relation to days. Rather, each moment held

Too much Tobasco maybe?

its own uniqueness. If the next hour passed without incident, we were grateful. We anticipated the worst and expected nothing in our daily existence. I thought of time as increments of a set unit: the daylight increments and the nighttime increments.

The only full day I had to be aware of was Sunday. Each Sunday, I distributed malaria pills to each of my men, and I had to sit and watch each and every one of those babies swallow his pill. Some marines did not want to take their medicine because of the tummy ache or a little diarrhea that it caused. However, I allowed no one to be overlooked, even if it meant cocking my pistol and making that individual gulp the tablet at gunpoint.

At night, the marines operated killer team patrols with fewer than six men in an ever-moving sweep to flush out the enemy. Some other company nicknamed us Killer Kilo, and the name affected the VC.

The KC scouts told us that the VC feared us and thus avoided contact with us. That became evident as the frequency of our firefights lessened; then our patrols tried to intensify to further scare Charlie.

On one such patrol in the deep jungles, we operated a two-day killer team ambush patrol. Somewhat craving for action— the addiction had already taken hold of me—I chose to walk point. As mundane as walking point might seem to the average civilian, I assure you that I found nothing mundane about it. I reviewed the coordinates with the lieutenant before venturing out early in the morning.

The map gave no indication of any trails; it just showed hill after hill. These topographical maps never showed what type of vegetation grew in a certain place or whether we should expect a swamp, a sand dune, or a rock pit. We had to always keep in mind that the maps were produced above the tops of the trees, by aerial reconnaissance only, leaving out the ground factor.

U.S. geological maps indicated streams, trails, swamps, forests and even buildings. These maps of Vietnam only told us, more or less, where we were in relation to the next hill or the ocean; very basic.

I will always remember the intensity of heading out into the jungle. Walking up the hills with all sorts of vines, thorny bushes, trees, and a never-ending supply of elephant grass in our faces made travel slow. That was acceptable as long as we found no booby traps.

The point man decided on which side of the growth to walk, when to advance, and when to stop. The rest of the team relied on him to catch most of the trip wires that detonated the anti-personnel mines. After spending some time out in the bush, a soldier always developed a sort of sixth sense. That sixth sense enabled even a city slicker to develop expert survival skills on the front.

The heat and humidity caused human skin to be more susceptible to the cuts and pricks that accompanied almost every foot of the jungle. My glasses constantly filled with sweat and steam, which clouded my vision. Pulling myself up by grabbing hold of a branch, discovering too late the thistles that covered it, was the rule rather than the exception.

My eyes constantly searched up and down, then side to side for the enemy, for booby traps, and for snakes, as deadly as any planted explosive. We had to learn about the two stepper, a bright green bamboo viper. The boa constrictor and the cobra required no introduction.

Usually, when we were out on patrol, someone back at the CP would monitor our movement. We filled radio messages with codes. On certain days, we used a special, wheeled decoder that changed letters into numbers in order to give our location according to the grid marks on the map. If we misplaced the decoder, we used the words "black horse" as a code, because of its ten letters.

The radio language was also unique. The military alphabet was alpha, bravo, Charlie, delta, echo, gulf, and so forth. Suggesting various innuendoes using military format became an art. Mike developed into a genius—a true artist—at that feat.

"Roger, this is alpha 1-6 in for a Romeo Charlie; how do you copy?"

"I copy you, luscious Charlotte…" and so on. This meant I was checking in for a radio check, and Mike communicated that he could hear me loud and clear.

On that particular day, after several hours of trudging through the underbrush, my hands swollen from the puncture wounds and my forearms bleeding from the multiple superficial cuts of the elephant grass, I decided to stop for a break. After sitting still for a few moments, we heard a very slight rustle through the grass.

We seasoned veterans all turned in unison, with our weapons aimed at the origin of the muffled noise. The green troops froze, wondering what was going on. We always seemed to ignore the new guys. Juan Gallegos moved quickly towards the suspected spot, with the rest of our fine-tuned squad encircling the area. We saw no VC—apparently they left in a hurry. The prospect of encountering the enemy excited us even more, so we quickly ended the break, proceeding quickly in pursuit of a real body. Again, we tramped through the thick, thick jungle.

A good length of time passed in the pursuit. Almost giving up out of exhaustion, I stopped to contemplate my next move. Out the corner of my eye, I saw something moving. It appeared yellow and big—*naw*, it couldn't be anything. It was something! This time, with my eyes fixed upon the position, I spotted a yellow hammock. Frozen still, and with the rest of the team following suit, I carefully and very slowly crept in the direction of the hammock.

After a few minutes which seemed like a few hours, we had crawled within visual distance of a VC camp! My heart pounded so loud that I thought everyone would hear it. Ready to shoot and ready to yell, I wondered what I would actually do. That blasted adrenaline was pumping through me like a fire hose. "Chu Hoi!" I screamed.

I had wanted to say, "Surrender!" Instead I said, "Open arms!" Chu Hoi was a program which recruited VC to become Kit Carson scouts. They got the message anyway. In an instant, my whole team was in the camp, a rifle aimed at each VC. We had captured four of Charlie and they held their hands high in the air. This time there was no rage or anger to cloud my head. We called in choppers to take these men for interrogation.

"Good job," everyone congratulated me—what a relief to finally redeem myself. I had not forgotten those ten kids back at Hill 124.

The relative simplicity of the VC camp did not surprise us. Their supplies had to be brought in by foot. Most of their food came from local villages, but the VC humped in the bulk of the rice from villages of key communist sympathizers. We never knew which villages these were.

The VC cooked their rice over small, open fires, giving off little smoke. Most of their equipment consisted of weaponry which they placed in various designated caches. This allowed for a quick grouping of VC to set up an attack and a way for quick retreat. They hid their weapons, and that allowed them to disperse without being questioned since they could be mistaken for local farmers. Their sleeping places were comfortable hammocks with ponchos for when it rained. After fifteen years of fighting the French and Americans, our enemy had jungle warfare completely figured out.

The choppers arrived, and we loaded Charlie on board. We decided to stay at the VC camp a while to pick up any stragglers. Actually, we just sat and relaxed for a moment. Juan Gallegos from the Los Angeles area, stayed with us. He had been trained in a CAG unit like his compatriot, Jose Gonzales. Juan was not an enthusiastic commando like Jose, but more relaxed and down-to-earth. He stood out, however, as an outstanding marine, and having him along comforted us.

Sitting in the VC camp, we envisioned ourselves as Viet Cong. Compared to these poor souls, we led a plush life. Their small, meager bowls of rice left a lot to be desired in a square meal, even if the meal was just C-rations. Their Ho Chi Minh sandals were cut out of old tires, with rubber straps wedged into the soles. Most of the VC did not wear uniforms nor black pajamas, as we had been told by the ever-knowing rear echelon. They wore the clothes all other Vietnamese wore. Sometimes they did have black pajama-type clothes, but so did other non-VC. Some donned the traditional straw hat because of its practicality in that particular environment.

Viet Cong usually carried bolt-action, Czechoslovakian SKSs or Chinese Communist (Chicom) AK-47's. On many occasions, however, they used American M-16s, since these were more plentiful and ammunition more easily accessible. They usually captured the M-16s from ARVN (Army of the Republic of Vietnam) soldiers or bought them in the black market. The VC often humped rice sacks weighing up to a hundred pounds for many miles at a time so they could eat. Our respect definitely went out to these "little people."

It was a no-show for the expected stragglers, but they probably knew what was going on, as the VC almost always seemed to. We had to move our position that evening so that we would not be captured.

The rains poured that night and for many nights following.

While a marine was on his watch in the rain, he wore his poncho with the hood on. It was quite cozy under that thing. Also under the poncho, even in a deluge of rain, the never-ending nocturnal mosquito kept us company. We hated those pests.

When we lay down to sleep, we placed our insulated poncho liners under the poncho and covered ourselves. Usually, a puddle accumulated under us. I slept on one side one night and the other side the next to alternate sides under water. It is no wonder that to this day, my joints still become stiff very easily.

Every night in the bush, minutes advanced very slowly. Although often sleepy, the sobering thoughts of getting my neck slit or being caught off guard in an assault kept me wide awake. I always welcomed the dawn. It meant I was not dead nor unconscious but still alive, though in the style of Dante's inferno. Dawn also meant that I would have to try to survive another day. Surviving the day was not really a primary thought; rather, getting through the next moment.

As the sun tried to show its scorching face, I noticed a body (of sorts) moving through the bush in front of me—a rock ape. "It's payback time!" I thought. I still had not forgiven the one that threw the frag back at me when I first arrived in Vietnam. I took out my .45 and fired a round. The ape was still moving.

"Bang, bang!" Two more shots. The beast was still alive.

"Bang, bang, bang, bang!" The .45 magazine held only seven rounds.

I waited a few moments while reloading to see if there was any movement. Nothing. It appeared safe to go and see what I had just terminated, as stories I had heard many stories about rock apes that had beaten up soldiers and left them in very bad shape.

As I made my way through the brush, I kept my eyes out for VC. No one could rest from anticipating an assault from the enemy, even if he was having a little fun for a brief second. To my surprise I found nothing! There was a little blood but no monkey. I was looking forward to getting about three hundred dollars from a local ville for the medicinal monkey meat. The Vietnamese believed the monkey meat carried healing properties and were more than willing to pay well for it.

What had happened? The .45 had been designed during World War II to stop the Filipino mountain men, a stout people who did not succumb to conventional weapons. Seven rounds and nothing? I would have expected that of a gorilla but not a mere monkey. I guess I was no Joshua Potter who could shoot the head off of a cobra at thirty feet. In any event, everyone awoke and, as usual, no one made a big deal of all the gunfire. We seemed to know without a word whether it was appropriate to get excited.

The rains of the night before made it another humid, hot day. We made our way back to Hill 111 by way of many swamps and jungle. If we saw a swamp in front of us we did not question whether to walk around it or through it; the answer was always through it. Whenever I walked up on a swamp, I wondered about its depth and which deadly creatures we would discover in it. Usually the swamps were waist to chest deep and about fifty feet in length. Sometimes during a very hot day, the swamp was the only thing cool we encountered.

Evening arrived after what seemed like an eternity. We still had not reached the hill. We set up another ambush since we were too tired to run a night patrol. None of us really slept much that night, sensing an uneasiness out in the periphery. We felt movement, but where?

Our trainers had told us that the enemy could smell Americans because of the food we ate. Well, the same was true on the other side of the coin. We could smell them for the fish and spices they ate. That night, all six of us detected the fish-like scent of the VCs. We also heard the quiet crushing of grass and the brushing of branches against clothing.

Suddenly we realized that we had positioned our ambush wrong! The VC trail passed about twenty feet from our position. The frustrating part of the whole mess was that we could not move to better our position since that would likely cause us to walk into one of their ambushes.

As the slow, slow minutes passed, it became obvious that the movement we were so anxious to confront was no small VC squad. More and more bodies moved through the grass and thick jungle only a few feet in front of us. Closer and closer they got to us. Then a flank of them walked right into our ambush. What should we do? We were ridiculously outnumbered; to engage meant suicide, but not to engage meant capture.

Juan Gallegos broke the silence and yelled, "Make a run for it—south!"

Taking only our weapons, in one accord we dashed southward. Running, tripping, getting slapped and cut by branches made invisible in the pitch black of the night, we ran hard and furiously.

Gunfire erupted! Tracer rounds passed around us as we came up on a rocky slope. It felt as though we were being chased by a thousand NVA regulars; we heard and felt the intimidating pounding of their Ho Chi Minh sandals at our heels. Remembering what the Kit Carson scouts had taught us, we hid between the rocks. Someone who resembled Juan stood and threw a grenade down to the bottom of the hill.

"Boom!" I knew then that he was trying to make it look as though one of us had tripped a booby trap down there to cause the enemy to overlook our meager protection.

I tried to sit motionless, hiding between two undersized boulders, but I quivered down to my toes. I thought of my life in the world and how meaningless it had seemed. I thought of the impending eternal God I might meet at any moment. The thought of eternity frightened me; I did not want to go just yet.

My family came to mind. My mother and father always thought that I would finish college; now they would ponder on what they did wrong to lose me. The mystery of my death would haunt them forever. My sister and her husband, Tom, came to mind, with their new baby, Leonard who would never know his uncle. Then I thought of my dear brother, Edward.

Tears began to flow. We had been so close; I dearly loved my brother. How could I do this to him? I had wanted to come to this place for the "adventure." Yeah, sure! What a letdown I had been to my family and to God.

I was so scared; it felt like I had not breathed a single breath. The sound of the Ho Chi Minh sandals on the rocks made it seem like at least a hundred NVA were searching for us. How many were really there? Because of my limited field of vision, I wanted to stick my head out from between the rocks to find out, but dared not move my head. In the darkness of the night, I imagined the worst.

My mind played tricks on me. Had my eyes seen the North Vietnamese regulars all looking at me? I blinked constantly to bring myself to reality. The specter of the obscurity of the night causes fear in all humans.

I expected but heard no shouts, no voices of American prisoners. In what seemed like an eternity, the enemy's swarming all around us slowly faded until there was dead silence, except for the usual sounds of the jungle. Still, I dared not move.

More time passed, and my bones became stiff and achy. When could I, or rather, when would I move? I could not tell by the night sounds of the jungle whether or not the enemy was still out there. My eyes continued to deceive me as visions of figures permeated the darkness.

After many hours had surely passed, I made myself move my stiff body out of the rocks and see what was out there. The dawn, in its cool dampness had already begun to appear. My joints hurt with each attempted movement. On a rock, Juan sat staring into the brush below.

"Where's everyone?" I asked. Juan continued to stare. As I looked around, each member of that "killer" team slowly crawled out of his hiding place and made way for our position. The sun was already up by the time all had presented themselves. That morning we spoke very few words, if any. After we thought we had collected ourselves, we returned to our original ambush site, attempting to recover at least some of our equipment. We definitely would not want to have had the radio taken by the NVA.

The surrounding area looked quite different during the day than it had in the darkness. At the ambush site, surprisingly enough, we found everything we had left in our flight, including the radio. Where did the NVA go? Why did they not return? How many of them were there? Why were we still alive? These philosophical questions would be thought of and asked by each of us at a different time and in a different country.

As we marched back to Hill 111, fatigue began to set in. Sometimes it seemed possible to sleep while walking, but that was more imagined than real. My eyes closed and for only a brief moment, a short period of rest ensued. I had been deceived into thinking that I actually had slept, if only for a short while.

Off in the distance, we heard an air attack: the driving cobra gunships using their "mini" guns in a continuous, loud, low roar. I could not help but wonder why the name, "mini," since the guns were Gatling guns mounted on the helicopters. Those guns could fire eleven-hundred rounds each minute, which is more than eighteen rounds per second. In the dark, the gunfire looked like a red beam of light, with every fourth round a tracer round. Our radio did not intercept any information about what was going on, but it took no genius to figure out that our pursuers had found themselves in big trouble.

Hill 111 was finally within sight, and soon Killer Kilo stood in front of the command post. After giving report of our little encounter and eating a tasteless C-rat dinner, I collapsed into a deep state of unconsciousness. When I awoke, rain poured and Mike cooked—I don't remember just what— probably some kind of stew. "Welcome to 'Nam, Doc. How about letting you and I drink some Kool Aid?"

Chapter 4
Settling In

That night the air activity continued as "bronco" airplanes dropped "basketball illums," very large flares with parachutes so bright that a person on the ground could read a newspaper by the light. The activity occurred at a distance, and we were not running any patrols in that area, so we remained ignorant of what transpired in the illuminated region.

That night Mike told me all about the characters in his Agatha Christy novels and about a few of his favorite stories. To this day, every time I see or hear anything about Hercule Perot or any other Agatha Christy character, I compare it to my first mental images formed that night.

I told Mike of various daydreams that I had developed over the years, mainly ideas of science fiction, like spaceless travel and a true perpetual motion machine. Also, about that time, I began to include a Mike character in a cartoon series I drew for the letters I sent home.

Also during the time period, our platoon began to receive a small but steady stream of replacements. Some of them had returned to Vietnam as second-tour vets. Two such newcomers, our platoon sergeant and the company gunnery sergeant, or "Gunny" as everyone referred to him, were Filipino.

Our platoon sergeant, Sgt. Tino, acted very unhappy about being back in "the 'Nam" but otherwise was an excellent soldier. However, the gunny, Ernesto La Fifi, proved to be one of the most outstanding men I have ever met. We called him Gunny La Fifi. La Fifi was a model of physical fitness, with noteworthy charisma and leadership. We all trembled in our boots when La Fifi gave us a silent stare. Marines "hopped to it" without question at his simplest command. La Fifi loved to be out with his men and patrolled with us when no other officer or NCO bothered.

Even with the influx of new bodies, it was business as usual—except they sent us on more operations and always to different locations. Our superiors suspended our "killer team" tactics for awhile. Increasing the numbers of troops running patrols seemed important again. Our leaders usually sent us out in one- and two-squad patrols.

Supplies arrived as long as the weather permitted, but the monsoon season had commenced so getting the choppers in was difficult. For mysterious reasons, contact with the enemy decreased. That did not deter our activity, however. We seemed to encounter casualties from natural causes almost as often as we had from Charlie in the past.

Some of the mishaps were absolutely ridiculous. In one instance, we were running a sweep through a narrow valley full of swamps. In the bush, everyone maintained silence all of the time, day or night—at least we were supposed to.

Once, as I walked through the deep mud, it became increasingly difficult to pick up my feet. After a few more steps, my right leg stuck and began to sink more with every effort I made to free it. After I had sunk to about waist deep, it finally dawned on me that I stood in quick sand. My initial instinct was to remain silent but the desire for survival got the best of me, and I shouted for help. I heard those behind and in front of me telling me, "Shhhhh shhhhh."

"I don't care about the noise; just get me outta here and *apurale* (Spanish for *hurry up*)!" I exclaimed.

My imagination went wild, thinking of the birds having a feast on my trapped body. Although three marines nearly pulled both of my arms out of their sockets, my comrades finally yanked me to safety.

"That's all we need, Doc, to lose you to quick sand. If it's not falling in a stream upside down, it's going down a cliff on a rope that's too short. Doc, you're gonna give all of us gray hair," Jose joked with me.

During the monsoon season, we continually waded through water, and some of the new guys had developed a cockiness about them as they refined their techniques for looking cool during a patrol. One such fellow, Private Coats, could walk through the water as if he were strolling down a sidewalk. One time, as Coats pranced through a stream like he owned it, he tripped and went under. None of us could keep a straight face. However, Coats had dropped his rifle and could not find it.

We continued our slow march and without thinking, left Coats behind. After all, he was only a new guy—but a smart one. As we broke trail from the stream and headed up the steep hill, we hit a dead end and decided to turn around. Returning down the same path, we heard noise. Cautiously, we approached the origin of the voice and prepared to spring an attack when someone commented loudly, "He's talking in English!"

All of a sudden, we saw Coats still looking for his rifle. When he had finally found it, he yelled an obscenity. As we approached him, Coats sarcastically remarked, "Thanks guys, for waiting for me." Angered at his carelessness and laughing at his foolishness, we kept quiet.

On returning from the patrol, we came upon some marines from our platoon who had stayed behind. They had decided they were tired of C-rations—which we all were—and went hunting. As we approached, we heard shooting and rushed toward the possible firefight, hoping to save our countrymen. We heard extensive gunfire, ranging from M-60 machine gun fire down to .45 caliber pistols. Our adrenaline pumped overtime. Upon arriving on the scene, we found our fellow grunts struggling to carry a 600-pound, wild boar.

"Is it safe to cook him, Doc?" they asked.

"What do you think, Doc?" Jose asked.

This huge, wild monster, with long tusks and sharp teeth had required at least forty M-16 rounds and several M-60 machine gun bursts to bring down. For a brief moment, the war seemed to take a back seat; preparing for a feast actually seemed like fun. As the hunter/soldiers scurried to build a pit fire to cook the beast, my thoughts quickly reflected back home to a matanza, where a family would butcher a pig or a goat and then invite friends for a party.

"We can eat him only if he's cooked to the bone," I remarked. Even with that recommendation, Lt. Winter did not permit us to do anything with the trophy. So much the better. I really had not wanted to chance our getting sick out here and then having to depend on each other while battling diarrhea or cramps.

Seeing our disappointment, Lt. Winter decided that we should test fire our weapons again, probably to prevent a mutiny. The lieutenant really did not know us as well as he thought he did. We would have never thought of, much less carried out, even the slightest resemblance of a mutinous act.

Mike challenged me to the mortar rounds. That really was not fair, since I had fired those things only once, and then, I nearly had blasted my fingers off. Someone fired a Willie Peter (white phosphorous) round, and declared that the closest mortar fired to the smoking round would win. I lost.

Sgt. Tino then spotted a deer out in the distance and tried to shoot it, but missed. Mike, the lieutenant, and everyone else also missed. After one single shot whistled out of my M-16's muzzle, the poor deer never knew what hit him. No stranger to deer hunting, I did not surprise myself. And no one ever regarded this Navy Corpsman any less a foot soldier from that point forward.

The shooting continued until a mishap befell one of the machine gunners. A gunpowder blast hit his face when the machine gunner's weapon went into a "cook off." This occurs when the barrel is so hot that a round being automatically inserted into the chamber fires prematurely and back blasts the person firing the weapon. I treated the marine with a little peroxide and he went on his way. However, that incident brought our entertainment time to an abrupt end.

A day or so later, a chopper arrived, surprising us all. As the huge, double-propped helicopter landed, we stared in confusion and wondered why we got the unexpected visit. Each time one of those things landed, it had sandblasted everything around with its typhoon-like wind.

Several young marines exited the chopper carrying three covered vats. Those "rear pogues," as we called them, appeared very unhappy at being sent out to serve us grunts. Gunny La Fifi had arranged for the rear echelon cooks to bring out T-bone steaks for our whole platoon. He had heard of our boar incident and rendered compassion on us. However, he bestowed absolutely no compassion on any of the rear personnel—they had to watch us eat.

We carried no mess kits or eating utensils, and the chopper had not brought any, so watching us eat was like viewing the Wild Kingdom lions consume a carcass. Our bellies went to hog heaven, and I can still vividly remember the taste of those steaks. They had not been grilled indoors, but had been sprinkled with spices and pepper for flavor. The gunny never slacked off at making sure that we were well taken care of. The only other item on the chopper was mail. The choppers would resupply other needs the following week.

After we finished devouring the steaks, and while some chewed the bones, Gunny La Fifi held a conference with the lieutenant and Sgt. Tino. The lieutenant's face looked excited while the sergeant's seemed worried—probably another operation, I thought. However, I reminded myself that the only thing worth paying any mind to was what was occurring in the present.

La Fifi then airlifted with the cooks to serve the other platoons, carrying steaks as well as that mysterious message. After they left, the area became very quiet, as we read our mail. We always read our letters immediately after receiving them, and told each other the highlights of our letters, sometimes even letting our "Ps" (slang for *partners* or *pals*) read them. Soldiers became essentially useless during those letter reading times.

One of the mortar team who hailed from the Caribbean, had been in the merchant marines before he enlisted in the Marines. His letters were very interesting, as his family's lifestyle was quite different from ours who were from the mainland.

We found that letters to the southern hill boys from states like Tennessee, Alabama, Georgia, and South Carolina were the most interesting. Even in their serious moments, their dialect had us in stitches. The few married men among us kept their letters very secret.

Some of the marines who had been "in country" for awhile often asked me to draw a cartoon or two for them, since they had the least to write in response to their loved ones' letters. The lover-boy types enjoyed flaunting their perfume-laden envelopes in front of us all; but as statistics would have it, the longer a man stayed in that pit called Vietnam, the less frequently those perfumed letters arrived.

The more I dwelled on it, the more it became obvious that being forgotten was the price paid for being patriotic and loyal to one's country. On arriving home, we discovered that most Americans of the era regarded us as outcasts. At least for the here and now, we could cling to each other. The present was our only reality.

Our dealings with the surrounding villagers had come to a halt; perhaps because of the incident with the children on Hill 124, or maybe because the NVA had moved into the ville's territory. We never found out.

Occasionally, we came upon small groups of farmers out in their fields. They seemed friendly, but we both remained suspicious of each other. Sometimes, the townspeople traded miniature bananas or small pineapples in exchange for a cigarette or two, but we thought it best not to carry on a conversation; likewise, they carefully did not answer any questions. One could readily see the uneasiness in the peasants who, at one time, had befriended us.

The days became routine again; running patrols still occupied our time. After a while, a marine could accurately guess where a booby trap might be planted. The VC adeptly created those mines, but eventually, their handiwork became predictable.

The NVA, however, comprised a mixed group of men, like the American military—some soldiers lacked combat experience and some were longtime vets, making them unpredictable. Actually, when we sensed the NVA to be near, we executed erratic, unusual patrols, causing our movement to be slower and forcing us to exhibit more caution than usual.

On one of those non-routine days, we patrolled past our old Hill 124, and at the foot of the hill, a small pond had positioned itself across the trail. Crossing it had never been a problem before, but on that particular day, the pond seemed deeper than usual. Instead of knee-deep, the water had become waist-high, which signaled us to prepare for monsoon season.

Before crossing the small body of water, the reformed Mackovich thought it wise to first throw a grenade into the water to test the pond for mines. He tossed the frag, and sure enough, it set off two additional blasts. We felt lucky to have been associated with the new Mackovich. Just as we recovered from the shock of what could have happened, formidable sounds greeted us—the sounds of blasts being spit from a hollow tube. That noise meant only one thing—incoming!

"Splash, splash, splash" Trying to get out of the water in a hurry reminded me of being chased (in a nightmare) by a monster and not being able to move my feet.

"BOOM! BOOM!" The mortar rounds hit all around us, and we laid low—the only protection possible when experiencing a mortar barrage. However, only five rounds bombarded us. The barrage must have come from a single assailant, as one person could carry only three to five rounds. The helmet of one of the marines earned a purple heart as it deflected a chunk of shrapnel. Another's flak jacket caught a couple of the flying metal pieces.

"Pump, pump, pump, pump," our hearts resounded in response to the adrenaline. Each of us had his own personal way of reacting in the aftermath of a little excitement. I usually got hungry, while Mike would want to take a leak. Regardless of what we did, caution always ruled. With each of us talking more rapidly than before and with unsteady movements, we pressed on.

I'm sure that we would each rather have gone back to the camp, but we patrolled on. The comedy of trying to guess where the mortar rounds originated took our minds off of our nervousness. Everyone was certain he knew from where the mortars were fired—and of course, the enemy never revealed the answer; Charlie just sat and waited for us to find him.

The day's strange weather made us edgy, too. In one

Get a load of this...
My dad got all bent outta shape cuz it rained after he washed the car. He says
they got over 0.75 inches or so. Wow!

Maybe I should change my socks more often.

moment, rain poured and in the next, hot steam rose from the ground. We welcomed the rains with their clouds because of the accompanying coolness. Although I had become well acclimatized, the heat, always seemed unbearable.

As expected, we never found our mortar man. Mike and I began pulling double watch with each other that night, just like some of the other men had already done. Double watch meant that Mike and I kept each other awake on his watch and on mine. We helped each other stay awake and stay alive. As friends, each day we continued our joking criticism of each other as a sort of protection against the possible grief that could follow if one of us became a statistic on the KIA or WIA list. But that night, there was no joking.

The night of double watches passed more securely than other nights had, since we executed our jobs with four eyes and four ears. Our hearing resembled a German shepherd's. Mike and I jumped at even the normal sounds of the animals that crept all around us, sounding like humans. Eventually, an animal would show itself or make a distinctive noise, and we would be relieved.

As usual, but especially that night, we allowed ourselves no talking and little moving. And of course, we battled those blasted mosquitoes. On each patrol, we continued the never-ending war with those God-forsaken pests. I will always hate them. Nevertheless, the whole patrol thought we would encounter more contact that night, but we never did.

At the appointed time, our weary patrol hesitantly and cautiously headed back to Hill 111, and my foot began to hurt. It felt like an ingrown toenail, but I was not absolutely sure. When we finally arrived at our base camp, I took off my boot. I had made it a rule to take off my boots for at least a ten minute period each day to avoid trench foot and for general hygiene. When I took off my boot, if my only other pair of socks was dry, I changed socks; otherwise, the ten-minute air treatment would suffice. I drew a cartoon for the incident which depicted the character which represented me finding plants and mushrooms growing from my feet.

That night as I took off my boot, I was somewhat apprehensive about what I would find. It had been more than a week since I had even unlaced one of my boots, breaking my own rule of pedal hygiene. On removing the wet boot from the painful foot, I discovered a sock full of blood.

"Oh no! I've been hit by shrapnel! Where's the hole?" I started to become faint, but bravely continued to conduct the exam. Then I removed the blood-soaked sock from my foot and cringed at the sight of the unexpected.

A fat leech had latched onto my ankle, and the loathsome creature had eaten itself to death. Most of the time, one had to put insect repellent on a leech or touch it with a lighted cigarette in order to extract it, but that gigantic parasite was so big that it just fell off. I do not know how it escaped getting squashed. I think there was probably another one that did explode, leaving all the blood. But finding the leech did not solve the mystery of the pain I felt. After further examination, I discovered that I had been right the first time—an ingrown toenail.

I decided to take care of it like the macho grunt that I was. Actually, my toe hurt so bad that I needed to do something with it immediately. I needed to cut out the nail, but I did not carry any local anesthetic such as Lidocaine or Novocaine.

I wondered, "What should I do?" Then I remembered my earlier days at Catholic mass—kneeling and sitting at the same time caused my legs to become numb. I would do that! I could kneel and sit on my foot to cause it to become numb, and then operate.

As I got situated, I took out my field surgical kit and

selected my instruments for the operation. The toe throbbed with extreme pain! I cleansed the toe as best I could, then knelt down, forcing my rump and my weight to rest on the foot with the throbbing toe. The foot was becoming numb all too slowly; then all of a sudden, I realized that the deadening process had worked. In a rush, I cut away the painful piece of my body. Then I stood up and the feeling began to return.

"Sit on it again," I thought. So I did. And sure enough, my foot went to sleep again. Actually, the pain did not go away altogether, but that was life in the bush. Drenched with perspiration, light headed, and gritting my teeth with pain, I finally completed the surgical procedure. For several days, I limped around like a cripple. However, in about a week, the lacerated phalanx had healed, and I walked normally.

Since our food supply was diminishing, and Mike knew the choppers were not running because of poor weather conditions, we began rationing our food. How we hated restricting the only enjoyment left in our lives!

Within a few days, the rain's fury had increased, with harsh winds like I had never seen—they called it a typhoon. The winds blew up to eighty miles an hour, carrying a nonstop deluge. To prevent our meager poncho hooches from blowing away, we had to tie them so low to the ground that the occupant would have to crawl on his belly to enter.

To walk was definitely a challenge. To be even partially mobile, one had to lean toward the wind at a 45-degree angle. Even at that angle, being tossed by the wind was the rule rather than the exception.

Gradually, we ate all of our food. Some tried boiling water with less than a morsel of food in the pot, trying to make the liquid seem like soup. The rest of us who had no food simply heated a little water to warm our stomachs for the little comfort it would render.

Two days had passed without a pause in that relentless storm. Then we monitored a radio message about a disaster. We understood that another platoon had a patrol out at the same time of the storm's onset. When they tried to cross the same pond that we had crossed when the mortar barraged us, the water was so high that it was practically impassable. In an attempt to cross, an unfortunate marine got caught in an undercurrent and couldn't be found.

We read the lieutenant's and the platoon sergeant's anxiety in the radio communication. After an hour or so of continuous suspense, they found their comrade, but it was too late—he had drowned. We knew of no way we could help them, even though Lt. Winter offered several times. Without a plan or an objective, he would have endangered his own men.

Three days passed ever so slowly. Finally, there seemed to be a break in the winds. Our hunger caused even the grass and trees to look appetizing. The water had soaked us so that our skin was blanched and wrinkled from our fingertips to our elbows and from our toes to our knees.

Then the order came for us to break camp. The Marines would airlift us out! In fewer than six minutes, everyone was packed and ready to go. Shivering, hungry, tired, and numbed, we waited for our chopper. Behind the sounds of the wind and the rain came the familiar, "Whap pa pa pa pa pa" sounds of the helicopter blades whirring in the distance.

Like little orphans, we stood waiting with anticipation for the overgrown grasshopper to land. The chopper touched down, bigger than life. We were headed back to the rear! It had been more than sixty days since any of us had showered, eaten a hot square meal that had not come from a can, with the exception of the steaks, or had even been indoors. Two months in the bush—was that the norm or an exception?

As I stood there watching and waiting, I felt my wet face

with its thick beard and realized that I had already forgotten what I looked like. The helicopter landed, and without the engines ever stopping, we boarded through the rear ramp in single file and in an orderly fashion. Solemn faces with an occasional half-hearted smile dotted the interior of the noisy but soberly taciturn aircraft. We were lifted up, as on angels' wings, out of that miserably wet, awful place.

Chapter 5
The Rear

The helicopter landed in the foothills somewhere west of Da Nang, at the base for the 3rd Battalion, 1st Regimen. Settled in, with its wooden and occasionally sandbagged buildings, the base had been there for about two and a half years. Khe Sahn and the Tet offensive of 1968 had become mere echoes in the memories of previous marines who had occupied these quarters.

We were relatively safe in that rear fortress, with racial quarrels among the ranks or an occasional sapper—a VC commando sabotage of a helicopter or a jeep—the only combat that occurred. We referred to the rear personnel, the marines who had rotated from the bush, and those whose jobs had kept them in the rear for their whole tour as "rear pogues." Because of potential strife between the grunts and the rear pogues, the brass separated us in our lodging and in the evening USO shows.

On arrival, we marched to our hooch, a plywood, tin-roofed building, with canvas cots lining the two sides of the length of its rectangular shape. Someone dumped a pile of clean clothes for us outside the showers, and in a very short time, the whole platoon was inside the shower building.

On the few mirrors inside, I watched the expressions on faces when the men first saw how they appeared. When I saw myself, it was like looking at a stranger. Who was that bearded, scroungy-looking man staring at my face?

After my heavenly shower, I borrowed some scissors to first cut the beard, and then a razor to shave it. After sifting through the pile of clean but worn uniforms, I found, more or less, the right size, and in the wave of a hand, I was a new man. Mike and I almost did not recognize each other.

Then we made a beeline to the chow hall. As we neared it, those in line stood off to one side and invited us to cut in. Actually, we would have cut in anyway, and they knew that. With our metal trays in hand, we demanded double servings. As we inhaled our food, we discovered that our eyes had been bigger than our stomachs. Rationing our meals to one and one-half meals per day out in the bush and being without food for more than three days had caused our stomachs to shrink. None of us could finish the food on his tray; regardless, we could justify the double servings.

At our table sat one of the KC scouts who had been wounded by the boobytrap that Dino had tripped. He showed us the scar on his belly, left after the operation. It covered half his abdomen. He acted glad to see us and told us that he had already been assigned to another unit, but that we were the best and he wished he was still with us.

That night, the USO show had been canceled because of the storm, but Gunny La Fifi brought several cases of beer to our hooch. We were all so worn out that few of us drank. To sleep indoors on a cot was like a fairy tale come true. Before long, the whole hooch was silent—except for the snoring.

The trumpet's sounding of reveille woke us the next morning. During the morning roll call, officers told us we had two days to spend in the rear before we returned to the field. For security reasons, they never told us where we would go, but the VC always knew, especially since many of them had mothers or sisters working for the marine officers as house maids and wash women. We did not care, however.

That day, as soon as we ate some real bacon and eggs, with real bread, and drank some real milk, we were out of there and off to Freedom Hill.

Going to Freedom Hill made us feel like humans again. It was an Air Force installation with a giant PX store, a bowling alley, a movie theater, a Chinese restaurant, a steam bath, and probably more. We never seemed to have enough time to see all of it.

We hitchhiked out to "the hill," which was no problem, since trucks and jeeps always stopped for us. Even though we had advanced to the rear, we were still in Vietnam and still needed our weapons.

The trip to Freedom Hill took us through the outlying villages of the outskirts of Da Nang. Along the way, we passed crowded Vietnamese homes. Little stands lined the road. The villagers sold food, clothes, and gasoline in soda bottles for the countless motor scooters that the locals used as a primary source of transportation.

Being just in from the bush, we felt uneasy about the crowded conditions. We feared we could be fired upon without ever knowing the origin of the sniper. It was a different world from that in bush, but the heat, humidity and some of the smells were the same.

Although ecstatic about the short but sweet rehab time granted to us, we did not talk much. The present—getting to Freedom Hill—was foremost on our minds. In other words, we did not even expect to arrive at "the hill" but would be glad if we did.

While riding in the back of a truck en route to Freedom Hill, I recalled a war movie in which the older soldiers told a new guy to whistle for a dog that was following them. This new guy thought that it would be nice to have a mascot, so he whistled, and as the dog approached their moving truck, a soldier took aim with his rifle and shot the dog. As we rode to Freedom Hill, a strange inclination came over me to pull the same stunt on one of our new guys, but I never saw a candidate dog. I knew for sure then, that the prophecy of that corpsman lying on the dirt floor of the hooch when I first arrived had truly come to pass.

We finally arrived at the haven of rest. Even as we jumped off of the large military truck, we automatically created a perimeter of protection like we were accustomed to doing when we disembarked from the choppers. At the gate, in order to enter, we were required to check our weapons. We found that extremely unnerving. To be without a "piece" was to be without a right arm. For each gun, the gatekeeper gave us a pink slip, which became worth more than the all money we carried.

Mike and I stayed together, along with a couple of other grunts with whom we had become close. It was like being a country kid attending a county fair. First we saw the PX, which was nothing more than a huge metal barn with too many booths crowded inside, selling absolutely useless junk. Then we passed jewelers with their watches and earrings for sentimental fools, Hong Kong tailors with their fancy suits for daydreamers, the electronics section with the latest in stereos for music connoisseurs, and of course, the portrait center for the rear echelon soldiers to have their only chance to be photographed wearing a phony helmet.

We saw much more, but it was all useless, cheap merchandise. For my mother, I managed to buy a pair of earrings—jade ones, which was her favorite stone. Embarrassingly enough, I also bought myself a Hong Kong suit that I never did wear since we were country bumpkins.

Next, we were off to the movies. "What show do you gutless swine wanna see?" asked Mike, with his usual mannerism.

"Let's see a real war movie," commented another.

"What are those like?" someone else quipped.

We all laughed. There was only one movie showing and I cannot remember its name. All I remember was that the show seemed to take place in the real world and we seemed to be the ones making believe. We had become accustomed to calling the U.S. the "world" or at times, the "real world."

We all left the movie in silence, somewhat disturbed by being reminded of the place we had left behind, half the globe away. A little later, however, we remarked to one another, "It don't mean nuthin'," which was one of those sayings a soldier adopted when he chose to shove a potential feeling under the rug and become a little more hardened.

The only way to top downtown after seeing a movie, was to eat at a good restaurant. There just so happened to be one on Freedom Hill. That restaurant experience must be the most memorable of my life.

Mike and I being the oldest, and of course, the most mature, led the way with our knowledge of the world. As we entered the restaurant, I made sure everyone took off his hat and signed in. While waiting to be seated, we folded our hands and spoke to one another in low tones.

Then Lieutenant Winter entered the restaurant with another officer and greeted us formally, "Good day, gentlemen."

"Good afternoon, sir," we replied. Their boots were polished while ours had never even seen shoe polish. Most of us had just had our hair cut, so we were even at that point in our etiquette battle. Our names were called ahead of the officers, a minor victory because seldom did enlisted men ever mix with officers during any type of social event.

Once we were in the restaurant proper and were seated, a Vietnamese waitress actually acted quite cordial towards the scroungy-looking group of bush grunts. We looked over the menu, and I said, "I'm getting sweet and sour pork. What are you getting?"

In an effort to appear sophisticated, Mike ordered some obscure oriental dinner. The other two ordered what Mike and I had. One of our other comrades found what he thought was a leftover menu but we discovered that it had only wine listed on it.

"That's a wine list, you fool. Let me see that thing," Mike remarked. "This Mateus stuff is pretty good, right Doc?"

"Man, that is good stuff. You mean they serve that here?" I responded. With a snap of Mike's fingers, the waitress made her way back to us, still smiling.

"What GI find?" she asked.

"GI find beaucoupe number one wine. You bring, yes?" Mike answered.

Before the waitress had brought the first part of our meals to us, we had finished our first bottle of wine and were already ordering another. Mike lifted the bottle to show the lieutenant and his friend what classy people drank, since Winter and his friends had just been seated next to us. By the time the food was completely served, we had imbibed three bottles of Mateus. Our systems had remained void of any type of intoxicants during those months in the field, so we were purified in a manner of speaking.

When the food finally arrived, sophistication was just a forgotten memory. We tried using chopsticks, but only knew how to shovel in food, like the villagers had taught us. The dishes became blurry, and after a while, it made no difference what we ate. Everything was full of humor, so we celebrated with two more bottles of Mateus. The next day, all I could remember was the MPs helping us find our way out of the restaurant after we had paid, I think.

We literally rolled on the ground, laughing at anything that moved. We had to collect our weapons and hitch a ride back to the battalion base. Brushing each other off and trying to put on a sober and serious look, we eased our way to the weapons shed.

Mike acquired his weapon first, but only after some discussion with the private in charge. Then Mike stood next to the shed, staring at the soldier; not actually threatening him, but letting him know that we wanted no trouble—just our weapons. A loaded gun in the hands of a loaded marine made a dangerous combination. That poor soul at the gate must have dealt with hundreds of wild young soldiers, so I guess he handled himself fairly well.

Once we had our weapons, we happily made our way to the road to hitch a ride. A truck stopped for us and we tried to quickly climb on board. We were not very successful, so the driver became quite impatient. We were all in except for me; I was still trying to climb in. As the truck began to take off, I shouted for my friends to let go of me so the truck would not drag me. They would not hear of it; they tried even harder to pull me up. My feet still touched the ground.

I ran as fast as I could, but my loyal friends would not let me go. Before I knew it, they had everyone in the truck pulling me on board. It was embarrassing. Umph! I flopped up on the truck bed like a dead seal. I felt no pain, anyway.

The Mateus began to peak in its victims, and we could barely recognize where we were supposed to get off. The driver seemed to know; however, so he stopped at the appropriate place and was kind enough, that time, to wait until we all fell out of his vehicle.

The memory of the remainder of that evening is scant and foggy, not like the memory of the next morning. Along with the bugle sounds of the wake-up call, sour mouth and a pounding head awakened me. Sergeant La Fifi came in, bright-eyed and bushy-tailed, and shook us out of our racks.

"Good news!" he proclaimed. "We get to go back to the bush today, gentlemen." We thought he was joking, but no such luck. It was a very very long morning.

Chapter 6
Between

Breakfast tasted like sour Mateus, and our heads were splitting. La Fifi tried to make good on his promise of at least two days of rehab, but apparently ol' Charlie was on the prowl, and our new colonel wanted to look good politically. Of course, he had marines as tough as nails, used nails, that is.

All I remember is packing up the few belongings I cared to lug around. The next moment, soaked to my bones, I was marching up a hill. I do not even remember being resupplied nor the helicopter ride to our position—or was it a truck ride? Many lost their breakfasts that morning; I wished I could have.

In the state we were in, we found it next to impossible to keep alert. That is why we almost never allowed ourselves to use anything intoxicating unless we knew we would spend two or three days in the rear. Needless to say, we were some upset foot soldiers that morning.

Thankfully, the day ended with no enemy contact. What a relief! The rains had let up and the heat was already making its way back before the sun set. Just as we began to make plans for the evening ambushes and patrols, we heard the familiar "pum-pum-pum" sounds of mortar rounds being launched at us from the distant mountains.

"Kapoom! Kapoom!" The rounds exploded a good fifty yards away.

Not feeling up to chasing after Mister Victor Charlie, Lt.

Winter told us, "Sorry men, I'm gonna let the fly boys have this one." Needless to say, Winter was just as tired as we were.

Actually, the lieutenant provided us with some well-deserved entertainment that evening. In 'Nam, when an air strike was called in, an abundance of fancy footwork took place. First we had to be unmistakably sure that our map coordinates (grids) were correct so that we were not the ones being fired upon. Next, we had to be sure that Charlie did not move before the strike occurred. This was accomplished by making him think that we were disabled, thereby luring him to come a little bit closer or at least to make himself visible.

Then came the air strike—a true piece of artistry. The radio communication was always a thriller, too. The pilot came on the air, "Kilo two alpha, this is Range Rover; please acknowledge."

"Range Rover, this is kilo two alpha. We copy you loud and clear. The yellow brick road will guide your path to the wicked witch of the north." Then we tossed a yellow smoke grenade out in front of us.

"Here comes the Wizard of Oz on his broomstick, so keep your heads low." We then heard the Phantom jet from the south, heading north to claim his victim. The 20 mm canons began firing as they discharged their empty shells over us. The jet drew small arms fire from our enemy mortar team—a bad mistake. The jet circled and came back.

"Wheeeeeee! Here I come again," the pilot chuckled. This time he dove down to his target. He dislodged a 250-pound bomb and quickly made a sharp turn upwards.

"Ka Booom!" The bomb exploded gloriously.

"How's that for an ol' timer?" As the pilot continued his ascent, he performed his "victory roll," in which the jet rolled 360 degrees.

On the ground, we all applauded and replied, "Good show,

ol' chap, good show." The pilot then sailed off to a hot meal and a dry bed. "C'*est la guerre,*" as the French would say. Yes, such was war.

"At least now we can be miserable in peace," we all observed. Heated C-rations under a poncho became our gourmet course for the evening.

What a life! Who could ask for more? A roof over your head—even if it was plastic. Solid ground to sit on—even if it sat under two inches of water. A nice hot meal—even if the heat tab used to cook it made your eyes burn. Friends sharing the good times with you—even if being their friend made you feel very uneasy. And lastly—who could ask for more?—You could sleep securely, knowing that Uncle Sam was out there protecting you, even if, at the moment, you yourself were Uncle Sam. Yes, it was a great life that year.

After dining at that exquisite country club, savoring the succulent duck under glass (chicken stew C-ration), it was off to the fox hunt (an ambush)! As was our custom on those hunts, I carried only a poncho, a poncho liner, a canteen, battle dressings, and a weapon. Except for the helmet and flak jacket that were becoming permanent attachments to our bodies, those items were the only conveniences we took. The thoughts of the previous day at Freedom Hill had already faded into a distant memory.

The ambush passed uneventfully, but the accompanying vigilance, anxiety, and stress did not pass (just like in all other ambushes, whether we had contact or not.) Statistics determined that fewer than one in one-hundred such ambushes resulted in a firefight. However, once a soldier had withstood one encounter, he would regard each subsequent ambush with the same anticipation and anxiety.

The rains of the monsoons made those evenings' endeavors all the more interesting. Due to the constant sound of the rain, we, instead of relying mainly on sound and occasionally on sight, as when the weather was drier, had to narrow our perception and use only our vision.

The rain on an uncovered head was like a Chinese water torture that would drive anyone insane. I think that on one occasion, I may have tolerated a whole thirty minutes of the water drops pounding my bare head before covering my crown.

Sometimes we covered our heads with unique bush hats. Even though today, the style is common, back then, the semi-wide floppy brim was peculiar for military attire. Since we were not used to it, we improvised by redesigning it. First, we frayed the nylon bands, making the hats look like frizzed fur bands. Then, we rolled the brims downwards, creating sort of a reversed cowboy style. This was the method I adopted from the very beginning when it was shown to me by welcoming KC scouts.

Some of the back hill boys created a type of cowboy hat, but their ears usually sunburned. The southern and inner city brothers put wire into the borders of theirs, creating a type of Panama hat; however, it did not hold up to the thick jungles well.

Then there were the Lt. Winters who believed that the government issue bush hat was not meant to be altered. They insisted on leaving it au naturale. Most of us did not pay attention to the lieutenant on that issue, because we liked our authentic bush style hats with the brim turned down on the sides, unique to Vietnam vets and ultimately, the most practical for the jungle. Making a fashion statement was not anyone's intention.

Once at near dusk, while walking to our ambush site, Mike looked down and saw gigantic footprints. Becoming quite alarmed, he exclaimed, "My God, monsters!" We both laughed almost immediately upon discovering that we had seen our own tracks created by our boots thick with muddy clay.

We're sunk! Look at these monster NVA footprints!

In one of his cartoons, Bill Mauldin had the same thing happen to his *Stars and Stripes* characters, Willie and Joe. This prompted spontaneous laughter as we recalled that scene while looking down at our own feet.

Bill Mauldin was a cartoonist for the *Stars and Stripes*, a serviceman's newspaper in Europe during WW II. At that time, Bill was in his early twenties, much like us. Mauldin wrote a book about his cartoons after the war, and reproduced many of his cartoons in it. His two characters, Willie and Joe, were two infantry men, drafted into a war they did not fully understand. Their bearded faces, eyes with bags under them, and their shabby clothes made them the common foot soldier who has fought a nation's wars for thousands of years. History books write of famous battles, prominent generals, and courageous captains, but few remember the soldiers, who are the real heroes.

Mike and Bob are the characters I drew in the small series of cartoons in this book. Most of the incidents drawn here are true and are pretty close to the events that Bill Mauldin drew about in his book, *Up Front with Willie and Joe.*

I do not remember all the sketches I drew in my letters, but the ones included here are among those still etched in my memory. The clothes that the characters, Mike and Bob wore were very baggy, just like our uniforms.

On that first mini-operation after Freedom Hill, five days passed with no further contact. The typhoon was long gone, but the monsoons it left behind were still very much present. The temperature never decreased, but at least the weather was tolerable due to the sun's rays being hidden by the low-lying clouds.

One day we measured rainfall with crude, makeshift devices, and recorded twelve inches in less than one hour. One wise cracker suggested that if anyone wanted to commit suicide by drowning, all he would have had to do was look up. To have a pair of dry socks on hand, I would wring out one pair and tuck them underneath my clothing. Alternating the pair I wore with the dry ones I carried was a necessity to prevent trenchfoot. Leather goods, such as wallets or watch bands would rot in one to two weeks. Metal watch bands would rust, so cheap, nylon bands were the most practical. Wallets were merely plastic "Baggies." Our boots, though made of canvas with nylon had leather as the main support for their lower halves. Juan Gallegos' boots actually rotted through, making it almost impossible for him to walk in the jungle.

With the mini-operation coming to an end, we thought we would resume our little rehab time back in the rear. Our hopes were up, but we had learned not to expect anything. With a break in the rains, a chopper landed for us; off we flew to the rear—our poor man's paradise. No sooner had we landed than we were herded to our bare hooches again. There Gunny La Fifi greeted us with a big smile; however, it lacked the enthusiasm he usually conveyed.

"You people sure are in demand," he said, knowing how we would react.

"Not another operation?" we asked in unison.

"This one's a big one. It'll involve several companies and guess which platoon will spearhead the OP!"

"When?—In about an hour," Sgt. Tino remarked sarcastically.

We were all very angry. It was like being Cinderella, except that we had weapons and we were not very nice—nor would any special favors from the fairy godmother ever come our way.

La Fifi quietly corrected Tino, "Tomorrow morning."

It was too late to go to Freedom Hill, but we could see a USO show at our own rear base that night—at least a show had

been scheduled. But the rains were not aware of any sched-
ules—or maybe they were. The brass had canceled the show
because the stage and wooden benches sat outdoors in the rain.

We showered, but did not bother to shave. Not shaving
may have been a small gesture of rebellion or perhaps just a
statement to set ourselves apart from the rear pogues. The LT
shaved, of course.

A strange feeling began to take hold of me while we were
there—a sort of impending doom. I could not explain or even
fully understand what I was feeling. I only knew that something was about to happen and that something would occur on
the next operation. At first, I did not share that gut feeling with
anyone, mainly because I realized that I would have a tremendous responsibility being the only corpsman for my platoon. If
something has to happen to me, what would become of them?

I had made it a point during the course of the past few
months with these thugs to teach them basic battlefield first
aid. Most knew enough to stop the bleeding until the choppers
arrived. Most of the wounded would survive.

My next question was, "Who could be entrusted with my
unit one?" Mike had to carry his sixty-pound radio along with
his own rucksack. His responsibilities as a radioman always
demanded all of his attention, so Mike could not divide himself
between the radio and the wounded during those crucial
moments of combat.

The next obvious choice was between Jose and Juan. I
chose Juan because he was not a squad leader and yet was
extremely reliable. Jose himself was a squad leader, making
him also somewhat indispensable. I decided not to mention
anything that night, mainly because I wanted to see whether
my sense of ill fate would subside.

That evening, most of the platoon played cards, wrote
letters, or just horsed around. I remember some of the John

Wayne-type movies depicting soldiers on the evening before a battle. Everyone became philosophical or nostalgic. The cinema gave no insight on what actually occurred. Survival meant to numb out or risk becoming a statistic for the psychiatrists.

We used candles for lighting since our remote hooch had no electricity. We melted a whole candle in a C-ration can and placed a rolled up piece of paper in it as a giant wick. This yielded about three candles of light. Some played poker, an exciting game that seemed to cause the players to forget just about anything. I played hearts or rummy with Mike and others.

The night passed with each of us grateful that none of us had to pull patrol or ambush duty. That in itself, was an occasion for celebration.

Later, as I loaded myself with extra battle dressings and other medical essentials as well as extra ammo for my M-16, I scrutinized each man in our close quarters. I couldn't decipher whether anyone else shared the same feeling that I had. Mike acted his old sarcastic self. Mackovich always seemed nervous, so he was no barometer. Jose prepared himself, oiling and cleaning his weapon like he always had when he was in the rear. Juan busily lost his money to the wheeler-dealer, Lizzio, and the rest of the band of young warriors were carrying on just like always.

It was comforting that few, if any, were nervous, so I brushed off my premonition as sheer superstition. I thought to myself that it had been so long since I had experienced any kind of feeling, that perhaps the emotion was just a spontaneous burst of unused synaptic charges within the confines of my numbed-out brain—something like a spark in a dying fire. With that, I was able to sleep. The sleep, however, was disturbed by my continual waking, which was natural for us who had spent any time out in the bush.

Morning arrived, and after breakfast we neatly placed all of our combat gear together, ready for boarding to the unknown destination. Before departing, we were called, in full combat dress, to an assembly—an awards ceremony.

During the ceremony, several of our group were given citations and bronze star medals with combat "V" devices for valor. Most of the recipients were transfers from other units, but as their heroic deeds were read to us, we stood proudly as their only audience.

These marines shared an air of expectation, believing that they would each receive the same, if not greater, recognition back in the world. Of course, the truth was that the ceremony was the only time anyone would ever give the young warriors any kind of honor for risking their lives for each other. Hostility towards the military filled the world during those days and for many years to come.

We were their families and were the only beings on the face of the earth that cared. Their families back home cared, but more in sympathy than in any other way. As much as all the heroes wanted to get out of that place, their memories of Vietnam would carry the brotherhood and closeness that in no other time would be equaled.

Our country considered us outcasts for having a sense of duty to God and country. The remainder of the nation enjoyed, even took for granted, the freedoms paid for by many before us, as we ourselves were paying at that moment. We were proud of these comrades who shared the same fears, apprehension, and anguish that we experienced every day and every night.

When the assembly was over, a crowd gathered around the medal winners. Admiring Crowder's Bronze Star with its combat "V" made me very proud of him. This was the first awards ceremony for valor that I had ever attended. A chill shot up my spine as we were dispersed to our gear and told to start boarding the choppers.

"Don't worry, Doc. You'll end up with one of those things on your chest—or on your coffin! Corpsmen always end up getting awards for doing stupid things," Mike reassured me.

We heard the word that a major NVA movement had been sighted north of us and we were supposed to intercept them at a bottleneck. Of course, as a security measure, we did not know that location. As we all knew, the VC and the NVA usually knew what we would attempt, even before any of us grunts would.

As we resupplied, the feelings of impending doom again permeated my thoughts. I asked Juan to take my unit one and to take charge of basic first aid during an assault if something happened to me. He did not look surprised at my request but regarded it a logical choice, just as I had. Mike, too, was in agreement with that request. I felt better after that and actually did not feel afraid at all. If I got hit, whether wounded or killed, it was just one of those things.

As I looked out at the battalion LZ, I saw several companies of marines in formation, waiting to depart for our destination. It was a gloomy, cloudy morning. At least we were not the only platoon to be sent out there as we often were the majority of the time. The high shrill of the jet engines and the loud flutter of the blades were the only sounds to be heard that morning. The presence of jet and diesel fuel was so pronounced that our skin became oily.

"Would this be my last chopper ride? Was this my last day as a complete human?" I wondered.

Our turn came to board the chopper! We double-timed it towards the rear ramp of the double-bladed beast. As we jogged in formation, I realized that I had become somewhat accustomed to the quick cadence while carrying over sixty pounds of gear. One of these days, I would be able to jog wearing only a T-shirt, trunks and tennis shoes. Actually, I could not fully remember what it was like to run in that manner.

Inside the chopper, I ran straight to my usual seat. Only the newcomers did not know where to sit. In just a few seconds, we were airborne. The tremendously loud noise seemed to become ghostly silent, as I reviewed the faces of each marine seated opposite me. We were already hundreds of feet in the air and many miles from our base when I began to notice small holes appearing in the floor board. This was the reason we each had our own particular sitting place.

We were being shot at and it was impossible to tell where the fire was coming from. If we sat in the same position each time, our chances of being hit lessened. Probably a gambler of some sort developed that superstition; it sounded just valid enough to convince all of us of its truth. That was why the new guys scrambled to any of the empty seats, usually a different one each time, until they caught on.

As I reviewed the faces again, the predictable occurred. A new guy named Parker sat slumped in his webbed canvas seat with opened eyes and an opened mouth. I made my way towards him and lay his lifeless body on the cold metal belly of the chopper.

I filled out the ID tag from the information on his dog tag and signaled to the helicopter crew chief that I had completed my part. He gave me the OK sign and that was that. The crew chief covered Parker with a poncho. Those deadly rounds had found their way to a randomly selected slot in that giant manned roulette wheel.

This occurrence became an omen to what I had felt previously. I would not let it get the best of me; I was determined. It seemed like hours in flight before we approached our drop-off point, although I am sure it was only minutes. We began to circle as the choppers ahead of us landed. I could not make out much detail from the little porthole situated behind me.

The ramp began to lower. Even though we had not fully landed, we had to stand up to get ready to disembark. The first marine jumped off. We still had not landed; nor had the pilot intended on landing completely. The second marine jumped off. It was my turn next.

Standing on the edge of the tailgate ramp, I could see that we were averaging between four and ten feet off the ground as the helicopter hovered and bounced over the elephant grass. My knees began wobbling and buckling under the weight of my battle equipment. Just then, out to my left from the thicket of trees, a rocket propelled grenade (RPG) streamed out towards the craft I was trying to leave.

Still not able to hear anything because of the loud rotors, I felt a huge blow to my left side which catapulted me off my feet like a human cannon ball onto the earth below. As the ground approached me, my head became the spearhead. My helmet lacked chin straps, so it fit loosely and fell off easily. Upon ground contact, my head was met by that loose helmet with its front lip instantly digging into the cartilage of my nose.

"Crunch," echoed through the confines of my skull. The remainder of my body followed, as if I flew in slow motion. The metal helmet's ripping through my nose sent a jolt of intense pain down my spine and to my feet. My head hurt as it hit the ground. My body came to a final halt in a face up position. The pulsating pain hammered at my nose and radiated to the very back of my head. I could not remember where I was at that moment. My eyes opened to a cloud of warm, dark red fluid that I could not see.

As I tried to sit up, Sgt. Pierce came to me and yelled out to the other marines, "Doc's hit! His face is full of blood! Doc, speak to me!"

"God, he got it bad!" another said.

"Doc, you all right?" spoke Mike's voice.

"No, I'm not okay!" I said.

After cleaning off the blood from my eyes, I sat up and looked around quite dazed.

A sudden fury of rage overran my consciousness in its already clouded state. All I could think of was teaching that chopper pilot a lesson for throwing me off. I grabbed my M-16, placed a clip in, cocked it and began to take aim at the hovering aircraft.

Sgt. Pierce cried, "Doc! No!" Then he snatched the rifle out of my hands saying, "You don't want to do that, Doc."

Not realizing what I was doing, I responded, "Oh yeah?"

I was laid down and a battle dressing was slapped over my nose, too tight, of course.

Still with my pack on, I looked for my unit one, found it and called for Juan. Juan's eyes were very wide and he said with a relieved voice "Man, Doc! At least you're alive." I gave him the unit one and he took it staring at me as if to say that he had changed his mind but he did not.

Mike and Sgt. Pierce walked me to another chopper that had fully landed in the field. They left my helmet behind, as I was quite upset at that cursed piece of equipment anyway. Sgt. Pierce had removed my rifle clip and told me jokingly but seriously not to replace it.

Upon boarding that chopper, I noticed that my own chopper was not smoking nor did it look damaged. Apparently the RPG set off an incomplete explosion, a dud of sorts. My head throbbed and my knees began trembling.

Sitting alone with the crew chief in the chopper's fuselage, I still felt hostile, but I refrained from replacing the M-16 magazine. My mind was in disarray, but I knew we were airborne once more.

Chapter 7
The USS Sanctuary

At what seemed like a hundred miles an hour, thoughts raced through my damaged mind. I could decipher a few of those thoughts, however. I thought that it would be nice to sleep in a hospital with real mattresses and linen sheets. I had not even seen a bed for months. Perhaps I would be medevaced to First Med and see my friend, Amarante. My hands were trembling. My face felt every pulse my heart pumped through its arteries.

What was that? Ocean below me? It seemed as if we were traveling two feet above the open sea's surface at a minimum of one hundred miles an hour.

Up ahead, I saw several ships. I knew that we were headed for the big white one with the red cross—which was actually a target—on its side. Da Nang Bay had become target practice for rocket launchers in the hillsides. Several times before, while looking from a tall mountain, I had seen the white hospital ship slowly slip out into the open seas.

The distant vessel soon lay just beneath us as we slowly descended. The deck of the ship moved up and down as the pilot attempted to land. The rear ramp lowered as if daring me to jump off. The deck was still slowly bouncing; we had not yet touched down. I looked back at the crew chief saying, "No way." Of course, he could not hear me.

Anxiety began to take over my almost stuporous state as I

froze at the edge of the helicopter ramp. I could not bring myself to step off, because I envisioned waking up in the jungle again.

We did land safely, and two ship marines approached me and gently helped me down. I was not dreaming; I truly was on the ship and I truly was still in pain. The chopper, with its tornado-like wind ascended, abandoning me in an entirely new world. I felt like a country kid visiting the city for the first time.

After I stepped on the landing pad, these marines took off my pack and my flak jacket, but I held on to my rifle. As I was escorted inside the ship to a small office where I checked my gear, including the M-16, the marines assured me that everything would be safe; I had my doubts. These were rear pogues, you know.

I must have looked pathetic because the next thing I can remember is lying on an operating room table still fully clothed. I allowed someone to remove my battle dressing. An ear, nose, and throat doctor (otolaryngologist) with thin, graying hair and probably in his fifties leaned over me and asked me questions, like how I was injured. I honestly could not remember what had happened. I could only curse that helicopter. The doctor mentioned something about a concussion and an extremely dirty wound.

The following events thoroughly awoke me. I vividly remember, to this day, the smallest detail of that brief time. The doctor instructed his helpers to clean my face with Betadine. This iodine solution stung greatly. Every muscle in my body began to tense up. Then the assistant draped my face with a fenestrated sterile cloth. The doctor commenced injecting a local anesthetic into my already tender nose. I had thought I knew pain before that took place, but I had no idea what real pain was until he started injecting.

"There, that should be enough," the surgeon commented.

The suture needle began to pierce my skin. "Ouch!" I exclaimed. "It really and truly smarts."

"Okay, I'll inject some more," he said reluctantly.

"Ouch! Man, it still hurts," I groaned.

"Give this marine another shot," the frustrated doctor commanded.

By that time, I realized that the gray haired man probably did not believe me, but the pain was worse than ever.

"The nose is not numb yet. I can feel everything that you're doing," I said emphatically.

"Can you feel this?" the doctor asked.

"Yes," I replied.

"What about this?" he asked again.

"No." (I knew that he was testing to see if I was faking.)

"I guess he's telling the truth. Sorry, son, but I can't put any more juice in you. You must have some sort of tolerance to lidocaine. Grit your teeth like a good soldier." I recoiled at those unpleasant words.

I felt each and every bite the surgical needle took into my flesh. I even felt the doctor trimming the skin with scissors. It seemed as if hours had passed and my muscles remained hard as rocks during the whole procedure. Even though the OR suite was air conditioned, I was drenched in sweat from the pain of the ordeal.

Out of the fenestration, I could see the instruments as they sewed my nose. The sharp suture needle pierced my skin with a sting that radiated to the center of my head.

"There, that should do it." It was over.

"I felt everyone of those stitches, Doctor," I remarked somewhat angrily.

"Well it's done, son. How's your head?"

"Things are still cloudy and my whole head hurts."

The doctor finished examining me and continued to carry

on a simple meaningless dialog. When he had completed his exam, I was placed in a wheelchair and wheeled to my ward. My head had not ceased pounding.

On arriving at the ENT ward, someone introduced me to the nurse in charge, Lt. Wagner, and I sensed our immediate dislike for each other. The lieutenant was a medium-sized, stocky blonde, with a round, featureless face. The first words out of her mouth were not choice words.

"Oh, here comes Wallace Beary," said the WAVE.

My mind focused on Wallace Beary, an old-time movie star with a big, red nose, who was half drunk most of the time. As with the chopper pilot incident, indignation began festering in the confines of my headache-laden thoughts. That did it! I let loose.

An undiscovered hand grenade had remained in a pocket of my jungle shirt. I reached into my shirt and pulled it out, grabbing hold of the pin with my forefinger. As I coldly stared at the nurse, I gradually pulled the pin from its safety slot.

"Call the marines, quick!" she commanded.

I was not aware of anyone else in the ward, although there were many. I had no idea what I was doing. The room became cloudy and my vision obscure, and then all turned black. Before I hit the deck, the ship's security had arrived to disarm me. They met no resistance.

That incident set the stage for a wonderful time on the USS Sanctuary. The ward corpsmen carried me into the shower and bathed me as best they could.

"These grunts always stink and take so long to get clean. I hate doing this," remarked of one of the pogues.

"Do you fairies always treat fellow corpsmen like this?" I muttered.

"You ain't no corpsman—are you?" said the other.

"Look at the insignia on my collar, you jerks," I said, still furious.

"Hey man, we're really sorry. We thought you was a common grunt," the same pogue said.

"There's no such thing as a 'common grunt'," I growled through clenched teeth. "Get outta here and leave me alone!" I shouted that time.

I managed to finish my shower alone and put on a clean set of dark blue pajamas. They sent away my clothes for safekeeping, by way of the laundry for wayward jungle attire.

With great effort, my feeble body made its way to my assigned rack, the top of three bunks. After struggling to climb to my reserved spot, laying on those clean sheets and mattress felt like sleeping on a cloud—as if nothing was beneath me. I was not used to being comfortable at all. Unless I slept on hard ground embedded with small hills and rocks, I guess I could not be secure enough to get comfortable. However, the concussion overtook me, and I finally fell asleep.

That night drew a total blank; I must have been unconscious. Two days later, Nurse Wagner told me that I had been hallucinating and had to have an IV since I could not or would not eat. When I did come to, it was morning and the IV had been removed, but I still had a headache.

Steve, another corpsman from the bush now occupied the bunk below me. Enemy machine gun fire had kicked up sand, spraying his eyes with it. Steve told me about walking on patrol when he came upon a lone VC, face to face. For a brief second, he said, they both froze and then Charlie decided to fire first.

"It was like a John Wayne movie, seeing the ground kicking up like a snake and rushing towards me. Before I knew it, dirt had kicked up into my face. I couldn't see, so I fired straight to where I had last seen him. The rest of the squad fired too. I stopped so that I wouldn't hit any of my own people." Steve told his story as if talking about a movie he had just seen.

There was no other patient in the ward who had seen combat other than Steve and myself. We formed an instant camaraderie in which no one else could partake. Some of the others sat and listened to us exchange war stories, and we would not mind, for the most part, but usually we preferred to be alone.

I asked Steve, "Do you find that your feelings are drifting away and that you may never get them back?"

"Yeah, I do. Actually, I had thought it was just me and that there was something wrong with me," he replied.

"What kind of unit are you with?" I asked.

"I'm with a CAG unit. We were living in this ville and actually having a pretty good time. I was getting the lingo down pat and learning how to cook Vietnamese food. It seemed as if the people liked us. I'm sure there were a lot of VC sympathizers in that ville, but our contact was dropping low," Steve said almost disappointedly.

"The same thing with us. We have noticed our rate of contact dropping, too. It's almost like everyone is playing a psychological game with us, including our own people. Wouldn't you agree?" I was becoming philosophical.

"Who knows? You know, Bob, I feel as though I've become part of this country. I don't even know if I miss the world anymore. People here seem to be more real than those back home. What do you think?"

"I've never really thought of it that much. Actually, I don't think I've thought of much of anything lately. Now that you mention it, though, I think you've got a point. Back stateside, when you went out with a girl, you never really knew whether she liked you because that was exactly the mind game she wanted to play with you. You never knew what it would take for a so-called best friend to turn his back on you. And people over you—forget it, man! No one ever knew what they were up to. They could fire you or flunk you in a second. "

"The people here don't seem to be concerned with all that petty junk. If they like you, you know it. If they don't like you, there's no question about that, either. You know who your enemies are and you know who your friends are, too." That was about as far as I was capable of reaching into the world of philosophy, so we stopped talking for awhile.

Initially, the staff brought meals to Steve and me, since the doctor wanted us to stay in bed for a couple of days.

After about two days, the USS Sanctuary put out to sea, heading east, away from Vietnam's coast, toward safety. During our time out at sea, a tropical storm began building. The ship rocked slowly at first, then as the storm grew, the ship responded by increasing her motion. I had always heard about being seasick, but thought it a shortcoming of the fainthearted.

Nurse Wagner took the opportunity to present an offering of good ol' American pay back. "Stay calm there, soldier. The ship's just gonna rock baaack and forth…baaack and forth…baaack and forth…baaack and forth…" She kept on until she had produced the desired effect.

With my head still aching and my insides in a state of tremulous nausea, I staggered to the head. It felt as if my toenails would be projected out of my throat. I was genuinely sick. That commode stayed by my side for the entire three days of the storm; however, I did sleep a little bit. The burning of the bile being forced out of my nose, accompanied by the nausea and cramping of my empty stomach seemed endless. As most things do, the vomiting finally did cease, and I was able to face up to another of Nurse Wagner's revenges.

Steve's company brought a refreshing break from the

already confining quarters of the floating metal cubicle. No sooner was I able to make friends, not fearing that he might die at any given time, than Steve received word that he was being transferred to a Naval hospital in Japan.

Japan seemed like Disneyland at that moment, and I wished that I, too, would be shipped there. I went to the galley for lunch and rushed back to see Steve off, but by the time I returned, Steve had already left. At least he was not dead. Life went on here, just as it had in the bush, so I cannot say that I spent any emotion on Steve's leaving.

My head finally cleared, and I could ambulate without difficulty, so I took the opportunity to fulfill a childhood dream—exploring a real ship. While exploring the ship I met a fellow from Colorado whose name was Carlos. Carlos was a machinist aboard the vessel and really had no place for sick people. He was able to show me around to all the interesting places as there were no restricted areas aboard.

By exploring most of the time, I could stay clear of Nurse Wagner until her shift ended, so she and I had no further confrontation. Even though the temperature was the same out in the ocean as it was inland, on the ship we endured no mosquitoes at night, and that was truly heaven.

The air conditioned cabins might have been most welcome, but I avoided the air conditioning as much as I could because I knew that soon, I would have to return to the bush. I could not afford to become too soft. Besides, the refrigerated air gave me a headache when it blew on my head.

When I awoke each morning, the nurse took my temperature via the humiliating manner. Then I had to wait for the doctor to make his early morning rounds. Every day, I would ask him if I was well enough to return to my unit. I felt that the platoon must really be having a hard time without me. Doc would just laugh and say, "No son, not yet."

Each day after the doctor's visit, I exercised and made a short trip to the chow hall or the galley, as the Navy called it. Mealtime, too, should have brought delight, but partaking in the pleasure of warm, balanced meals took on an air of prohibition. I resented everyone on that ship for being able to eat on clean tables, using sparkling utensils and sterile trays, and eating food prepared by cooks. The food was delicious, but I found no enjoyment in it.

The whole idea of diverse conditions while some were being denied the bare essentials, such as a roof, safety, electric lights—or any kind of light, for that matter—and the antithesis of taking all these things for granted overwhelmed my simple mind at that time. I guess the only recourse was for me to become defiant. Each day started out with the question of when I would be allowed to go back to my unit.

My conversations with Carlos, the machinist from Colorado were limited, since we did not have much in common, other than being Chicanos from neighboring states. We talked often during his off duty hours or played an occasional game of cards.

Another young corpsman with whom I felt very comfortable was a fellow grunt named Kim. Kim was a member of the feared R.O.K. Marines, the Korean marines of the Republic of Korea. Kim had limited mastery of the English language, but that didn't matter since his function on the vessel was liaison to any wounded R.O.K. Marine shipped here. We shared our bush experiences, including funny stories and events that had happened to us or to our comrades. Also, Kim told me of old Korean legends of battles with their arch enemy, Japan.

I remember one such story about a turtle ship Korea used to invade Japan. It was one of the first armored ships in Naval history. Kim told me of how it had weathered a storm and saved some soldiers stranded on an island or something similar.

Other stories included the occupation of both countries in each other's homeland and stories of various national heroes.

As was expected, Kim was also an expert in Tae Kwan Do karate. Having a little knowledge of Japanese Shotokahn karate, we exchanged moves only. Kim was gracious enough to not humiliate me by saying that he did not want to cause further injury to my nose or head.

My stay on the USS Sanctuary was not the vacation that I had expected. Even with my new-found friends, I was awful lonely there. The mail continued arriving just as it had in the jungles. I found it even harder to find things to write about in the fortress of safety than out on the guerrilla-infested, tropical mainland. I had stopped writing just long enough for the American Red Cross to send me a subtle message which said, "Write home!"

I guess I really did not want to have to explain, mainly to my mother, the real reason I recuperated in a hospital ship. I received a few care packages, but the thrill of their contents did not mean the same as they had during those times of destitution.

There was a ham radio operator on board who could patch telephone calls back to the world, so I got a chance to call home one evening. The operator told me to use proper radio procedure and to guard what I said; otherwise, my message would be censored.

In using proper radio procedure, I had to use the terms *over* and *over and out* when ending a sentence or message in order to signal operators both overseas and in the states to turn on their sets, to transmit, or to receive.

Of course, my family was totally confused, but the operators were kind enough to compensate. In my superficial, brief message, I tried to reassure everyone that I really was in no danger at all. It seemed like they could not decide whether to believe me or not, but they played along anyway. However, the short, three-minute conversation set me in the nostalgic mode for a few hours.

I thought pleasant thoughts of New Mexico and of everyone I knew, but still I had not yet recaptured any true feelings. At the time, it really did not bother me, but it amused me to realize that I was void of feelings.

I could not burn my letters on the ship and I was still paranoid about leaving them in the trash. I thought that if the letters lay in waste piles, they could be retrieved later by the enemy, even if the enemy was not at sea. So I ripped up and threw the torn letters overboard.

Letting those cherished letters go into the China Sea was frighteningly easy. I had not realized that I had not yet made a transition from the war to civilization. I had remained barbaric without ever knowing it, even though I truly thought that I was as normal and as well-adjusted as the next guy.

Resupplying a floating hospital was a spectacular sight. It required the efforts of everyone on board except the patients. One method transferred supplies from ship to ship. As a supply ship docked parallel to ours, a small cord with a ball attached to its end was shot at us. Someone on our ship picked it up and hoisted in the attached cords. Progressively heavier ropes were tied to the cord and then finally, a cable came over.

Sailors attached the cable to our ship and used a basket on pulleys for transferring the goods. Occasionally the goods were people. Seeing the person getting dunked as the waves rocked the two vessels closer together was well worth the watch through the porthole.

The Navy seemed to take care of its own quite well. In the other method, workers formed human chains from the helicopter pad down to the lower storage decks. As all those materials passed through the hands of the sailors and marines, nothing slipped into any pockets or hiding places. This may have been because officers supervised the operation, but I believe that there was still honor among the crew.

One day, while waiting in line for a meal, I spotted a marine I recognized from another platoon in our same company. Seeing him excited me, and I couldn't wait to hear how things were going for my platoon. This young man had acquired a case of trench foot from his feet remaining wet for extended periods of time. His corpsman was definitely not doing his duty in keeping his men healthy.

"Did you guys get into it much?" I asked.

"Are you kidding? It's been raining so hard. I think we were the only ones dumb enough to be out there. We haven't see one blessed VC soul." That pretty much ended our conversation.

So much the better, I thought. At least I would not feel guilty for being where I was. It seemed from that point on, I began to actually enjoy my stay on the flotilla.

That night, I asked Kim to meet me on the top deck, as *War and Peace*, with Henry Fonda was coming out. Jane Fonda's trip to Hanoi may have already occurred at that time—I cannot fully remember—but Henry Fonda himself was not being boycotted. As we sat down for the movie, Kim handed me a wrapped package.

"This gift for fellow marine," he said, with a big grin.

Opening the gift, I discovered a brand new R.O.K. Marine uniform. I was speechless. He told me that he already had an American marine uniform and that he knew that I could not give him anything in return. I certainly appreciated Kim. I have that uniform to this day.

The movie lasted three hours, and for a moment, I thought that the story had war all figured out. I even wrote a letter to my dad of how the movie impressed me and of how war was philosophically reasoned. My dad later told me that he had figured I was "under the influence" by the garbage I wrote. I swear, I had had nothing to drink, as alcohol was forbidden among the patients. I had a chance to see the movie again in 1992, and I could not figure out how I came to my original conclusion. Maybe the water was spiked; who knows?

The remainder of my stay on the USS Sanctuary was fairly mundane, as the days began to blend with one another. I did get a chance to visit the dentist, and was quite apprehensive about seeing him. I knew for sure that my teeth would have to all come out. Prior to arriving on the Sanctuary, I never brushed my teeth more than a half dozen times in country. Surely they were rotting away.

The toothpaste carried a long-traveling fragrance which was dangerous in the bush. All hygiene that is taken for granted by most people had been lost on the front. My teeth were cleaned; the dentist said that I had hard enamel—all that worry for nothing. Initially, I did not believe him and thought it as another plot against us enlisted men.

I found most of the other patients in my ward quite boring. One foul-mouthed tub of lard (a crew member on the ship) probably knew more war stories than I could dream of—typical of the noncombatant—so brave back in the rear. I think these people are the same ones who must have cousins who are occasional hunters and never served in the military but know all there is to know about war, just ask them.

We did have an Aussie with us, however. This "ol' chap" who had some kind of nose problem was from the Australian Navy. These boys were really dedicated. Their normal tour in the military lasted twelve long years. He had already been in four and had just eight more to go. I had not realized that the Australians had committed troops to the Vietnam War.

"The blooming rats would be crawling all over us if we didn't stop 'em. Wouldn't yer say there, yank?"

"You mean like the domino effect?" I replied.

"I guess yer could say that. Yer see, this is our neck o' the woods an' we'd like to keep it a little tidy. The Japs had themselves a bloody good time with our colonies an' we ain't goin' to let that happen ag'in with any of these slimy commies." Johnny became a little excited over his patriotism,

"You yanks have got some fat politicians who butt into everyone's business; that's quite obvious. But you grunts are gutsy and yer know something? Our people in the coast, outback, north, south—we all thank God for the whole lot o' ya. Yer are welcome to come stay with us any time ya please," Johnny concluded.

I did not realize it then, but that was one of the very few times anyone ever thanked us for making the biggest sacrifice anyone could ever make. Even nurse Wagner was silent and teary eyed listening to Johnny's remarks. I learned later that the Aussies had a number of ground troops in 'Nam and carried a pretty good reputation. I never met any of them, though.

Each morning, I followed an established routine. I consistently asked the doctor if I could be released back to my unit.

"Son, don't you want to be transferred to this beautiful ship? Just think. No more hot, filthy jungles. No more shooting. What do you say?"

"No thanks, sir. I belong out in the bush and I really want to get back as soon as I can." I did not conceal my disdain for that man, that ship, and its crew very well at that particular moment.

"You just had a psuedomonas infection in your nose. Normally, you would've healed in a week instead of the two and a half it's taken you. You barely hiccup in the bush and you could come down with God knows what. It's dangerous out there," the doctor pleaded.

"I'll have my orders to return to my unit whenever you

think I'm ready, sir." That was all that I could say to the officer who had no earthly idea what he was talking about.

My thoughts reverted to the members of my platoon. These boys had had to become men overnight—all on account of the sins of two governing powers, each as corrupt as the other. If I had been born in Hanoi, I would be fighting the Americans. I felt that regardless of whether my country was right or wrong, it was my duty to be loyal to it. I had enjoyed its benefits and fruits, and now I had become just one of the laborers asked to perform an unpleasant duty for it. If my dad had asked me to complete some ridiculous and unpleasant task, I probably would not like it, but I would do it just the same, out of respect and honor.

I never admired or even liked freeloaders. I felt like the only people who really cared about the grunts out in the bush were the grunts themselves. It seemed that the ship's doctor did not wish us to be out in the swamps and rice paddies, but he did not bother to find out what it was like out there. He never asked, so we never discussed it.

The doctor seemed to want to keep his evening socials unspoiled, not ever having to think twice about what went on in the jungles of Vietnam. It seemed that he was reminded that we grunts actually existed only when facing the likes of Willie or Joe—or Mike or Bob.

I realized that if I stayed as a crew member aboard the USS Sanctuary, I would become nothing more than a notch in the belt of that self-righteous *saviour* of the troops. Nope, I really did not want to remain there.

"Okay, we'll see about next week," said the plump, relaxed officer.

"Why not tomorrow, sir?" Again only a few words could be uttered.

"Ha! Tomorrow's Thanksgiving Day, son."

"If that's the only reason, then, I'd rather be with my friends, sir." Not even a hint of a smile feigned from my lips.

"Okay. I'll let you go." Whether out of defeat or genuine concern, the doctor gave in; I will never know his reasoning, but that was the best news I had heard in eighteen days. It felt like I had just been granted parole.

I ran to the various decks trying to locate Kim or Carlos, but could find neither. I felt no disappointment, as I had been accustomed to losing buddies. This time, however, I was consoled by there being no injury involved.

That evening, the reverie of donning my battle gear excited me. I fantasized riding off like a gallant knight. It was like I had obtained permission to return home. I recollected my dad's telling me of the time he was wounded and of how he could not wait to get back to his unit. Only he could understand how I felt that night.

The next morning arrived none too soon. I woke early, showered, and rushed down for a breakfast of two eggs, bacon, toast, and juice. Next, I hurried to collect my gear. Marines on the ship issued me a clean, camouflage uniform, my same boots, a new helmet (with straps), my own rifle, and my old pack and flak jacket. Juan carried my unit one.

I looked through my pack, and of course, most of my C-rations were gone. I thought sarcastically, "If these rear echelon warriors feel they are part of the war effort by eating some wounded marine's C-rations, then more power to them. I don't mind helping them daydream."

Lieutenant Wagner handed my orders to me with, "Happy Thanksgiving. Keep your nose out of trouble." She too had grown accustomed to not growing too attached to her patients, especially if they were returning to the front. Her coldness was just as much of a protection for her as it had been for us.

Kim greeted me on the deck that morning. "I will remember you, Doc Bob. Good luck."

We saluted each other out of respect and in simultaneous mockery of the officers. Then, as I climbed down to a launch at the ship's side I knew that my easy days had once again become a thing of the past.

I exchanged no words with the other people on the small motor boat, since I was the only combatant on board among sailors, officers and several Vietnamese civilians. After the boat docked, and we all disembarked, I stood on the dock all alone.

Everyone except this marine had a place to go. The realization that the hospital ship's responsibility for my welfare stopped the moment I set foot on dry land made me feel all the more like an outcast. No one had bothered to inform me that I would have to find my own transportation to my unit. At least I was lost in the middle of a military base.

Because of the holiday, most of the administrative offices were closed, so I made way for the barracks. After being misinformed by the ever-present rear echelon, I found an older sergeant who looked like he had seen combat at some time in his career.

After I explained my situation to the sergeant, he stood, put on a sort of mischievous grin, and said, "Come with me, son. We'll get you back to your unit."

We walked to the transport area and found an unsuspecting private taking a nap. "Jones! Fire up a truck and take this soldier where he wants to go."

Jones, not in his best humor, made the occasion even more enjoyable for me. After some bustling about fueling and filling out papers—and after plenty of grumbling—Jones told me to get in. This was my first time to ride in the cab of a vehicle since I arrived in country four months earlier. I told Jones that I was with the 1st Marine Division 3/1, but that I had no idea where it was from there.

By the way that poor boy was prepared, I doubt it if he had ever been in any type of action situation. He had no helmet, flak jacket, or rifle. He did carry a .38 caliber revolver which was essentially useless in the bush. After driving around lost for some time, we finally saw the sign on the gates: *3/1 1st MARDIV.*

I sincerely thanked Jones, and he recognized that as he also wished me an earnest, "God speed." It was getting late in the afternoon and I hoped Jones would have a safe trip back. (I must have gotten soft on the ship; I was beginning to show some early signs of having feelings.)

My throat developed a lump in it as I gazed upon the compound entrance. Safety was now a thing of the past; I had not even allowed myself to enjoy it fully when it was plentiful. Too late now.

Chapter 8
Welcome Home

"Here are my orders to return to Kilo Company, 2nd Platoon, sir," I told the officer of the day.

"Where did you come from, soldier?" I could tell he really enjoyed working on Thanksgiving.

When I told him the USS Sanctuary, he gave me a cold stare and muttered, "We'll see what we can do."

What was that supposed to mean? I sat and waited.

"You had dinner yet?" the officer asked.

"Only breakfast," I replied.

"They probably have turkey out there for you guys," he said with only semi-concern.

Darkness had not yet set in; it was around five o'clock or so. The officer finally came out and told me to go outside and wait for a jeep. By that time I was feeling like a pinball being bounced across the countryside. Two marines in a jeep showed up to escort me to my unit, which was surprising since I had only been trucked to my unit once before and that was to the observation posts. I thought, "Maybe the platoon is now at an OP!"

One of the drivers, Garcia, had formerly been a corporal in my platoon. We had not been well acquainted but did recognize each other.

"Where you been, Doc?" Garcia asked, with a big grin. After the small talk, we raced through the villages. I thought it somewhat foolish to send a jeep out that late and virtually unprotected. As the condensed villages of the outer Da Nang area began to thin out, we took an exit up a hill to a small band of armed bodies. As we approached them, an air of familiarity struck me—that was my platoon!

"Hey, lookie here guys. It's Doc!" remarked one of the band members.

"Get over here and carry my stuff, you slime buckets."

We had a short and sweet reunion. Seldom did anyone come back after being wounded, at least not to his same unit.

First, I asked for some turkey. "Hey man! Sorry, it's all gone, but here's some C-rats, Doc." I was starved, so even disappointment-laden as the C-rations were, they still tasted good to my empty stomach.

After grilling everyone about what had taken place while I had been away, I learned one of the hardest lessons I have ever learned. The message hit so deeply that to this day, I can feel my heart sink whenever I recall the memory. I learned that I was not indispensable. The platoon got along without me just fine!

As humbled as I was at that moment, I experienced elation on returning. This was my home and these sorry, sad sacks had become my family. Here, the name of the game was survival and to be dependent on any one person broke the first rule of survival. I should have realized that.

Maybe I did become soft on the ship, after all. All the responsibility I had carried in nurturing the men physically and emotionally had made me feel somewhat deified among their ranks. That sense of urgency in returning to their rescue resulted only from my own ego. Because I knew that, I never did feel let down by my platoon nor did I ever resent them for not missing me. Rather, I actually began new growth in the ever-progressing metamorphosis of an infantry soldier during wartime.

I soon replaced the hollow consciousness I initially felt with the numbed out but comfortable feeling I lived with prior to my hospitalization.

"Hey Mike, what are we doing here on this hill so close to the villes?" I yelled.

"Well, thanks for asking how I'm doing and even for checking to see if I was alive or not, Doc. You missed some hairy action out there. We killed a bamboo viper and found two hornets' nests set up by the VC as booby traps. It has been boring with a capital B," Mike answered in his usual manner.

Then he added, "We're supposed to be protecting Hill 190 against any holiday attacks while the jerks on the hill enjoy their Thanksgiving. You remember how they treat Killer Kilo, don't you? We're the dispensable ones, and of course, the VC are supposed to fear our sorry little faces."

"What is this Hil! 190?" I asked Mike.

"It's like a base for a whole company out there beyond those two small hills over there," Mike said, pointing north.

"They have hooches, showers, a mess hall with cooks, and even a stage for USO shows. Man, it's like the rear!" Mike sounded like a kid describing Santa Clause. "One good thing, though—they still don't have electricity," he added with a snicker.

"So what! Are they such pansies that they can't even protect themselves?" I snapped, getting a little perturbed.

"Hey man, don't get all bent out of shape. In a couple of days, we get to take over the hill. Of course, we'll have to do our own protecting." Mike quickly tried to calm me down.

"There's gotta be a catch, right? They're probably gonna make us tear it down like we did 124." I had reverted to my old pessimistic self.

"What did they put in your head on that ship, a radar? That's the only reason they would let us set foot on anything like that. LT says he'll give us a week or so to enjoy it before it comes down. Besides, I hear the NVA are moving in, so we won't be so lonely."

"So, what are we doing now—patrols or what?" I really was not in the mood for patrols just yet but I did not care all that much at that stage of the game. As it was, constant patrols were sent out of our position, most through the villes. The villes were not free fire zones like the jungles. Also, they were safer since the VC would not plant booby traps where the locals trafficked about. Of course, the rice paddies and jungles needed patrolling, so it was not a complete vacation.

I spent the night in the familiar poncho hooch on the ground that I had thought I missed. Maybe those soft, mattressed beds were not so bad after all. I had also forgotten about those miserable mosquitoes after sundown.

This was like starting all over. The constant sweating, the heat and humidity, the insects, and most importantly, the pervasive threat of attack—all the former demons had reappeared to make life unbearable. Somehow, it had passed my memory banks how a person's stomach could be so intensely bound up with adrenaline which stimulated a steady flow of hydrochloric acid into the empty organ.

Yes, I was back in the 'Nam, in all its reality. My short leave of absence from that pit had given me a break from the ever-present thoughts and existence of mortality and morbidity. Now again, those thoughts were as real and as solid as the ground I slept on. I passionately hated that place—the product of America's blundering politics.

Had we been fighting the Germans or the Japanese, I don't know whether I would have felt any different at that particular moment. I really did not despise my homeland; I just hated the war. Being a sentry for a country or a kingdom of any generation would be lonely, as I was. While trying to sleep the standard two-hour increments, I had long forgotten that it was Thanksgiving Day.

By the next day, we had begun running patrols into the villes, rice paddies, and countryside. Here I started to realize the full impact of being a foreign soldier in a far-away country. Never before had we spent so much time in the midst of Vietnamese culture. I began to pick up on the language, family structure, religious customs, and foods. Actually, I was enjoying myself here, sort of like a tourist, barring the war, of course. My learning phrases such as *chou ahn, cam ahn,* and *manjoi cahn* brought smiles to suspicious eyes. Of course, that did not come to pass in one day, but at least the trend toward my Vietnamization began here.

The war still raged, however. On one particular day, we received three, badly-needed, new guys after our platoon had dwindled to about nineteen men. A platoon stateside usually comprised up to fifty-six men. These new boys acted somewhat cocky since back home, rumor had it that the war was at a standstill with very little action. I think the press got weary of covering our events, so they slowed down their reporting. Since our platoon was short on men, the LT put me in charge of taking a new squad out on their first patrol.

With my well-oiled tongue, I hollered, "Get your fat, stateside faces in gear an' let's get a move on! Where's your flak jackets?"

"Man, there ain't nothin' out there," the most vocal new guy answered.

"Listen stateside, I don't even care to know your name, much less care if you catch shrapnel or not. Out here, we say things just once; if you don't listen and obey, you usually get hurt. If you want to change your minds, it's too late 'cause we're heading out right now. Move it!"

For some reason my temper had snapped. I wondered why;

I almost never blew up. Even though I had just come from a rest of sorts, the metamorphosis continued.

The squad leader had told us to perform a perimeter patrol and then, right at dusk, to change our positions for an ambush. Being with these new guys made me feel very uneasy. They were loud in their walk, clumsy, easily distracted, and quite useless.

About a click away from our CP, in broad daylight, after thrashing through some elephant grass and bamboo, we walked up on an open field. The new guys breathed a sigh of relief and instead of stopping at the edge of the vegetation, they continued to march out into the open.

"Get back in here, you idiots!" I whispered as loud as I could, trying not to break silence. It was like a nightmare to have everything go wrong.

Just then, I heard that familiar hollow tube popping in the distance. "Get down!" I shouted to deaf ears. On seeing that they did not immediately respond, I ran out and tackled two of them. The third froze, and as I raised up to pull him down, "BOOM!" The mortar round hit. Thud, thud—two blows hit my chest, as if someone had jabbed me with a sharp rod. My heart sank with fear.

"Not again!" I thought.

"BOOM! BOOM!" The next two rounds hit. A few seconds passed with my face in the dirt. No more rounds fired.

I sat up, dreading to look down at my chest; then I spied two small holes in the front of my flak jacket only.

"Only!" I uttered. "No holes in my chest!" The flak jacket had worked!

"Anybody hurt?" I asked. No one answered, but they obviously were unharmed. Realizing that we should return fire to the most probable origin of the mortar rounds, I decided not to chance anything that might involve common sense with these losers.

"Hey man, you got hit," my frozen partner stuttered. "I ain't never goin' nowhere widout my flak, man," he continued. Actually, none of the trio ever left without their flak jackets after that evening.

The gaze of these boys' on my flak jacket amused me. Their eyes were filled with fear and embarrassment. None of them could say anything—so much the better. At least after that incident, it was easy to herd them like little puppies with all their cockiness drained out of their egos. Blood would have been more effective but I was glad there was none, especially none of mine.

We set up our ambush uneventfully. The night passed with our turns at our watch being faithfully performed. The next morning the boys remained silent since they had passed through a sleepless vigil, pondering their mortality. They had not yet seen anything. Soon they would blend in with the rest of our ranks of distraught men.

We spent only a few days on that unnamed hill anticipating the taking over of Hill 190. It would be a bloodless overrunning but an overrunning just the same. The other two platoons from Kilo Company would be joining us, along with our commanding officer (CO), Capt. Stubb, Gunny La Fifi, the mortar squad, and a communications team. There would be even a head corpsman even though I had never met him. This would be a real invasion.

From a distance, Hill 190 seemed quite vulnerable. Our mentality had evolved to that of guerrilla warfare and all of us were uneasy with the idea of congregating a whole company on one small hill. It seemed to be asking for trouble—as if we were inviting an unfriendly takeover. Could that be the real, underlying plan of our rear echelon warriors? Was Kilo Company becoming bait to draw out the enemy? The foot soldier is the last to know anybody's plans.

The day finally arrived. Lima Company had a myriad of trucks and helicopters at the hill to transfer them from their little paradise. I had secretly hoped, along with the rest of my platoon, that Lima Company would get the deep bush as their next assignment. They had lived on that hill as long as I had been Vietnam.

We had to "quick time it" in to secure the place before any VC would have a chance to sneak in and booby trap the area. We arrived in no time at all, with smiles from ear to ear. All the faces of the departing crew reflected gloom and doom. We jeered the former residents while they boarded their choppers and trucks. They had accumulated too many useless objects, we thought; on our backs sat the only possessions we owned. Christmas had arrived early for us.

The hill was not totally abandoned because the 82 mm mortar team stayed. This specialty team consisted of what seemed to be two or three squads. The team had set its roots deep on that hill. They had decorated the interior of their hooch like an opium den—with parachutes on the ceiling, beaded string curtains as room dividers, nets, strobe lights, black lights, posters and cubbyholes all over. This single hooch even had a generator to supply it with electricity.

Most of the team's members were cocky, loud, arrogant, and disorderly, and had grown soft and ugly, and some of our own potheads were attracted to them. However, we were too busy to allow any corruption by the decadence of the hippie-like gang.

If that was not enough, the rest of our company arrived in all its glamour. Surprisingly, Capt. Stubb made order out of the chaos. The first night, he chose one squad out of each platoon to pull perimeter duty. The rest of us cleaned up while the captain discussed operations with the lieutenants and sergeants. Before long, we all had our assignments and were reviewing

our maps for our patrols which would commence on the
following day.

The men of Kilo Company were thrilled with the setup of
the compound. A couple of cooks had remained behind for a
few days to cook hot meals for us; however, we knew that
"heaven" wouldn't last long. I think everyone took a shower
that night after the hot meal. Since we had no fuel to warm up
the water, it was cold, but no one cared.

I was sure there was some reason the captain took a special
interest in that hill; otherwise, he would have remained back in
the rear. Perhaps it was because that place was so much like the
rear that he felt safe here. That was what I initially thought, but
soon enough, I found out that the captain had wanted to head
our company so he could accomplish something with his tour
of duty. Captain Stubb had once been an enlisted man himself
and had previously served a tour in Vietnam as a sergeant.

Word had it that a major NVA thrust would begin here and
push onward towards Da Nang itself. The battalion chiefs
decided that they could not entrust a defense of such magnitude
to a company gone soft, so they called in Killer Kilo to save the
day. At the time, few of us even suspected what was going on,
much less knew of such threats.

Captain Stubb, in his early forties, always smiling and soft
spoken in his speech, seemed to be able to relate to his men and
to cause them to want to follow him—quite a change from your
average lieutenant. In the days that followed, the captain
patrolled many times with his troops. He wanted to get to know
the terrain first hand so he could create his master plan.

Meanwhile, we became accustomed to working out of a
central compound and coordinating our actions with numerous
other troops. Initially, the leaders had divided the surrounding
areas into sectors, with each platoon responsible for patrolling
its own particular zone. This allowed each platoon to become

familiar with its own territory during planned operations. The patrolling of these sectors would be coordinated by the brass at the CP on Hill 190.

The very day after arriving at the hill, we were out patrolling through the villes and rice paddies. This was, of course, for propaganda purposes, since we wanted our visibility to send a direct message to the VC and the NVA; we were not there for a vacation.

The ville closest to our hill was different from the villes we had visited out in the jungles; it portrayed an obvious French influence. The cemeteries appeared pure French, with their stucco walls, bright colors, square facades, and tile roofs. The public buildings, such as schools and churches, had been built in the same fashion.

In the villes, we even saw motorized vehicles like the common, three-wheeled Lambrettas, glorified motor scooters with a mounted cab. Some of these Lambrettas could carry close to a dozen people with all their produce as they transported it to the city to sell—what a sight! The citizens peddled food from portable stands in much the same way that hot dogs are sold in large city parks.

During the initial show of force, Tran, a Vietnamese boy around twelve years old approached our patrolling squad. Tran wore remnants of American and ARVN uniforms and spoke fluent English. Tran realized that since we did not know him, we would automatically be suspicious of him, so he waited until we took a break before he talked to us. He understood the reality of VC spies of any age and was careful not to ask us very many questions. Rather, Tran explained to some older, more seasoned marines how Lima Company had allowed him to stay on their hill and had paid him to do odd jobs and offered to serve us also. Actually, the boy was quite skilled at diplomacy, as he quickly won the confidence of at least the younger marines in our two-squad patrol.

Tran tried to convince us that he would be invaluable because he could tell us who was who in the ville. One of the squad leaders asked Tran if he was well-liked in his community. Tran answered correctly by saying that since he was an orphan and had previously been involved with American GIs, he was a marked boy among the VC. Nobody trusted him, he said, with any type of local gossip or news that might pertain to the conflict.

Tran had sold his soul and we had the lease whether we wanted it or not. Tran also realized that it would take some time and effort to win our confidence. He was a shrewd and very intelligent person, not a child and still not a man. Tran would never see his childhood like some of us would never see our youth.

"I help you marines out *beau coups* good. Lima Company like me number one. You go ask lieutenant if I can visit number one squad, okay? I not let you down. No way. I know area here, where it safe, where booby trap are. Sometimes I find out where VC hide. When we find VC, you let me blast with Claymore. Click, click, boom—they history, man!" Tran rambled on.

"Listen Tran, you can't go out on any patrols with us. If you try to come with us, we will have to assume that you're a VC spy and you know what that means, right?" Gonzales made his point.

"Hey, Killer Kilo no pushover, just like everyone say. I know you GIs ten minute, and already I like you." Tran was smiling more now than before.

"What does everyone say about Killer Kilo, Tran?" asked Cooper, one of the transfers decorated before our last operation.

"Hey man, keep cool. VC afraid of you. They stay away

when you come. They like Army. Army easy to fight. They like Lima, too. Lima Company lazy. VC can do anything and Lima never know." Tran acted excited.

Was that a put on or what? We told Tran to *didi mau* (leave) and that we would catch him later. In talking with each other, the new guys were all taken in by Tran. We older ones remained much more skeptical. Eventually, time would tell.

If he was genuine, Tran would come around and prove himself in some way. If a stoolie, he would continue to ask inappropriate questions and insist on going out on patrols with us. We cut our talk short and continued conducting our show of force. There was no action that day just like on many other days, but adrenaline ran high on patrol, as usual.

When we arrived back at Hill 190, lo and behold, the cooks had prepared a hot meal for us. This just did not seem right, but what the heck, we enjoyed it anyway. Still no replacement had been sent for Doc Potter, so being the only corpsman for the platoon, I had to participate in most of the patrols and ambushes. Initially, we set up our ambushes within a half to a full click from the hill to catch any curious Charlie that might hope we would be lazy; however, no contact.

On the top of our hill sat the CP (command post), where the captain and his crew planned out their strategy. Also, a huge starlight scope and a strong radio were set up there. Actually, we were led by a whole slew of command personnel that I was never aware of at the time—six or seven sergeants including Gunny La Fifi, a whole radio crew, our lieutenants, of course, and our obscure chief corpsman.

On one occasion, Gunny La Fifi asked me if I would consider being the chief corpsman. I asked him where he thought I would do the most good. He only answered that he did not think the present chief Doc was worth anything and thought I would do a much better job.

"If you give me the rank, I'll be more than glad to take the job. But you know as well as I do that all of this business is nothing but politics, and we're nothing but pawns. No one is going to promote a front line grunt corpsman. I don't even like anyone at the top, except you," I responded.

Nothing ever became of that conversation, as I remained the platoon's Doc. Our discussion did let me know that the gunny was watching over us, but we all knew that anyway.

The ensuing days were anything but mundane. The brass allowed us about five days of hot meals before sending the cooks to the rear and tearing down the mess hall. Also, the showers had to come down. The captain did not think it appropriate for us to literally be caught with our pants down.

One day a USO show was allowed to visit us. A helicopter arrived carrying an American USO troop. American girls? Most of the company had not seen a round eyed girl in months. Early in the afternoon, long before the sun even thought of setting, the show began. First, the band played all the familiar rock songs. Then the girls appeared. Exciting? No! Disappointing? Yes! Those weren't girls; they were dogs. When you saw starved, crazy marines shaking their heads and becoming nauseated, you knew the entertainment was definitely, very, very sorry. Mike and I started laughing so much, we almost suffocated. We left early out of embarrassment.

Taylor, another transferred squad leader, always tried to come up with of interesting ways to entertain us. His squad wore black T-shirts as their symbol of uniqueness. On one occasion, Taylor arranged a boxing match between the squads on Hill 190. We formed a human circle and, one by one, each marine challenged another marine to a round.

There were no grudge matches here since we had grown accustomed to depending upon each other; we overlooked each others' shortcomings and kept no scores. The fights were fun and very interesting. Some of the boys boxed quite well, while others had a long ways to go. One wise character asked a very muscular black fellow named Carver to challenge me to a match.

"Uh uh. No way, man. I've been here long enough to know about Doc! You can fight him yourself, but I ain't that dumb."

At first, I had no idea what Carver was talking about. Then I remembered the unsubstantiated rumors about me that I had heard about way back when I first arrived. That's when Corporal Joe made up one of his stories about me, and it had stuck. It did give me the edge, however, in some especially uncomfortable situations. I was quite grateful that I did not have to fight Carver as he was solid muscle.

Boxing reminds me of a new sergeant named Vaughn who just did not fit in. He seemed to not like me in particular, for reasons unknown. I thought it was probably jealousy; he did not think corpsmen should receive the honor and respect that I had attained.

I did not like the sergeant much either. Vaughn had fought in country once before for about four months before he was medevaced out because he had caught some shrapnel in his chest which needed surgery.

One day, I challenged Vaughn to a boxing match, but he declined, saying that it was not becoming for NCOs to engage in that kind of activity. The real reason had to do with yellowness. His refusing to box turned out to be a bad move on his part; from that point on, Vaughn lost credibility with his men. However, he was still the sergeant; we still followed his orders. Military training had instilled in our minds to obey first and ask questions later—maybe.

So much for fun and games on Hill 190. While we conducted endless patrols, the command played its hand at espionage. Tran proved quite useful, as he supplied us the names of village officials and probable VC contacts. The price on Tran's head grew as word got out that he spent lots of time—many late hours—with the Americans. The captain was up to something big. We all sensed it, even though, at that point, we knew nothing.

Although earlier, cheerful village people had befriended us as we patrolled their territory, now obviously fearful locals passed our patrols. One morning, we stopped a group of school children for simple questioning and their unusual quietness heightened our suspicions. I asked one young boy his age, but he shook his head which meant that he could not understand me. I held up several fingers to indicate I was twenty one and then some more to indicate the marine next to me was nineteen. Then with a questioning gesture, I pointed to the boy who held up ten fingers and two more.

I noticed that the 12-year-old carried some books and an ink bottle for his fountain pen and I asked if I could look at one of the books. He showed it to me and was I ever surprised!

The book contained half blank pages and half filled with carefully handwritten words and numbers that could have won prizes for penmanship. He had written numerous formulas with Greek letters like π ε ψ α and β. This not-yet-teenaged boy studied calculus! I barely knew my time tables at his age. To top it off, these kids had to write their own texts—amazing!

The machine gunner displayed his weapon to another student and asked if he had ever seen one before. The young boy answered no, obviously understanding English. The gunner commenced breaking down his M-60 machine gun, then put it back together—no small feat. He invited the boy to do the same.

The boy looked a little puzzled at first and then, with a serious expression, began working. His busy little hands moved as fast as they could and the weapon was completely disassembled. Without a break in his concentrating eyes, the boy put the machine gun back together almost as fast as he had taken it apart. The whole group of students erupted in excited applause. They had won a victory against the technically advanced Americans.

The marine said kindly, "*Cam ahn em. Didi mau.*," which meant, "Thank you, son; go now." We continued on our patrol, which carried us through a graveyard and next to a schoolhouse. Working around buildings particularly produced anxiety in us, as buildings held too many hiding places and too many civilians, even though the VC did not usually operate in towns.

For some reason, the area remained quiet and appeared ghostly. I kept the forefinger of my sweaty, unsteady hand near the trigger the whole time. The unfamiliar backdrop of civilization caused an increase in our anxiety level. We kept our customary staggered formation with its proper distance; still nothing.

We stopped to have lunch in a cemetery of ornate monuments with multicolored trimmings. The mold and mildew marred most of their beauty, however. It was like sitting in an ancient, archeological dig, because the humid jungles had caused everything to age prematurely with fungus and an overgrowth of vegetation. White sand covered the terrain. Even though it appeared nice and cool, it was still Southeast Asia with all its heat.

As we saddled up, out in the distance a figure carrying what looked like a rifle made a dash towards the brush. Immediately, we fanned out, trying to encircle the person. We ran as fast as we could without losing caution or our awareness of booby traps or ambushes.

I could just picture myself setting off a trip wire. Then I heard, "Pop!" Was a round being fired or what?

Carlson, one of the new guys, yelled. He had stepped on a

toe popper, a booby trap made from a bamboo tube just shorter than an M-16 round. The tube contained a small nail at the center of the closed end with a round placed so that pressure would cause the nail to set off the rear cap of the round. The toe popper had been buried just deep enough to accomplish its job. The trap put a hole in Carlson's foot.

I told Gonzales to hurry before our adversary got too far; that Carlson and I would be fine. We stayed back, while the squad hastily ran in pursuit.

While dressing Carlson's foot, I noticed the rifle-bearing Viet Cong coming out of the brush, heading into the clearing near the schoolhouse. "That coward!" I exclaimed. "Wait here. I'm going to get Charlie." Leaving Carlson behind, I rushed cautiously toward the schoolhouse.

From behind a tree, I aimed at the windows and yelled, "*Lai dai*, Viet Cong!" ("Come out, VC.") No answer. I dashed to the only door.

"Gotta save those children," I thought, as my heart beat frantically. I grabbed the door handle, opened it, and took cover off to the side, hoping that the children would have sense enough to run out to safety. They did. Screaming, those war-torn children ran for cover, taking quick advantage of their only chance for liberty. Then, I pointed my rifle into an open window and quickly searched inside.

There, at gun point, he had taken the schoolmaster and a few children hostage. "*Chou hoi*, you scum!" I said sternly. Through the darkness in the schoolroom, I thought I could see Charlie preparing to throw a grenade at me. I quickly moved out of the window opening and lay prone.

It sounded like a rock had hit the school's inside wall. "One thousand, two thousand, three thousand, four thousand…," I counted the standard four seconds for a grenade to detonate.

"BOOM!" The small enemy had indeed thrown a grenade

at me, but he missed the window and hit the inside wall bouncing the grenade back inside the schoolroom.

Black smoke and debris shot out of the window. "I don't wanna look inside," I thought.

The rest of the squad came out of the brush, taking positions, not knowing what to expect. Trembling, I tried to find the strength to stand up and look inside. Sliding my back up the wall, I finally pushed myself up to a standing position. I pointed my rifle inside and followed it with my eyes. All lay on the floor of the shattered, one-room schoolhouse. I signaled for the squad to come out of their positions and waited for them before I entered the school.

Two little boys lay together, stunned but alive. We saw three holes in one of them; in his arm, in his leg, and one in his abdomen. The child with him had a laceration across his forehead.

The school teacher was dead, and Charlie had multiple wounds and an obviously fractured leg. I exercised tremendous restraint in not finishing him off. I spent most of my time applying battle dressings to the two boys. As I administered aid to these people, I could not ignore my attitude that they seemed like mere pieces of living tissue to me at the time. The dead schoolteacher was a carcass and nothing more. What had become of the person I used to be? I had completely numbed out. I tried to present a caring attitude, but I only feigned it for the children's family.

By the time the chopper arrived at the scene, the whole community had also. The boys' parents and grandparents hovered over their little treasures. A Vietnamese liaison came in the chopper, already aware of the incident. The rules allowed two family members to accompany the children to a military hospital that accepted civilian casualties. Charlie would go also but to a POW (prisoners of war) hospital. Carlson would be sent to a military hospital, probably First Med, and that would likely be the last time we would see that new grunt. Who knows when a replacement teacher would be sent to these gifted children?

Usually no one among our ranks spoke much during the first moments after an event like that. It felt like we had been hauled away by a giant eagle, had been carried along, then released, fallen, and hit the ground; and then tried to carry on as if nothing had ever happened. The moment something like that happened, we had to shove aside the totally unnatural occurrence in order to continue functioning. It always took a while for the adrenaline to settle down—sometimes a day or two. I was not surprised that psychologists, much later, developed the diagnosis of Post Traumatic Stress Disorder to fit many Vietnam veterans.

The lieutenant allowed us to return to our base instead of setting up ambush that night. I wondered about his rationale for making that decision, because at other times, he would have had us stay and conduct business as usual. It was still early in the afternoon when we arrived at base camp, and soon after, the captain called a meeting of all the troops.

"I want you men to know that among the companies of the 3rd Battalion, you are the most respected because of your courage and loyalty to one another. You have kept your recreation away from the bush; we have had almost no problem with drugs or alcohol in firefights. I know that some of you smoke mama sahn's weed and I won't say anything unless the safety of another marine is at risk. Enough of that. As I said, there is really no problem like that with you people."

"I hope you have enjoyed your little stay here, and I'm sorry that the compound has to come down, but you are no strangers to the great outdoors. We are here to do a special job, and for now you will have to trust me in that some of you will be called to do things that you have never done before. The rest of you will have to stay extra alert—look for the unexpected; I hope to bring in some big fish soon. I'm glad I have you men under my command, and if any of you have any problems, please feel free to see me at any time."

The captain's unique words touched me. I had never heard a marine officer take the time to speak with his men like Captain Stubb did that day. The lieutenants and some of the sergeants also tossed in their two bits. For once, however, the captain had set the pace for communication.

That evening, I was eager to sleep in our plywood hooch. With makeshift shades, we could cover the windows enough to have a little candle light inside. We appreciated being able to see and talk during those dark hours. Also, I wrote a few short letters before lights out.

As I dozed off, a very strange sensation woke me. I felt an uneasy presence of something unnatural in my hooch. My eyes opened but nothing was there. I was awake; I knew that for sure. I was about to sit up but fearfully discovered that my body was paralyzed.

I could not move a single muscle! As I attempted to break the pseudoparalysis, my body began to levitate. "No, this is not happening to me," I thought. My body raised slowly upwards, still in a reclined position and totally helpless. "What is going on!" No voice, no movement, no stopping. I became quite frightened.

"God? Where are You? If I continue to float, I'm afraid I won't be able to return, so help me please." I began to pray. I barely was able to gaze back at the cot I had been sleeping on; when I did, lo' and behold, I viewed my body! Just then, instantaneously, without any obvious movement, I lay back in my cot and felt full motion of all my extremities. My heart pounded loudly and rapidly. Sweat poured from my pores as fast as my heart was beating.

"What just happened?" I whispered in the standard bush fashion.

Not knowing what to do with the seemingly supernatural experience, I remained at the edge of my cot, totally confused. Was the experience real or was it just a nightmare? I felt that it was no nightmare, since I still had my rational thinking.

The only person I could confide in without being regarded as a pure lunatic was Jose Gonzales. Jose, a religious man, seemed to have conviction, even if he did engage in swearing every now and then. It took very little to wake up Jose, as he was a seasoned combat veteran.

"*Que pasa, amigo?*" Jose asked.

"Man, I don't know how to tell you, but you gotta listen," I said hesitantly.

"Just spit it out, Doc. I'm right here. *Digame.*"

"You see, I was just getting to sleep when I felt my body rise up. I was in thin air and I looked back and actually saw my own body out on the rack. I thought I was gonna die if I didn't start moving fast." I was sure he heard the fear in my voice.

"*El diablo*! Man, we gotta pray right now and hope that God will listen to us. We ain't such great people, you know."

One of the few prayers I knew was the *Our Father* that my dad had taught me as a little boy. So we prayed as well as we could. I felt very awkward then; we both promised not to mention it to anyone. I was able to sleep after that, but I woke up many times out of habit. The specter of that night never bothered me again.

Chapter 9
Nathaniel Victor

Morning arrived, and the command sent word for us to saddle up; the day had arrived for us to begin the captain's private operation. No matter when or where dispatched, we were always ready to go since our small rucksacks, which held all our earthly belongings, could be loaded at a moment's notice.

We saw no familiar helicopters or trucks ready to ship us out to an unknown destination. We saw only troops bearing maps, loaded packs, and weapons heading out from our own backyard towards the jungles in the background. The captain, in surprisingly good physical condition, also saddled up and walked with us.

Thick mud comprised the terrain since the monsoons were very much upon us. We made a beeline towards the mountains without a stop. At the foothills of these mountains, we continued on a forced march of sorts, straight up the steep inclines.

We pressed on all day, making very few stops. The sun would come out with a steaming vengeance for a while, then the skies would darken and drench us. These feuding forces continued all day long, which was unusual during the monsoons. The rains customarily poured for days at a time without ever allowing the sun to shine. Once we began our ascent, we had no relief of a flat surface.

Hours passed, but we had not completed our force march.

If that march was supposed to terminate in a surprise attack, I did not think any of us would have the strength to do any surprising.

Onward! I had not been that exhausted since cross country training in high school. Still, no stopping. We each added to the burden of our already-wearied legs by carrying a 15 to 20 pound mortar round. Sometimes, up higher on the mountain, a soldier at the front of the line would slip on the mud and then slide down, knocking everyone down like bowling pins. This was irritating and hilarious at the same time, and really made us consider the weight we carried. Eating one and one-half meals a day helped some, but the needed water and ammo comprised the bulk of those torturing pounds.

Panting like overworked sheep dogs, we finally came to a halt. I could not believe how tired I was. We assumed that Capt. Stubb and the lieutenants must have been so fatigued that they decided to stop for the night, even though we would sleep (sic) on a high-grade slope. Mike and I decided to share a meal since we could not even begin to imagine our each cooking a meal without help from the other. Long Range Rats (LRPRs) it would be.

I took out a packet of something au gratin and attempted to tear the edge of the pack so I could remove the plastic bag which contained the food. It would not open. With my teeth I tried unsuccessfully to rip it open. Then Mike tried his hand at it, but he became a one-man cartoon show as he tried to open that bag.

Becoming very frustrated and dying of starvation, I grabbed the food pack, took out my bayonet, and began to thrust the sharp-pointed instrument of war through the top edge of that demon-possessed packet. Still, I did not have the strength to penetrate it. I fell backwards, gazing up into the rain as it fell on my face. There was not one ounce of strength left in any of my muscles that evening. I had already resolved that we just would not eat when with a shout, Mike exclaimed, "I did it! I did it! I got it open!"

We finally cooked the food and to this day, I remember how good it tasted. Even though I ate only one half of a meal, it was enough to satisfy my weary bones. After finishing our meals, we were ordered to set up the perimeter, but only for our protection; not for ambushes or much else.

I stretched out on the ground with a tree between my legs to prevent me from rolling down the mountain. No one else set up poncho hooches either. We each just threw our ponchos over us to keep out at least a little rain. And of course, we slept in the most uncomfortable positions we could drum up. Occasionally, the night's peace was disturbed by a marine's rolling down the hill in his sleep and being stopped by a tree or another marine.

That night, as always, I took my turn on watch. Thankfully, we had no contact, which was not surprising. Who in his right mind would be patrolling that mountain at night—or for that matter, even in the day?

I do not know whether I should have welcomed the morning or cursed it. We were still dead dog tired, but from lack of sleep, not due to physical exertion. To add to our misery, the rain had completely soaked each of us. I tried my best to get the other marines to change their socks to prevent trench foot. Some did; some did not. Once we began moving again, our bodies' heat somehow compensated for our being saturated in the shivering wetness of those monsoons.

On a whim, I took off both my helmet and my hat for about thirty minutes. I could not believe the misery that resulted. The continuously falling drops of water played pitter patter on my head and made of me a believer in the old Chinese water torture. Before long, I had to put my hat back on. I just could not take it any more. It felt like the inside of my brain echoed with the roar of rainfall, vibrating to the point of numbing pain. This experience clearly affirmed the value of a head cover.

About mid day while taking a break, I looked down at my hands and arms. As to be expected, the palms and fingertips had become pale and wrinkled. As I began to inspect further, I discovered that the back sides of my hands were also wrinkled. Further examination of my arms revealed that I was being pickled alive. Not only were my hands white and wrinkled, but all the way up past my elbows, it looked as if I had been stricken with leprosy. A quick look at my legs told the same story—I was changing into an Egyptian mummy.

Of course, for those of us who lived in the bush, that skin condition was nothing unique—it had become an everyday occurrence during the monsoons. However, I had never noticed the extent of our being water logged until that particular rain. This experience was an eye opener; I actually had envisioned the hide sloughing off of my bones at any time.

During the nights, whether on ambush or back at the CP, we invariably slept in a puddle of water. One evening, I slept on one side and the following night, I slept on the other side. With the sophisticated medical knowledge acquired over my short military career, I rationalized that by switching sides each night, I could prevent arthritis from setting in later. I was no doctor and I was wrong; my bones have been stiff ever since, despite those rotations. At least it helped lessen the aches on the following mornings.

There, in the middle of the monsoon season, it rained twelve inches an hour at times. New Mexico's average annual rainfall never exceeded eight inches for the whole year. Since it rained practically every night, the temperature finally dropped to tolerable levels.

Unfortunately, my favorite enemy, the mosquito, didn't seem to care. His unmistakable, high-pitched buzzing seemed to scream above all other jungle sounds during those dark hours. Of course, my poncho served as all mosquitoes' favorite shelter. And their favorite companion was, of course, yours truly. Also, we discovered that our insect repellent washed away during rain. Oh, how I hated those God-forsaken, persistent creatures! I hated their noise that kept me awake, I hated the intense itching they caused, and I hated the very thought of their existence. I hated mosquitoes!

Another disgusting facet of the jungles during monsoon season was how the foliage attacked our pruney skin. Anytime we walked through the jungles, those nasty, razor-sharp edges on the elephant grass and the forever-present thorns found soft, soggy, easily penetrable skin to force their way into. The ease of entry was due to the days of our soaking in crystal pure water before that malicious vegetation could feast on our marinated skin. Ah, yes—truly paradise on earth!

During that time of inundation, our platoons split up so we could encircle a certain alleged NVA territory. So far, the information on the enemy had been incomplete, but the captain thought that by probing in the vicinity of Nathaniel Victor, we could better assess the terrain that Nathaniel had had to traverse in his attempt to overrun us. The lieutenants and sergeants worked frantically over their maps to coordinate the platoon sections for the operation. The captain chose to stay with our part of the platoon.

After the first platoon departed, we readied ourselves for the evening. Darkness followed shortly, signaling the whole platoon to saddle up. The whole platoon? The security of working with small groups and without the officers was gone. We enlisted marines were at a definite disadvantage.

The pitch black night offered no moon or starlight to

illuminate even the tips of our noses. Once on the move, we discovered how hard it was to determine the position of the marine in front of you. All we needed was for some new guy to get lost and take half the platoon with him.

Walking through unfamiliar soil, we crossed hills, streams, swamps and jungle. It was hard enough during the daylight to keep good footing, but during the night, we found it next to impossible. Walking through the water was very agitating. Half the time, the water was deeper than expected; and the other half, it was shallower.

At one point, I saw the captain walking several men in front of me, and when he went under with a splash, I almost laughed out loud. Had I been drinking a coke, the whole can would have come out my nose. Needless to say, my turn at going under also came. Sometime late into the evening, we set up a line of ambushes according to squads. If I hadn't know better, I would have thought that we were being trained for something.

Despite our anticipation, we did not run into Nathaniel Victor that night. No one could really criticize the captain for what he was doing as we all figured that his plan was to engage the enemy.

The captain was no dummy, either. He knew that we lacked experience in operating as a big group. We all knew how to function in conventional war strategies, but none of us had ever been tested in combat using these maneuvers. Captain Stubb knew that we were good soldiers and that we would not let him nor each other down when it came to fighting. The captain did not want any of us to get hurt acquiring a little hands-on experience in a relatively safe zone.

He knew that the experience would build the important tools required for us to successfully pull off his larger plan. The captain did not actually tell anyone what he was doing, but we were no dummies either. At least Mike, myself, and several of the squad leaders figured it out after the first night.

The following day, we walked half a day and then set up a command post so we could patrol the area during the day and at night. When night came, however, our whole platoon changed positions before setting out for our evening patrol. Charlie and the NVA were as accustomed to running night patrols as we were to running them by day. As we reversed the procedure, it became exciting.

I set out with Alpha squad that night. Even though it was training, we were still in the 'Nam, and the adrenaline pumped as hard as it had every night in the bush. The night was not well suited for movement; there was no way one could catch even a glimmer of a trip wire nor a glare from the metal barrel of an enemy's rifle.

Perspiration poured out of me due to the heat, humidity, and anxiety. Thankfully, no rain dampened us for the majority of that evening.

After a few hours, we broke through the thick grass and vines into a clearing. Cautiously, the point man slowly walked close to the edge of the growth, careful not to lead us through the center of the opening. We kept our staggered positions and we followed him with the same care and stealth.

"Crack-crack-crack-crack-crack!! Rat-ta-ta-ta-tat!" Immediately, I found myself face down in the mud, as did everyone else. Something seemed peculiar about the ambush. "Boom"—a grenade!

"Crack-crack-crack! Rat-ta-tat!" Something prevented me from returning fire. As I lifted my head and looked about me in those first seconds, I saw that no one else returned fire! Then I heard them—an M-16 rifle...an M-60 machine gun...an M-26 grenade—the sounds of American weapons!

I yelled at the top of my lungs, "Green clusters! Someone

shoot off a green cluster!" Before I could get all the words out, a marine fired off green cluster flares. The shooting stopped.

"Kilo two alpha, identify yourselves!" Our squad leader shouted.

"Kilo one bravo." After that chilling response, a dead silence covered the area.

"What, in heaven's name are you people doing here?" No one from kilo one answered.

As I lay there listening, I recalled realizing when the firing had started, that the tracers looked different, and it seemed like too many weapons being fired to be the enemy. Also, the VC did not tote around M-60 machine guns, even though they occasionally used captured or stolen M-16s.

The point man's walking close to the elephant grass perimeter made it difficult to see the shape of our silhouettes. Thank God that no one in our squad fired back; that would have given away our positions and the "enemy" would not have missed us. Our thinking alike had developed over time and it was so necessary for our survival that it was unexplainable.

"Anyone hit?" I began my survey.

"Doc, Spitzer here thinks he's caught some frag."

"Where does it hurt, Spitz?"

"Right on my right cheek bone, Doc. But it ain't nothin'. Jus' barely dinged me."

Spitzer was right, he had a very small shrapnel wound which only required a small patch. Friendly fire had not earned him a "slow badge," as everyone called a Purple Heart.

We did not know whether to be angry or just plain thankful. The two squads approached each other awkwardly. "Hey man, where you guys supposed to be? Besides, you're lousy shots." The humor was as dry as our mouths.

Their squad leader tried to explain where he thought they were and after comparing maps, it was obvious his whole platoon was off track. We told them to just stay put and we that would move to a different pos (position). That way, the mistake would not happen again that evening. At that point, we still did not care to talk with them, even if out of anger. Spitzer's wound could wait until the morning.

We felt a certain sickening that accompanied being involved in "friendly" fire—almost like a betrayal, but not as severe. For a long time, I was thankful that we had our act together and had not wounded or killed anyone from kilo one bravo. I gave even more thanks that none of us were hurt. We also felt somewhat vulnerable at that point since that time, our adrenaline had caused more depression than excitability like after an enemy encounter.

With permission from the lieutenant, we set up for an ambush instead of running a patrol. The LT thought, and we knew, that we would not be able to react quickly with our minds dwelling on what had just happened. The incident had foiled the planned night patrol, but only for the moment.

By the time morning had arrived, our nerves had moved back into position, and once more, we were ready to take on the world like good marines. The truth is that, that time, we needed a few hours, rather than the few minutes, it usually required to allow our numbing potions to anesthetize our minds. Those two words, *friendly fire*, were never good. But at least we were heading to the command post for a little rest.

On our way back to the CP—before we ever made it in—the "Top" (the captain) radioed us a new set of coordinates to patrol. Although prepared for an overnighter, we had not taken much food and water, but *c'est la guerre*. This was the day the sun decided to visit us after it had hidden out behind those cool clouds for the past few days. It became very hot.

Our maps did not display any blue lines which would indicate streams. Of course, we couldn't depend on those maps, as they had proved notoriously inaccurate, as stated before; most of them had been devised from air surveillance and not from ground observation.

We found ourselves in the middle of a lush green jungle in mid-monsoon season, with bodies of water around us in every direction. On the average day in the bush, we would be plagued with water everywhere, trying to think of ways to keep the water off of ourselves. So what surrounds us when we need water the most? That's right—Murphy's Law ruled again. Of course, we just had to patrol within walking distance of no remnant of a water hole. We had already exhausted all of our water and any water-containing foods from our C-rations. Our tongues began to swell as the symptoms of dehydration set in.

"Hey Doc! I'm beginning to feel sick. What does it mean?"

"Yeah, Doc. Me too; I can't even think straight."

"We gotta find water! I don't think we can make it any further. Think of something, man."

The mood turned desperate. I also worried. We walked some more, but that time, not on a mission to search and destroy, but rather to search and replenish. Necessity being the mother of invention revealed a brilliant idea, or so I thought at the time.

"Mike! Taylor! Stop!" I summoned the squad. "I've seen the locals carrying banana tree stocks to the market to sell for some kind of food they make. There's plenty around here. Let's go ahead and cut one down to see if they have enough water for us."

Thompson, a machine gunner, grabbed a machete and cut down a banana tree trunk, bringing a piece for me to inspect. But before I could look at it, his fellow gun team members yanked out chunks for themselves and began to devour the pulp. "This VC food tastes like cucumber! Gimme some more."

Havoc ensued. The whole squad consumed as much of the

banana stock as they could. Finally, I grabbed some to taste for myself. The white pulp tasted great—and very juicy. They were right, it did taste like cucumber. What a sweet savor we experienced as the pulp began to quench our thirst.

Before I could take any additional bites, one of Thompson's men began to yell, "My mouth! My mouth! Doc, my mouth's on fire!" Shortly after, in the same sequence in which the forbidden fruit had been eaten, the men began to complain. The daisy chain finally hit me, since I had been the last to partake.

"What is going on here?" It felt as if a thousand pins were being thrust into the mucous membranes of my mouth. My tongue experienced a pain unequaled by any jalapeño or green chili I had ever eaten. What should we do? Pandemonium ruled, as I scrambled for ideas.

"Xylocaine! Viscous Xylocaine!" Frantically searching through my medical bag, I found a bottle of Xylocaine and immediately squirted some into my mouth. Relief! What a relief! So I began squirting Xylocaine into all the mouths.

"What's that stuff, Doc?"

As I opened my mouth to answer, nothing but slurred jumble fell out! What next? That's right! No one could ever talk a straight sentence after visiting the dentist—and that day in the jungle was no different! The Xylocaine numbed our mouths! Not anything important, right? Wrong. What about the radio?

"Kilo two alpha, state your pos," the CP radioman beckoned to our squad.

Mike put his handset to his mouth and garbled out a noise. It sounded as though his tongue was the size of an orange. We all broke out laughing. For a few moments, we actually talked and laughed on patrol out in the middle of the bush. Our guard was down, but it was okay. "Oh forthethet." With that classic answer, Mike signed off.

Totally out of verbal communication, and nearly mute, we continued our search for water. Resorting to survival techniques that I had learned in the Boy Scouts and applying the same basic principles here, we finally found a stream that seemed to be filled with the sweetest coolest water I had ever tasted. I was surprised that the VC had not set up an ambush by the water. By the time we found that heavenly water, the effects of the Xylocaine and fortunately the banana tree stocks had worn off. We had accomplished nothing on that day, but what else was new?

Semi-lost but generally heading in the correct direction, we made it our goal to return to the CP before sundown. This time, I filled my six canteens of water, just in case we detoured again. The fact that we had eaten no food had not really mattered to any of us today. We had been well watered.

After a few hills and valleys, things began to look familiar and more like our maps. There it was, the CP, just like home again! At that moment, I thought to myself how warped my thinking had become. I had adhered to the philosophy of every nomadic person who had ever walked this earth. Finding refuge in a gathering of about twenty individuals whose homes were makeshift poncho tents and eating out of cans could not be called *coming home.*

We had become nomadic tribesmen, warlike in nature. We had ceased fighting for any country or for any idealistic endeavors. It had become a medieval sport in which we hunted and we were being hunted. There had long since ceased being any rationale to the conflict. The adrenaline rush in its subtle but complete addiction, had slowly overtaken each of us. Front lawns, birthday parties, flush toilets, and Saturday night cruising now seemed as foreign as Lithuania to most. We welcomed that home; it was not a memorable welcome but a welcome just the same.

"Welcome home men! We'll be saddling up in fifteen minutes."

"Just give me a can of beef 'n shrapnel and I'll be as good as new," I said, and then fell back to sleep for every one of those fifteen minutes.

I had already forgotten about Spitzer and his wound; he was a very quiet individual who seldom complained about anything. His wound ultimately healed itself out in the bush without any ritualistic medical magic of mine or of any of the people in the rear.

We were off. The whole nomadic platoon was on the move again. Usually, when within the confines of the platoon, most of us lost interest in our position or in where we were heading. That day was no different. Also, Mike was talkative, so during our short breaks—when we could speak in low tones—I was entertained by the latest news on dilapidation of the establishment with all its problems and woes. We Kool-Aid sharers argued playfully since Mike did not care for the Vietnamese people as I did. However, after a long time, I finally won out. Probably, my winning was due to Mike's having been in country so long that he finally became used to the Vietnamese presence rather than by my winning the on-going argument.

After walking a while, we took a short rest on the incline of a small hill, out of the thickness of the jungle but in an area thoroughly overgrown with elephant grass. Exhausted, I leaned back and dropped to a sitting position.

As soon as I realized what I had just done, I knew that I could not reverse my action. I was already on my way down to the ground, committing a grave wartime sin. It could have easily been a mortal sin, too, in every sense of the word, *mortal.* You see, I had not checked the area on which I had chosen to sit—definitely a felony!

"Clunk!" I hit ground with my buttocks. The clunking sound was metal, hollow metal. The only hollow metal that large that I was familiar with was a five-hundred pound bomb. And I knew of no safe five hundred pound bombs on the ground in the middle of the jungle. "Thank God I'm still alive to hear the clunk," I thought.

Mike saw the pale, distressed look on my face and knew right then that something serious had just happened.

"Doc! What's going on? Is it what I think it is?"

I could not speak. I shivered inside and out. My heart palpitated furiously. I dared not move even my eyeballs, much less my mouth and tongue, to answer Mike.

"Sarge! Captain! We've got a problem here!" Mike was as nervous as I was. I knew he was hating himself for befriending a potential dead man.

"Everyone take cover! I'm going to move to find out whether this thing's a dud." Mike just stood there. "Hey, that includes you, you pint-sized Greek!" I roared. I could not endure the thought of bringing the men down with me.

The whole ordeal reminded me of doing so many other things out on the front in 'Nam. Before engaging in some potentially lethal action, we just took a deep breath and proceeded blindly. *Hope for the best and expect the worst* was just about the only attitude one could have that would preserve any remnant of sanity in that pit.

"No, Doc. We're *Ps* and we're in this together. If there's no wire, then this probably ain't no booby trap."

"Take cover, Mike, or I'll kill you. If you want to give me instructions, just yell and I promise I'll do exactly what you say." Convinced that I would follow his instructions, Mike took

cover nearby. The rest of the platoon already had taken cover at
a safer distance.

"*Slowly* look for that wire, Doc." Ha! I was not about to
look for that wire *fast*!

My hands maneuvered slower than a snail. Every blade of
grass felt like a wire. "Thump, thump, thump, thump," my
heart became the only noise within a fifty-foot radius. The
fingers on both my right and left hands gradually inched their
way up and down each side of my rump in an ever-so-slow
sweep. I expected each second to be my last. My fingertips
trembled as they slowly proceeded across the hot metal bomb
casing.

"Wire!" I sort of shouted. Dead silence pierced the jungle.
My body was in complete tetany—hard as a rock. "Oh, God!
I'm yours. It's up to You," my prayer was not so silent.

Enough time had passed that my legs had begun to stiffen
which caused me to have a hard time moving. I knew I could
not stay in that position forever. I had to move to find out
whether that was a dud. Our battalion included no demolition
expert. It was a live bomb or a dead one, and that was the
whole story.

I took a deep breath and ordered myself to move. I obeyed.
One-fourth inch. Rest. One-half inch. Another rest. Three-
fourths of an inch. JUMP!

I lunged forward, hit the ground with a belly flop, threw
my arms over my head, and held my breath!

"One thousand, two thousand, three thousand, four thousand, five thousand."

"It's a dud!" exclaimed Mike.

"Don't move yet," I yelled in sheer terror.

"Doc, it's okay. The blasted thing's a dud. Get up." Mike's
voice of reassurance was just what the doctor had ordered. I
stood up and brushed off myself. Really though, I was check-

ing my pants to see if they were wet with anything other than sweat.

"Dry?...good," I thought.

When we had walked about a click—well out of harm's way—the captain ordered the mortar team to detonate the bomb. I remember hoping the mortar team was out of range. The boom caused a little shock wave that we felt even as far away as we had moved. "I could've been vapor," I thought, a little disconcerted.

As we sat and waited for the mortar team to catch up with us, no one said much. Mike offered me a swig of his Kool-Aid—one of any Marine's prize possessions to be saved for special occasions only. This was considered a special occasion.

We finished the captain's operation in about two additional days, and on the last one, we encountered a sniper who fired a couple of rounds at us. One of our men spotted him and a squad set chase after him. Coats saw the sniper disappear into the ground, which meant the enemy used tunnels.

The rest of the platoon caught up with the squad, and we set a perimeter around the tunnel opening. Most of the tunnels were south of us, so few of my platoon had ever ventured into one of them. A wide variety of stories about tunnels floated around and it was hard to know which to believe.

Mike volunteered to enter the tunnel, even though Gallegos was smaller. Mike had become like me—fully addicted to the adrenaline of uncertainty.

Gonzales threw in a concussion grenade followed by a smoke grenade. Mike got ready by rolling down his sleeves and buttoning his collar to protect himself from the burning powder left by the smoke bombs. Making sure he had his flashlight, his .45, his cap, and a bayonet, Mike was ready to descend.

"Look out gooks, 'cause here I come," Mike called ahead

with a nervous stutter. None of the rest of us joked or made any other comment.

Five long minutes passed and no sign of the Greek. I sat in the shade of a bamboo thicket and took a standard Vietnam issue, short, three-minute nap. When I awoke, my watch indicated that only eight minutes had passed since Mike entered the tunnel. However, it seemed like several hours.

No one stood at the mouth of the tunnel for fear of a back blast or something else unexpected. I made way for the tunnel entrance to see if I could hear something. I could hear what sounded like grunting and cursing mixed with other unexplainable noises. It had to be Mike.

Sure enough, Mike backed out of the tunnel complaining in his usual fashion, pulling something as he exited.

"Gonzales, where is your sorry little face? You should be doing this instead of me. You're the one that made this mess," Mike commented as he hauled out the body of our little VC killed by the concussion grenade.

Gonzales then rolled down his sleeves, taking Mike's remark personally. "How far did you get?" Jose asked Mike in an irritated tone.

"About thirty yards. I couldn't tell how much more tunnel was left. It didn't seem like a big one, but check it out for yourself." Mike was exhausted from pulling out the corpse.

Jose crawled in and after about ten minutes, crawled out backwards, fortunately empty-handed. He reported that the tunnel had ended a short distance from where Mike had found Charlie.

The rear geniuses told us to leave the body there and end our little excursion. All that we needed was another propaganda tool for the communists to use against us. We buried the brave comrade and headed back.

Hey kid! Watch out fer them elephant grass blades. They're pretty sharp, you know.

Chapter 10
The Encounter

After we arrived at Hill 190, the captain again busied himself making strategy. And we went back to our routine of playing bird dog trying to catch the skillful game. Tran was there to greet us as we returned, hoping that his information to the captain was fruitful. Tran knew that we would not give him any details, but he could tell by our faces, more or less, what had occurred.

Several evenings later, the captain summoned a few marines for a special meeting. The chosen ones included few of the squad leaders and some of the transfers from the 5th Marine Division, about six in all. After a short briefing, the special squad returned to their hooches and began applying camouflage makeup. It looked like those excited men were readying themselves for a high school talent show.

After the painted warriors departed, most of us were bewildered as to what was happening. "Let them play their games," we thought.

Several hours passed before the painted marauders passed back through our perimeter guards, carrying on as if they had just come back from trick or treating on Halloween night. Gonzales led the pack. My curiosity had gotten the best of me, so I asked, "Hey! What's going on out there with you Girl Scouts?"

"Hey, man! We really pulled one over on the village chief. Tran told us that the NVA were seen at the hooch of the chief several times. So the captain decided that the chief needed a friendly visit to see if he wanted to be patriotic enough to let us know what Nathaniel Victor's plans were. It was great! We staged a mock interrogation with one of the local friendlies, pretending to be real rough on him. With all our makeup, we really looked mean."

All the others who went were just as excited. Apparently for once, we had broken ground on intelligence. We had to act quickly and keep very quiet. Tran had been escorted away from the hill long before the "commandos" had gone into the village. Three days passed without anyone knowing about the captain's plans—so much the better, though. If we had known anything, you could rest assured that the VC also knew. I do not even think the lieutenants knew.

Our platoon was still shy one corpsman, but one of the other platoons had no corpsman, so, ever so often, my superiors volunteered me to help them. That meant that I pulled ambushes and patrols almost every night, whereas the rest of the platoon rested every second or third day.

For some reason, the captain had sent the first and third platoons out to base themselves somewhere else. The only reason I could come up with was that he used those platoons as false decoys to make both Charlie and Nathaniel think that there would be minimal security left on Hill 190. So by the third day, we comprised Hill 190 in its entirety.

The captain called for a platoon-wide night patrol, leaving virtually no one back at our hill. As dusk began, in full battle gear, we headed out to our pre-planned positions. It was not until then that we all finally received the full gist of the ol' captain's plans.

The NVA had planned a massive entry into a neighboring ville using our hill as a pathway. I had heard of hills becoming overrun, but had never seen that happen yet, thank God.

However, it seemed that Nathaniel had one Achilles' heel. In order to overtake our position, the NVA regulars had to cross a body of water, which made them sitting ducks for an ambush. And an ambush is exactly what we had planned for them.

"Make sure the first NVA regular who crosses over does so safely, 'cause he's just a scout trying to draw fire," Lieutenant Winter whispered nervously. Then he assigned certain times for each of us to fire. The marine at the front of the ambush and closest to the river would fire last to make sure that all the regulars had crossed.

Lying prone, under the cover of brush close to the banks of the wide river, we began our vigil. Anticipating where the enemy would enter and at what time I would fire were the only thoughts that occupied my head. We waited and waited—nothing new.

After about three hours, right in the middle of the river, a lone NVA scout waded. Pay dirt! "Come on in, come on in," I thought, silently beckoning other NVA to follow him.

Just then, somewhere to the south of us, the explosions of 105 mm artillery shells began sounding off. After each boom, the piercing jet-like sounds tore over our heads, "Boom! Boom!"

The rounds exploded in the water and on the bank opposite us! Cracking sounds pierced the atmosphere like jet aircraft and continued as long as the rounds persisted in their pounding of the bank. What was going on?

The captain frantically called on the radio, trying to find out who and why anyone was firing. It seemed that some forward observer spotted movement and carelessly called in artillery to his designated map coordinates.

Artillery never accomplished anything! Very seldom could any casualties be attributed to the big guns. The NVA just made a U-turn to safety and would just come back another time.

After the clumsy barrage of military waste ended, we all

maintained our set positions in hopes that Nathaniel would try to sneak in again, not realizing that we were waiting for him. The captain's long, thought-out plans had dissolved in just a few minutes. "What the heck," I thought. "This is just another foiled ambush. It don't mean nothin'."

The phrase, "It don't mean nothin'," was part of the coping mechanisms we grunts used when something did not develop according to plans. Why become angry or even frustrated? That never accomplished anything but ulcers or suicides.

We resumed our pattern of shared watches in two hour intervals. The enemy had exposed himself and very well might try to cross the river at that pre-planned juncture one more time. The night passed ever so slowly. Off in the distance, I could almost envision the NVA trying to cross again. Blinking hard helped vanish the illusions. Dawn appeared and Nathaniel Victor had once again proved himself an accomplished soldier.

The captain formed a scouting party early that morning, to see whether any casualties had been inflicted by the rear echelon artillery. On returning, they reported one small trace of a blood trail and nothing to indicate any mass injuries.

All night, something kept bothering my right forearm, so at first light, on self-examination, I discovered a painful knot about the size of a small plum. "Perhaps a scorpion bit me last night," I mused. Whatever it was, it would have to wait until we got back to the hill.

The captain again proved himself a worthy leader; he did not take the misfortune personally. He, like the rest of us, considered the major mess up as "just one of those things." Perhaps it was just meant to be. Perhaps we would have been outnumbered and ultimately suffered major losses. It was not for us to know those things, Capt. Stubb concluded. Maybe he was right.

Chapter 11
Yuletide

With our platoon still short one corpsman, I had to continue to pull double duty, even with fever caused by that "scorpion bite." Over the next few days, the knot on my arm became larger and increasingly more painful. Gradually, I realized that the "bite" was really a boil gone wild. My arm was swollen from my fingernails to my elbow. Moving enough to even bat an eyelash hurt bad. Knowing that I should either treat the infection on the spot or chance becoming septic, I took the only action I knew at the time.

I carried a meager supply of antibiotics—mainly horse pills called erythromycin—and a sharp bayonet. Mike cleaned off the bayonet and then, with his cigarette lighter, heated it until the tip became red hot. I cleansed the origin of the infection with a little bit of soap and water. Mike handed over the bayonet and then stepped back, not wishing to participate any further.

I grasped the bayonet (not so steadily) with my left hand and placed its sharp, sizzling tip over the head of the boil. I thrust the bayonet point into the skin. It really hurt! Out burst a deluge of thick pus. I had prepared some gauze pads to catch the molten lava from the volcano.

What a relief! Finally, the pain began to subside. After expressing as much of the poison as I could, I dressed the wound and placed my arm in a sling. Each day for the following week, I performed the same ritual, expressing as much debris as possible, with each session rendering more relief than the preceding time. Still, I had to accompany the squads on their ambushes just about every night. Luckily, during those times, we experienced hardly any activity, so I did not have to use my right arm much.

That experience with the boil took place around the middle of December, 1970. Thankfully, the monsoons seemed to be letting up. People were already receiving Christmas packages from home. The season of the year should have caused some nostalgia, but that was strangely absent for some reason.

In fact, as horrible and insensitive as it may sound, during that time, I received some significant mail from home—photos in which I could not recognize any of my family! The mail included a picture of my father holding a photo of me in his lap and another photo of my mother and brother. It was as if those photos were the first introductions I had ever had with my family. As was the custom, I did burn the letters, but I kept the pictures.

I felt that perhaps I was committing some sort of sin for not recognizing my own flesh and blood, but thought I would deal with that at a later time, just as I would subsequently deal with everything else. Confrontation with personal issues during combat was never in anyone's best interest. Sure, that was what the book said.

"This is so stupid," I thought. "I've become a functioning blob without a soul. I can't believe I cannot recognize my own family." My head began to buzz with an uncomfortable feeling, as if an unwelcome intruder was forcing its way inside me. I sat on the ground, staring again at those photographs. My eyes glazed over as I gazed off into space. My mind went blank. I ate very little for supper that evening.

The bush provided no stores to buy Christmas cards, so I

decided to make some. I chose only one idea, then did a mass production of the cards for my family, friends, and relatives.

"*Paz en la tierra a los hombres de buena voluntad*" means "Peace on earth, to men of good will." How ironic, now that I think of it. In fact, I do believe there was definite sarcasm in those cards drawn on cardboard torn from C-ration boxes. On a hill that overlooked a small village with a bright star above it, a modern soldier kneeled on one knee.

There was no peace, no hope, and no good will. Most of us blasphemed God daily, myself included. That Christmas was nothing more than a faint memory of a childhood tradition celebrated in the obscure past. The sooner the so-called holiday ended, the easier it would be to concentrate on achieving the objective at hand—body counts. Cold and cruel? No, that was just our way of life at the time.

Prior to the actual Christmas Day, we heard rumors that the NVA were mounting an offensive equal to that of the 1968 Tet Offensive. The idea was unsubstantiated, as only the rear people seemed to know anything about it. And of course, there were no braver warriors than the rear echelon. In any event, the superiors felt compelled to keep us on special alert. That was to ensure all those *heroic* men of the supporting ranks a safe and wholesome holiday festivity. I loved those rear clowns.

I participated in non-stop patrols. For about eight or ten days, I wore my arm in a sling. Daily, I squeezed thick, purulent material from the bayonet opening. Finally and uneventfully, the boil healed. The lack of enemy contact became a little worrisome. We, too, began to believe that those rumors were indeed true. Still, we found time for a little horsing around.

On one patrol, we stopped outside of a certain ville. A little boy stood next to us, watering his water buffalo. Those water buffalo were the workhorse and mainstay of Southeast Asian agriculture. Little boys often worked in the rice paddies, riding their huge, oxen-like animals. These beasts performed like well-trained dogs. The little boys rode on their backs, holding to the animals' tails for support. Often we observed a child fast asleep on top of a water buffalo while the animal itself responsibly carried on the farm work. When a stranger approached the two, the buffalo would lower its head in a charging stance and let out a big snort, scratching the ground with its front hoof to protect its master.

Once, Sergeant Tito, himself raised around the creatures, gave out a peculiar whistle which produced an irritating sound to one of the animals. Then our squad almost experienced an immediate charging of that bull.

The little boy who was watering his buffalo carried a cluster of small red peppers in his hand. "GI number ten. No can eat. *Beau coupe* hot. Five dollar no can eat."

A challenge! Being from New Mexico and raised on Southwest chili, both green and red, I thought I could eat anything. Also being quite familiar with the culinary delight called *perrers*, I knew that red was always more mild than the green categories. (At least that was the way it had been back home.)

Having spent over five months in country, I had grown accustomed to eating the wild little green chilies out in the bush to flavor the bland government issue food. No challenge—a steal!

"Ten dollars, baby *sahn*. Number one GI can eat, no problem." I had presented my bid.

"Twenty bucks says the doc can't eat it!" Loyalty dies quick when it comes to gambling.

"You're on. Go ahead, baby *sahn*, give the doc a big one." The squad was divided.

I selected a large, single, red pod, placed it in my mouth,

chewed it a few times, and swallowed it. Even the water buffalo was silent as we counted the seconds.

"Ha! Pay up, you sorry girl scout troop. That was like lettuce."

As I was collecting my loot, something inside of me began to happen. "This is very unusual," I thought, "Chili is always hot at the beginning—at the first bite."

That oriental chili was quite different—no sensation at first. Then, in a matter of fewer than three seconds, it hit me. Like napalm, the explosion of intense heat was merciless in its destruction of each cell of the mucous membranes of my mouth!

"Aaaaaah, water! Water! Water! Aaaaaah, ooooooh, heeeeeeh! Something sweet, candy, jelly, anything! Come on, gimme water!"

In a near state of panic, I downed six, one-quart canteens of water, at least that many candy bars, and several packages of cocoa mix. I remembered as a child, when I ate an extraordinarily hot bite of chili and my dad fed me a spoonful of jelly. It might have been just a placebo effect then, but with those peppers, eating something sweet was crucial.

I could not stand the intensity. I sat down, panting out of desperation. I had made my bed and so I had to sleep in it. The humiliation was not any problem because each one knew that I would deal with them later. All I wanted was relief. Ten long, torturing minutes passed. It was as if hot coals were sitting on my tongue, spilling down my throat, and into my stomach.

Then, with the same swiftness that the onset of the punishment took place, the pain left abruptly, leaving only a small remnant of pain in the pit of my stomach. Then it was over! As I look back, I think the abdominal pain came from the water and candy rather than the chili.

"Twenty bucks says I can do it again," I heard me say. Was

I stark raving mad? Who, in his right mind would even think of such a thing? A Marine Corps grunt, that's who.

No one bet that time, thank God. My stomach felt like Paul Newman's must have in the movie, *Cool Hand Luke*. The water I drank would soon dissipate, as our sweat always needed replenishing. Wow! What an experience! I never did quit eating those native miniature green chilies mixed with my C-rations, though, I just stayed away from the long red ones.

Despite the joking around we did with each other, we each knew we were still at war. Our platoon had been out on patrol for two days, and all seemed too quiet. We looked with suspicion upon each house, building, and any remnant of an edifice.

As Marines, we had learned not to disturb any objects on the ground for fear of booby traps. Even though we patrolled amid civilization, we still observed strict silence. Also, sometimes we would happen upon a group of families working in their back yards, thrashing rice. They became startled at our seemingly sudden appearance, which also made us wonder what was going on.

"*Chao ong. Ong manh gioi?*" ("Good morning. How are you?"), they would say nervously.

"*Cam on ong. Toi khoe lam,*" ("I am fine. Thank you."), we answered courteously. That would often break the ice, but still both sides showed an indication of suspicion.

"*Chao ong. Toi la bac si. Ahn dau chan?*" ("Hello sir, I am a medic. Does the boy's foot hurt?") I carried on a brief, choppy conversation.

"*Ti ti bac si. Thuc an, nuoc?*" ("A little bit, doc. Do you want some food, water?") The boy had no fear.

"*Cam on anh.*" ("Thank you boy.")

"*Khong co chi.*" ("You are welcome.") The language of manners is universal.

So, that one time, our squad sat and ate with the family.

The oriental pepper I had eaten, for some reason had made me hungry. However, my heart leaped in my chest when I noted something long and red in the bowl of rice and noodles the kind folks served me. Not wanting to insult the kindness of the family, I ate the whole meal.

The other members of the squad watched my reactions and snickered. I smiled back, and with my chopsticks shoved a pile of food into my mouth and ate it without flinching. Actually, I tasted no strong spiciness, so I did not have to engage in theatrics for the soldiers' sakes. Most of the squad followed suit and enjoyed the Vietnamese meal.

As we sat as guests of that impromptu host family, we heard several shots in the distance and a commotion in a nearby rice paddy. Our hosts were called out by a panic-stricken woman, yelling at the top of her lungs. We made haste to see what had happened.

Out in the middle of the water soaked field stood a lone water buffalo with a small lifeless body at its side.

"*Lai day, lai day, bac si, lai day!*" ("Come here, come here, doc, come here!") A woman beckoned me.

We made our way to the center of the field and found a young boy dead.

"*Toi xin loi ba.*" ("I'm very sorry, ma'am.")

One of the men pointed to a tree line, indicating that that had been the source of the shots. "*Di di, di di mau!*" We told the people to leave.

Spreading out in proper staggered formation, our squad slowly approached the edge of the rice paddy towards the tree line. We made ourselves sitting ducks if the VC were still there. Adrenaline shot through its familiar pathway (my veins) once more. Along with the adrenaline, we felt fully concentrated fear. With each step, it was as if I was looking down the barrel of a shotgun with the assailant's finger slowly squeezing the trigger.

The stench of the rice paddy seemed to fade away as fear gripped me from the depths of my bowels. I looked from side to side to see which way I would dive when the firing broke out. The water was waist high, and my boots sunk deeply into the soft, muddy underwater surface.

This was no dream, no comfortable movie theater, no book in an air conditioned room. This was reality in its rawest sense. I had long since forgotten how to experience comfort and safety. They were but faint echoes somewhere within my cerebral cortex. Our reluctant approach to the tree line made us feel like the tentacles of a monster were wrapped around our ankles during a nightmare. The flooded rice paddy was no friend to the American GI.

As we climbed up the final dike, I wondered why Charlie had not fired on us. "He has probably already left," I thought as I squatted down on dry land to wait for the rest of the squad to slosh out of the dung-laden paddy. We regrouped and quickly assaulted the jungle and the unknowns there.

Expecting the worst and hoping for the best, as usual, was the only sane attitude we could have. It wasn't long before we discovered three Americans sitting on the ground among the trees. The three marines—Coleson, the 50 caliber machine gunner, and his two cronies—seemed to be enjoying themselves.

"What are you idiots doing here?" Our squad leader asked angrily.

"Jus' havin' a good ol' time—need a little target practice, you know," Coleson snickered back. I had heard that Coleson had spent some time in a correctional institution and had been freed only to join the Marines.

"What do you think you're doing killing little kids?" I snapped at him as I boiled with anger.

I began to grab his head, but Coleson pulled his .45 caliber pistol on me. Now that I think of it, I really cannot blame Coleson, but at the time, I considered that he had given up all his rights for having intentionally murdered innocent children.

His pointing a gun at me was all I needed. I had rehearsed the scene many times before in karate and personal defense courses I had taken a couple of years earlier. Slowly, I raised my hands in the air to appear frightened so I could distract the coward.

Making sure I was a short distance from the muzzle of the gun, I looked Coleson straight in the eye. With a karate-like snap, I brought my left hand down and across the extended mid portion of my torso. My palm, cocked in striking position, slammed into his hand that held the pistol. That slapped his line of fire off to my right side where it could do no harm. Then I thrust my right hand down, whistling over the barrel of his military pistol. This forced the gun down over Coleson's fingers which caused him to let go or else to have the bones of his fingers splintered by the force of the hard trigger ring.

Coleson let go. Then I yanked the gun away from the murderer and shoved it, muzzle first, to the middle of his forehead. My left hand grasped and twisted his shirt collar. It was difficult to restrain myself for that short moment. Operating on automatic pilot, I moved very swiftly and surprised both Coleson and myself.

"How 'bout some good ol' target practice, Coleson?" I uttered through tightly clenched teeth.

My forefinger slowly applied tension to the trigger, and I was not sure when it would fire. All at once, like a breath of fresh air, words invaded my train of thought and were spoken to me somewhere within my mind.

The utterance asked me, "What are you doing? Are you aware of the consequences if you kill this man?"

Whether I heard my conscience or a supernatural voice intervening, I do not know. I am only thankful that I listened amid my almost dominant rage. After placing the hammer of the pistol back into the safety position, I shoved Coleson down onto the ground.

That poor excuse for a human being actually began to snicker, but the effort failed and ended in a nervous twitch. He sat on the dirt, speechless and gravely humiliated.

"Don't you ever get close to me in a firefight unless you want to see hell," I snapped.

Besides being effectively shamed, Coleson sat still, drenched with fear.

Regaining my composure, I looked around to see the expressions on the faces of the rest of the onlooking marines. It was obvious they agreed and were willing to back me if necessary. Off towards the rice paddy, three older Vietnamese men intently scrutinized us, nodding their heads with approval.

"*Cam on bac si.*" ("Thanks, Doc.")

We wondered but never determined how the VC would use the murder and what followed for their propaganda. I thought it likely that what those elders witnessed carried more credence than the lies of the communists.

None of our squad ever reported the incident to our superiors; we knew that justice would be best served if kept to our level. Results benefited the whole squad that way. Coleson could not handle being a marked man so he begged for and received a transfer to a rear unit. Some stoolie probably told the lieutenant the story so that those in charge would move Coleson to prevent harm coming to the poor criminal. But we knew that Coleson would have to live with himself and with God. None of us ever heard from him again.

We made our way back to Hill 190 with very little to report to the bosses. Coleson returned also, but not with us. Hill 190 did not have a shower, but did have enough clean water to at least wash our faces, hands, and teeth. Also, enjoying mail call made life a little bit more tolerable.

The interval between mail calls had become so erratic that sometimes I would get two or three letters at once, totally out of sequence. One letter would ask why I had not written while the next would be answering a previous letter. Packages from home always transformed us mean soldiers into cute little boys. Pudding in cans, Kool-Aid, beeny weenies, sardines, raisins, cashews, canned green chilies—these parcels produced heaven on earth.

The lieutenant informed us that shortly after Christmas, we would be leaving Hill 190 and would become what he called a Skylark unit. None of us had ever heard of a Skylark unit, so we did not know what to think. Skylark did not sound very exciting nor aggressive. Mike shook his head while the rest of us ho-hummed the whole idea. We were not moved with excitement or anticipation.

"When on the Skylark team, we will have our gear packed at all times, ready to depart, wherever and whenever we are called upon—which includes times we might be in the rear. That time will start as soon as we leave 190."

"Men, that may even mean going across the border to Laos or Cambodia. You are on your honor not to discuss this with anyone, including those back home to whom you write. Are there any questions?"

The lieutenant spoke while holding his hands behind his back, probably thinking he looked like General Patton or some hero of the past. Patton he was not.

"Are they gonna pass out little tiny wings like what the skylarks have?" someone blurted out. We were merciless, but the lieutenant, not all that stiff, also broke out in laughter with that inquiry.

He actually worried about us. This young officer, originally from Hawaii, had made a career of the Marine Corps, and tried to play the part most of the time. For some reason, he always felt that he was not seeing enough combat. Perhaps it was because this lieutenant never went out on routine patrols with the squads, nor did he wish to accompany us on our night ambushes. No one disliked him, but he did not demand or deserve the same respect we had given Gunny La Fifi.

That Skylark news made so much of an impression on each of us that most of us forgot all about it until later when someone had to remind us not to unpack. With Christmas approaching, talk within my little group was that the holiday merely meant that the time continued to pass, and that it was just a little bit closer to our going home to the states.

Our "in country" homes, however, consisted of makeshift bunkers of foxholes and sandbags. As Gonzales cleaned out his hole, he found a peculiar-looking piece of metal. When he tossed it out a little ways, a loud boom jolted us all. The bent-up scrap actually had been a disfigured M-79 round—a rifle grenade, blooper round.

After the explosion, we heard another one of many gasps of relief from Juan and then sighed ourselves. We may have been hardened to the concept of death but were not totally impervious, especially to the death of a friend. I thanked God that Gonzales was not hurt.

After one evening of rest at the hill, our platoon headed "back to the salt mines" for the next couple of days. We still had only one corpsman for our whole platoon, so I still pulled the standard double duty. The only comment that came to my mind about that was, "It don't mean nothin'."

During the early morning hours, we were usually out patrolling, fresh and frisky. Once, while in the middle of a rice paddy, we received a special radio message. Several booby traps had been detected in some dikes. Charlie knew that Americans did not particularly care for the manure-treated, wet rice paddies and figured that we would rather walk on top of the dry dikes than in the muck and mire. Wrong.

The message also said that we were to pick one marine from our platoon to go to Freedom Hill for the annual Bob Hope Christmas Show. The lieutenant picked our squad to choose from since we were out in the bush, and probably would have been left out otherwise—not bad reasoning.

"Okay, Doc, how we gonna choose?"

What an opportunity! The only "fair" way, I thought, would be to draw straws. The only problem was that when I was younger, I had studied magic and could easily "force" a card on most unsuspecting onlookers. Would the same thing work with straws? I'd find out.

I cut six straws of one length and left a seventh an inch longer. I showed the straws to the squad to their satisfaction. Then I turned around and arranged the seven straws in a certain order.

I turned back to the group and allowed each member to draw, of course leaving myself for last. It worked! I was left with the long straw! Or was it chance? I was not sure. As a matter of fact, I had been confused when I was trying to force the hand, but it did not matter. I was going to see the Bob Hope Show!

Initially, I was filled with disbelief, and then excitement. For years, most of America had seen Bob Hope's Christmas Special each year when he brought America's well wishes to the boys overseas—in Korea, Germany, and for the past several years, Vietnam. For me, I would never forget Christmas in Da Nang, 1970.

The rest of the squad was filled with both jealousy and happiness for me. With congratulations, they escorted me out of the flooded field and waited with me by a road until a truck came by to pick me up. I began to feel excited but never completely experienced that emotion.

As a military truck approached us, Mike flagged it down, and the driver was kind enough to stop. If a road was nearby, hitchhiking was the major form of transportation when it came time for an individual grunt to make his way back to the rear.

I quickly got picked up and was off to dreamland. The driver and the other passenger told me to sit in the back, as they had nothing in common with a dirty bush marine. My clothes did smell of the fresh rice paddy I had just left, you know, so I could not really blame them. I faced backward in the truck and sat stiffly.

Since that was the first time I had traveled through the outer villes without any protection, my hand held tightly to my rifle as I nervously made quick and thorough surveys of buildings, people, their positions, potential ambush sites and approaching motorcycles for possible saboteurs. That was becoming an impossible task, as we entered more increasingly congested streets. I gave up. If we got blown up, so what?

About half an hour passed before we arrived at the battalion rear. The truck stopped to let me off. "You got any orders, marine?" the guard asked me at the gate.

"I'm supposed to see the Bob Hope Show," I told him with a slight air of pride.

"Oh yeah, another one of you guys. Go on over to the CP and report in. Peace, man."

"Yeah sure, peace to you, too," I replied, thinking that the hippie thing had infiltrated all the way to the 'Nam.

The first thing the lifers said to me when I reported to them, was to get a haircut and to change my smelly clothes. So I blissfully scrubbed down in a nearby shower, and then spent seventy-five cents on a cheap, "high 'n tight" marine haircut.

My hair had grown too long for any rear military superior to tolerate.

The Vietnamese barber was old enough to be an ARVN (Army of the Republic of Vietnam) soldier or a Viet Cong. I recognized that automatically, and felt suspicious towards him. He gave me my first hair cut since my stay on the USS Sanctuary. I felt as if they were treating me like a six-year-old on Sunday. To those rear pogues, I was too dirty and shabby-looking to go out. I might bring shame to the Marine Corps. And like a six-year-old, I felt resentful. Nonetheless, I was going to see Bob Hope and those lifers in the upper echelon would not spoil that for me.

As I was up on a hill getting ready, I heard a loud crash followed by a commotion down by the little barber shop where I had just been. A large earth moving vehicle had just jumped a gear and rolled into the small shack, flattening the structure! Out of impulse, I ran down to see if I could render any assistance.

A crowd had gathered around the wreckage, so I had to force my way through it to get to the injured. There were two flattened bodies within the debris—the Vietnamese barber and an American. The American still had a flicker of life left in him, but the barber was dead . Even in the rear, my emotions were neutralized.

I did not understand what was going on with myself. Was I supposed to be a different person when removed from the combat environment? Would I ever regain the feelings I once had? What would I be like if I ever saw stateside soil again? My head was spinning with these philosophical renderings. I was a fish out of water.

As I walked away, the smell of fresh blood sent my thoughts back to the bush where I felt most comfortable, with Mike, Gonzales, and the rest of the platoon. Life was simple—

you either survived or you didn't. The enemy was *out there,* not sharing your C- rations. There was no back-stabbing, no deceit, no internal jealousy, no sabotage from within the ranks. I was glad to get a little break with the Bob Hope treat, but was looking forward to returning to my unit. The tragic accident faded into the background.

Once out of the compound, rides were easy to come by. In less than a minute, a personnel truck stopped just as I stuck out my thumb. I felt vulnerable as we seemed so unprotected. I felt like my little forty five was nothing more than a pea shooter but it was better than nothing.

Freedom Hill! As I jumped off the truck, the multitude of people who had congregated in such a confined area overwhelmed me. I felt hesitant to go up to the bleachers, so I found a spot close to the end. I did not know a soul in the vast mob. I sat next to what I thought were Army grunts who donned worn but clean uniforms and boots that were completely scuffed to a light tan.

My typically camouflaged Marine uniform, even though clean, made me stick out like a sore thumb. Also, they wore dry boots while mine were still wet with the sewer-like smell of the rice paddies. As they gave me a puzzled look, I knew that I had sat beside drug store cowboys—rear pogues pretending to be grunts.

How disgusting! Then I was glad I wore smelly boots since they were the only badge of the bush I possessed at the time. Only a true grunt would know the significance of the odor. I was glad those rear echelon phonies were offended.

Out to one side, I noticed a number of soldiers garbed in light blue pajamas—obviously patients. It was good to see them there. I saw no one I recognized. Suddenly I realized that I should stop looking around, as the show was about to start.

I could only think about what I would write back home. For the longest time, I had had very little to discuss, since I feared I would cause undue grief to my parents and family if I told them the truth. How do you tell your mother that you almost pulled the trigger on another American?

The letters from my friends were becoming less frequent, as I had expected. There were, however, the faithful few who kept me going the whole tour. And to them, I am forever indebted. I even received more CARE packages from them than I did from my own family. Of course, I did not embarrass my folks by telling them that since they supplied me well enough as it was.

As Bob Hope's theme song kicked off the show, I shot back to reality. The announcer presented his speil on how great it was to bring the show to men in uniform and so forth. I was getting to experience a real production, with all the fanfare of Hollywood.

First appeared The Gold Diggers, a female dance troupe often seen on TV back in the states. Then came Lola Falana, a singer and actress who had found time to be with us against the trend of anti-war sentiment that prevailed in the U.S. She was beautiful.

I wondered whether any of those stars had fears or reservations about coming to entertain the troops. To this day, just the mention of their names brings back fond memories of that hot December afternoon in 1970. Even several professional football stars appeared on the stage. Of course, none could show up the king of comedy himself, the man who, for years, had made his annual trek to the troops in the remote parts of the world performing their duty.

Bob Hope came out wearing his silly costume—an over-sized baseball cap with an army green top, sergeant's strips, khaki pants and Ho Chi Minh sandals. His skits hilariously poked fun at Washington, commanding officers, and career military personnel.

Mr. Hope began, "The term 'round eyes' has a particular meaning to you out here doesn't it? I know you are not referring to these American beauties who are gracious enough to join this year's Christmas tour. Okay, son. If you don't quit panting with your tongue hanging down to your toes, I'll tell the cameraman to film you for your girlfriend back home." The crowd roared.

As the Gold Diggers came out in their costumes and sang, the crowd stood up, sang along, and danced to the beat of the music. Lola Falana, the tall, dark beauty, walked out onto the stage, continued across the stage floor, and approached the audience. She caressed the hand of a young black soldier and led him up to the stage with her.

As the young man stood there with his hat in his hand, he was petrified with stage fright. Bob Hope asked the shivering enlistee for his name, and the young man came out with three different names. It could have been staged but it sure sounded authentic. After the interview, the actress kissed the soldier on the cheek, bringing about a standing ovation.

Some athletes came out—football and basketball were both represented. I cannot recall any of names. They too, received a warm welcome, but it was not even close to the women's welcome.

Bob Hope cracked jokes about his golfing in the vast greenery of Vietnam. "As I yelled out 'fore,' a marine raised his hand and asked if five came next," Hope quipped.

"When I bought these Ho Chi Minh sandals, the young boy gave me a road hazard warranty. Needless to say, the fine print excluded any intentional damage done to destroy the manufacturer's craftmanship."

The show also included bands playing the latest music and

many more one-liners by Hope and the others. By the huge smiles of the people on the stage, one almost forgot it was close to one hundred degrees with at least that percentage humidity.

Mr. Hope truly catered to the common enlisted man, both out on the front and in the rear. Needless to say, even though the show lasted two and one-half hours, it was over all too soon. Also, the audience bestowed the production two standing ovations.

The movie camera filmed the audience, and of course, everyone wanted to get into the picture to reassure folks back home that all was well. I waved frantically as the camera swept my way. I think the cameraman got a full view of my hand.

Of course, the officers swarmed the cast of the traveling goodwill show. Those higher-ups were used to pushing their weight around and no one's being able to contest anything they did. I remember wishing that Mr. Hope would not give in too much to their spoiled kid tactics. With the way he joked about these officers, I did not think the brass would get very far anyway.

It really did not matter. We had been paid tribute. I represented my whole platoon, the lieutenant included. That is what mattered right then. I wanted to yell, "Thanks a million you wonderful people." As time would ultimately unveil, there were not very many people we young veterans would ever be able to thank.

The crowd dispersed, and I was left with a little free time at Freedom Hill, so I made my way to the PX and then to the amusements. I was quite lonely without my buddies, so I did not enjoy any of the recreation offered. Besides, I was becoming anxious to tell my "Ps" about the Bob Hope Show and to start writing letters.

I waited in line at the gate to reclaim my weapon before

hitching a ride back to Battalion Headquarters. Once there, I had a good, hot meal and requested a ride back to my unit.

Luckily, Gunny La Fifi was at Battalion Headquarters and assigned a jeep driver to take me back but not until the morning, since the sun had begun to set. That night, the gunny took me to the NCO (Non-Commissioned Officer) Club as a gesture of friendship.

It seemed like the longer I stayed out in the bush, the more shy and introverted I became. I was very quiet that night which is really not my character. I thought about what a privilege it was to sit with that man. The gunny really understood infantrymen in the trenches.

Bright and early the next day, a jeep with two marines transported me and the mail back to Hill 190. I arrived just after the daily mine sweep had been performed by some of our rear crew members. That amounted to real combat for them.

I should not be too harsh on them, however, as many of those mine sweepers were former grunts who were spending their last months back in the rear before ending their tour in 'Nam. A good portion of them, though, were rear pogues from start to finish.

Back on the hill, I was like Santa Clause with news from the North Pole. Everyone wanted to hear about the show and about all the stars who performed. As to be expected, the female stars were of more interest than even Hope himself.

Four days remained until Christmas and a truce was expected for Christmas Eve. Traditionally, a truce had been on the books but was seldom fully honored. I remember hearing newscasts about those truces and thinking how thoughtful it was for both sides to remember the Savior's birthday. In reality, a truce was merely a short time period for reloading.

Later another jeep arrived from the rear carrying an officer and two enlisted men The officer was a young Chinese-

American doctor named Thomas Chang. Dr. Chang, an informal physician, had been drafted and did not want to be in the 'Nam any more than anyone else. His salutes revealed his disdain for the military.

Dr. Chang had arrived at the ville for a Med Cap. A Med Cap was a goodwill gesture by the Americans bringing medical care to the remote village people. He had a trunkload of medicines and supplies ready for action.

Someone asked me to accompany Chang and help out the team. I truly believe that the team expected me, a corpsman, to protect them, also corpsmen. I obliged. Thankfully, the platoon also provided the security of a squad. We discovered Dr. Chang to be a caring young man and he joked like he was one of us.

As we entered the ville, the people there realized that we were up to something different, as we were no routine patrol. We looked for a canopy or a booth of some sort so we could set up the makeshift clinic. Eventually, we found an abandoned vending stand and set up shop.

The village chief and his entourage approached us. They all greeted us and were obviously quite curious about what we were doing. They were equally curious about the Chinese doctor with us. Due to centuries of border wars, there had become racial resentments between the Chinese and the Indochinese.

We thought it weird that the Orientals had no difficulty recognizing characteristics of the different nationalities but had trouble distinguishing individual white or black people.

"*Ong bac si.*" I told them that the man was a doctor.

The village chief immediately took advantage of the situation and came up with a crop of physical ailments.

"*Dau dau,*" the chief said, pointing to his head. This meant that he had a headache.

Before long, it seemed that whole village had lined up to

see the *"Bac si."* The language barrier melted as they pointed to various parts of their bodies, to their *dau, dao tu,* and *chan,* that is, to their heads, stomachs, or feet.

About midday, the vendors in their bicycle-driven carts appeared, holding up hot food or ice cream. The patients broke from the line to take a lunch break and so did we. I bought an ice cream bar, hoping that it would not taste too bad so I wouldn't insult anyone if I couldn't finish it. Well, the ice cream had been made from water buffalo's milk and tasted like it too. I think I swallowed the whole bar in one gulp. I also bought some hot food with rice. We had eaten that type of food many times before so I knew what to expect.

Dr. Chang watched with amusement and stuck to his C-rations. To the doctor, C-rations were a novelty that in the rear, he seldom "had the opportunity" to partake of. He usually had to endure the food in the mess hall—such a hard luck story.

Out in the bush, we were so starved for variety, that we would have eaten rotten eggs if they had been offered. Come to think of it, the Vietnamese did regard rotten eggs as a delicacy and did offer them to us. Yup, and I ate one too, swallowing it whole, hoping not to taste it. I still smell and taste that black egg anytime I see a hard boiled egg.

The remainder of the afternoon was cut short by the rear crew wanting to get back well before sunset. We invited them to spend the night, but they graciously declined the offer and quickly departed. Dr. Chang had been the only doctor from our battalion to engage in a Med Cap, and for that among other reasons, we gave him credit. It was extremely refreshing to do something constructive and not destructive for a change. Never before had I seen so many smiles in one setting. In contrast, that night I accompanied a squad to set up an ambush. We had no contact—just lost sleep, as usual.

Christmas Eve arrived all too soon. We joked about having

no time to buy gifts! Ha! Mike and I pulled perimeter guard together that evening. To honor our side of the truce, the Americans sent no one out on ambush or patrol. We took cookies and Kool Aid to keep us company. Earlier that afternoon, the rear had sent out a shipment of turkey and egg nog. Even if we were sitting in a sandbag-encased hole with rain pouring down on us, it was a nice meal.

Mike and I did not talk much about Christmas. We decided we would leave celebrating for next year, God willing. We did share all our goodies, to the point of gluttony, feeling no remorse; we deserved it. Morning arrived again, without incident.

The lieutenant seemed unusually excited that particular morning right after mail call. He could not wait to make his announcement. Skylark was in force! "Get your gear ready, troops. The choppers will be here in twenty minutes. Squad leaders report to the CP for briefing."

"What has the crazy LT gotten us into this time?" It was Sgt. Pierce voicing a seldom questioning opinion. He sensed trouble, as we all did. This was not a prelude to danger nor a feeling of impending doom, but rather just a concern based on experience with our "gungie" lieutenant.

Putting Skylark in full swing also meant the final closing of Hill 190. Everything had already been completely torn down and all trash had been burned and buried. The only excess possessions we had were the CARE packages we had received recently. It was customary to share and use up the contents of the gifts to avoid having to haul unnecessary weight.

That morning, Tran arrived very sad. Tran had become part of the team and some of the platoon had grown quite attached to him. The ones who were the most moved were some of the new guys who had not yet mastered the skill of emotional shut down. Tran, of course, knew better but he still was just a twelve-year-old and an orphan at that. Since he was the only villager allowed on the compound, we gave him several empty sandbags full of foodstuffs and commodities we had to leave behind.

Tran would be the local "Wise Man," as there was no Santa Clause in Vietnam. Most everyone in country were either Catholics or Buddhists. The French left a large portion of the nation converted to Roman Catholicism and so they were able to celebrate Christmas with us.

Tran did not dare ask where we were going; he constantly feared interrogation by the VC. And besides, we could not tell him since we did not even know ourselves. A brief farewell was all the weeping boy could give us. Not only had our platoon befriended him but had also offered him a safe haven of refuge. Tran was marked with a price on his head for having collaborated with the "imperialists." The ville would have to protect him after we left, but they could hardly protect themselves, much less an orphan. It was like turning the page of a book and never finishing the story.

"Whomp whomp whomp whomp whomp whomp whomp," the chopper was making itself known. We sat savoring the last few seconds of peace before boarding to who only knew where or what.

Mike looked at me and said, "Merry Christmas, Doc."

"Merry Christmas, Mike." Neither one of us were joking.

Only one chopper was needed since our platoon had dwindled to only about nineteen brave young men. The jet engines did not even slow down as the craft landed and lowered its ramp. Against the sand blasting of the wind given off by the chopper, we single filed it to our usual self-assigned seats. I never did learn the name of the ville we were supposed to be protecting by "living" on Hill 190.

Chapter 12
Skylark

"Where are we going?" I shouted at the top of my lungs to the lieutenant.

"Elephant Valley. The A Shah," Lt. Winter had to yell three times before I could understand him.

Recently, according to skuttlebut, the Americal Division of the U.S. Army had been overrun around that area.

"What could one platoon do against the North Vietnamese Army?" I thought, knowing full well the answer.

At least after becoming airborne, it felt nice and cool up in the clouds. I looked down at my arm and rolled up my sleeve. For once, there was no sweat. I thanked God for life's little pleasures, sat back, and enjoyed the few minutes of refreshing high altitude. The helicopter machine gunner was eating an apple and tossed the core out his window opening.

"Good for him," I thought. I had decided not to think bad thoughts about the chopper crews. It was probably still Christmas, or close to it, anyway.

Down below and off to the south, we could see the hellish Que Son mountains. The area was also known as "Indian country." It was where the Fifth Marines had encountered much resistance. Mike, being a transfer from the Fifth, had told me about the NVA and VC infestation of that mountain range.

Our drop off point was not too far from what I observed—

just a few more miles to the west. I leaned back again, as I did not care to think about things like NVA and VC infestation. I closed my eyes and dosed off into a refreshing short nap that must have lasted every bit of four minutes—a well deserved rest, I would say.

Thump. We had landed. As I was about to jump off the ramp, I froze at the edge. I could not move. I had not yet psychologically resolved the incident that put me aboard the hospital ship. With a gentle shove from Mike, I was able to exit. Mike knew without my having to say anything what the source of the problem was.

The chopper took French leave and was out of sight before anyone could break out a map.

"What's our objective?" asked Gonzales.

"The NVA are on the move up this valley after doing some damage to our army. We'll try to intercept a regimen of them." Did the lieutenant realize what he was saying? We were not so polite as to remain quiet.

"What do you mean—a regimen? We have only nineteen bodies out here against a couple of hundred regulars. No way, man!" Again, we heard the rare voicing of Sgt. Pierce's opinion. However, we all shared the same concern.

"Hopefully, the Army is flanking them farther down the valley and we will just have to pick up stragglers," said the lieutenant, still not convincing us. We had never had any type of joint venture with the Army, so we were all very suspicious of the assistance we might receive.

Despite the brief verbal protest, we were still dedicated marines and followed orders. The Marine Corps was the ground fighting force of the Navy, which meant our total numbers were much fewer than any other military branch. Also we operated in smaller groups. Historically, the Marines had been the first to spearhead an invasion and were usually quite capable of accomplishing with smaller numbers what the army could with much larger ones. This, of course, was tradition.

During times like the night that the chopper dropped us off in the Que Son Mountains, one could look down at his hand, pinch it, and realize he was just flesh and blood like everyone else—nothing special, nothing different.

I was just a body that bled as much and easy as any soldier, pilot, or sailor. Marine training was more intense, but I could not see that it was all that much more intense than the Army's. A sense of vulnerability prevailed.

Instead of a pursuit, we set up an ambush. The terrain was that of a narrowing canyon. The canyon was about a mile wide where we had landed, so our genius platoon leader, in all his wisdom, had us pair up and set up ambush positions about five hundred feet apart. The elephant grass concealed us well.

As we set up, the familiar explosions from the hollow tubes began sounding off, followed shortly by ground blasts—a mortar barrage. Sergeant Pierce immediately positioned himself down on one knee, obviously up to something. He frantically waved his hand at another marine, while keeping his eye fixed on something.

Pierce had spotted the muzzle flash from the mortar tube. The other marine crawled up to him as the enemy's mortar rounds exploded, but Sgt. Pierce remained up on one knee. Someone handed a LAAW to Pierce, and the sergeant quickly set it up, un-telescoped it, and lifted the sites.

"BAAMM!" We witnessed a single explosion off in the hills, followed by several other blasts in quick succession. Since Pierce's LAAW hit its target, all the enemy's mortar rounds detonated. That was the best shot I had ever seen. We were amazed because odds were totally against the direct hit that occurred. A round of applause erupted for Sergeant Pierce, the hero of the moment.

As the dust settled from the short attack, I made my routine assessment to see if anyone was injured. One marine caught a little shrapnel wound to his arm, but it was nothing major.

"What is this?" I thought. "Oh no." I had discovered a lifeless body, face down on the ground.

"Who is it?" I questioned, not really wanting to know. It was one of the new guys. I had to read the name from his dog tags to find out who he was. We had told our new folks all the time to hit the dirt as soon as they even thought they heard mortar rounds.

"Why don't you stupid, pea-brained idiots listen to us when we tell you something? You are all going to end up like your friend here because you're too stupid to follow instructions!" I was fire mad.

A squad made a beeline towards the mortar site to investigate while the rest of us waited for a chopper to fly out our wounded and KIA.

The lieutenant began having second thoughts about his strategy. "Maybe we'd better stick closer together and just start a sweep."

The chopper came and left quickly with its load. If more of the enemy were nearby, we had no choice but to keep moving since we had already given away our position.

The curious squad reported no bodies but did find trails of blood. The NVA and the VC never intentionally left their dead or wounded because they believed that if we could be deprived of positive body counts, our morale would suffer. Maybe they were right. Maybe they were all wet, like our leaders. None of us really cared whether we had body counts or not. I think it was only a statistic about which the commanders in the rear could brag during their cocktail parties.

Although the visibility was low, we pushed on through the thick elephant grass. The flat valley was not so flat after all; we encountered hills, jungle, and swamps. Were we lost? No, not us Marines. We really weren't lost; our trusty map just did not have the descriptions of all the obstacles actually present. What else was new?

As we crawled out of a swampy area, we decided to halt for the day, and set up our ambushes. We knew we were still in a valley but wondered if it was the only valley around and whether the NVA were actually advancing up that particular one.

After we got situated, Cochran, a quiet rifleman who had been in country for several months, showed me a laceration on his forearm. It definitely would need suturing. I pulled out my field surgical set and began heating water in a steel helmet to sterilize the instruments as thoroughly as possible.

"We don't have anything to numb you with, soldier, so I can't have any crying, you hear?" I had excellent bedside manners.

I cleaned the wound fairly well with a little surgical soap that I kept hidden for rainy days. I did not carry any surgical gloves, so I washed my hands with the soap too. Suturing out in the field after patient and doctor had just climbed out of a swamp was about as crude as it comes. Piercing the curved suture needle through live skin stimulated the patient. He muttered a muffled grunt with each stitch I placed across his wound. Tying off the suture and cutting the excess length produced an array of impressive noises.

With the job complete, I applied an abundance of Neosporin and changed out the dressing twice daily. It was horribly dirty out in Indian Country. None of the injured men had problems with infection later, as long as I faithfully continued to observe and treat them. At the first sign of any redness, that person was immediately medevaced out of the bush.

Each time I would attend to one person, it seemed as if the rest of the platoon suddenly remembered that I was their corpsman and not just another grunt. Suddenly, it was sick call, with everyone complaining of one thing or another. Some of those complaints were weeks old, but the ailing persons had forgotten until they saw me doctoring another soldier. Maybe they were jealous because someone else was getting more attention than they were. Oh well, mending the sick and wounded was the only source of entertainment available, so why not humor the masses? I officially opened sick bay that afternoon.

As soon as I completed patching and passing out pills and potions, I was off to the ambushes. My personality altered like a light switch, turning itself on and off in a split second. Even though I tried to blend the two roles of corpsman and infantryman, they sharply contrasted with each other. In one of the roles, I played an instrument of helps and mercy, while in the other role, I had become a tool of destruction and bloodshed.

Most folks thought that corpsmen must be reasonably pacifist by nature. However, every individual who had spent time out in the bush had become an enthusiastically rapacious hawk. We had heard that the VC thought it beneficial to their war effort to decommission our officers and corpsmen and thereby demoralize the rest of the troops.

I do not know about doing without the officers, but leaving the troops with no corpsman certainly set us back. Our troops did not demoralize that easily, however. To me, the eighteen days I spent on the USS Sanctuary had not seemed to adversely affect our platoon.

Expecting that NVA regimen any time, we spent the subsequent three days fighting mosquitoes and leeches down in that swampy valley. However, our little platoon experienced no further contact with the enemy. We figured that the survivors of the VC mortar team must have somehow gotten word to the advancing NVA regimen, which allowed them to detour and avoid us.

After those three days, a single chopper (like before) flew in to airlift us to another covert destination. Supplies had been placed in the aircraft with us, which meant that we were not heading back to the rear. This Skylark business was losing its popularity fast. The scent of death permeated Indian Country, and we would all be quite content to take leave of its unwelcome doormat.

The chopper seemed to take an unusually long time to transfer us to our new but temporary home. While in flight, the squad leaders passed out our C-rats and LRPs, as we called the dehydrated food. Then someone distributed the ammo.

Usually when supplies came in, there would also be a red nylon bag containing our mail. We saw no red bag that time. However, during the flight, we noticed that someone had sent us somewhat of a gift—two more new guys. I think we were supposed to have over fifty members per platoon; these two pushed us up to nineteen again. Wow! Only thirty-one more to go and we would be a complete platoon for once.

Looking down, I could see rice paddies scattered below, with jungle between—no major villes or towns in those semi-boonies. In a field full of vegetation, our helicopter descended and then touched down.

As I approached the edge of the ramp, I stopped, looked down, and jumped. Since I had closed my eyes, I hadn't seen that it was a whole six inches before I finally hit the ground, almost losing my balance. If anyone had been paying attention, they would have laughed for thirty minutes straight, but no one was looking—I hope.

As we set up perimeter guard, our leader was busy on the radio, jotting down his coded coordinates for our upcoming mission. Our motions had become so routine that seldom, if ever, did anyone else bother to find out where we were at a given time. All I knew was that we had landed either in the mountainous jungles or were in the rice paddies surrounding some little ville.

Sometimes I felt as though we were fighting both the northern and the southern countries at the same time. There had to be a better way. It seemed as though the game of chess we were playing was never intended to have any winners.

As we humped it to our designated command post, it started to rain again—and it rained hard! That day, I had chosen to don my rainsuit instead of my poncho. Life sure was difficult, considering our plethoric wardrobe choices. I figured I would have my half of a hooch ready if I did not have to go out on ambush that night—what a dream!

I looked up at the rain and realized that I would not be able to breathe. If anyone had been suicidal, he could have merely looked up and would have drown in a short time. Even though as we humped through the pouring rain my mind wandered off in senseless thoughts, my eyes and ears continued in earnest to probe the area with radar-like beams, detecting any unusual movement or sound or any visual evidence of danger. "How far to that CP?" I wondered.

As we sloshed to our destination, marines began to slide off to the sides of hills. Of course, we stopped and helped them get back on course. We clambered up one hill—the last for the evening—that seemed impossible to ascend. It must have taken us two hours to advance only thirty feet, crawling on all fours all the way, eating mud, having absolutely no traction, on a seventy-five degree incline. At least the troops at the front of the platoon could step on the heads of the men below them for some sort of support. Disneyland was never so much fun!

Marines must be like sheep, when one goes over the cliff the rest follow.

Once on top of the hill, we set up the post, and again they asked me to go out on night patrol. How nice of them to ask me. What if I said no? How could I? I had become all Marine.

A few soldiers set up their hooches, under which in the downpour we could heat some food. The heat tabs created tear gas-like fumes that had the same effect, especially in close quarters like that evening's. I took two minutes to take a deep breath, then I was off to save the world.

Six of us set out on a routine ambush. We found a clearing voted most likely to host a parade of the enemy, and then formed an L-shaped trap. We had asked a machine gun team (three men) to go with us, as we did most evenings. They would keep their own watch, and we would keep ours.

Moving about seven meters from that machine gun team made it almost impossible to have visual or verbal contact with them because of the horrendous rain. I squatted down with my little team of three to help decide the watch schedule. Mike was back at the CP, so when to take my turn made no difference to me.

After being assigned second watch, I prepared my bed. First, I laid out my flak jacket for a mattress, then my canteen for a pillow, a poncho liner for the bedding, my poncho for a bedspread, mud and puddles underneath for my box spring, and, last but not least, my weapon and medical gear next to my hand for immediate access.

Oh yes, we shouldn't forget the music; I told the mosquitoes to come on in, since they would anyway. The final touch before collapsing was a quick look at my watch to set my internal clock to two hours.

A tap to my foot caused my eyelids to open and my body to sit up before my brain was aware that it had been aroused. It was my turn to man the radio on our side of the ambush. Rain still poured. I could not see more than ten feet in front of me. The machine gun team had moved out of communication range. Like well-oiled machines, my eyes scanned the few visible feet.

The marine before me had turned up the squelch a little louder than usual because of the roar of the showers as the radio enjoyed protection under my poncho.

"Romeo Charlie, Two Bravo, Hotel Mike? Over. (Radio check, squad two B, how do you read me?) I had broken radio silence. It was never in force anyway.

"Lima Charlie. Any Indians? Over." (Loud and clear. Any of the enemy?)

"Roger. That's an affirmative. Nathaniel reported one click from your pos with a beeline to your bull's eye. Report from friendlies down the road. Do you copy?" Mike was on the other end, trying to be as discreet as possible in his attempt to warn us of a potential disaster.

"Roger, I copy. Much grass. Over and out."

"I've got to communicate with John Boy," I thought. John Boy was a southern country kid and about as country as they come. I hoped that he would identify me before he opened fire. I had to tell him of the NVA sighting.

We were very ineffective without the gunners. John Boy had no radio, so I had to warn him in person before we gave away our position by firing at the enemy. At that moment, I wished that I had spent more time with Mr. Country so perhaps he could read my thoughts. There was no time for second guessing each other.

I slowly tapped Cooper's foot and told him what I had to do. Without hesitation, he arose and took position. I think Cooper was relieved that I had not told him to go warn the gunners instead. After transferring the radio, I stood up and heard and felt my water-logged joints squeak like rusty hinges.

Ever so slowly, I placed one foot in front of the other, heading towards the area I thought the machine gun team was located. "What if I'm going in the wrong direction? Worse yet, what if they think I'm Nathaniel Victor?"

My body fulfilled its duty, while my mind staunchly debated. My body was marine, but I still had a little human left in my mind. After about five steps that took forever to accomplish, I whispered, "John Boy, don't shoot. It's Doc!" No answer.

I took a few more steps. The rain continued to drown out my forced whispers. I stood and looked around me, trying to decide the best thing to do. If I did nothing and the gunners were caught off guard, we would all be killed. I just had to have faith in John Boy. I wished again that I had've gotten to know him a little better so I could feel a little more confident in approaching him.

Going down a cliff for the first time had been a whole lot easier than finding John Boy in the dark that night.

"John Boy, don't shoot! It's Doc!" Still no response. The rain sounded like a waterfall. I took in a deep breath, anticipating the machine gun crew's opening fire on me.

Mentally, I prepared myself to hit the ground as fast as possible. I could take only two more steps before I had to pause and call out again to John Boy. Still no answer. I just knew that I was walking in the wrong direction. How could I have gotten so turned around? I was becoming quite frustrated.

I thought I'd heard something. My body froze solid—not even my eyelashes moved. There it was again!

"John Boy, it's me, Doc. Don't shoot!" I whispered a little louder that time.

"Halt! Who goes there?" Thank God for boot camp rituals which called for strict sentry procedures.

Beyond the wall of water, I could make out a faint semblance of what seemed to be someone crouching down behind a machine gun on a stand. I swore it was pointing directly at me. Since the rain distorted everything, it was almost as if an evil spirit stared at me from behind that ghostly shadow.

"This is it," I thought, as I predicted the specter opening fire at any moment.

"It's me, Doc. Don't shoot," again I whispered loudly.

"Halt! Who goes there?"

"What? Had he not heard me?" I thought, as my heart raced about five-hundred beats per minute. "Do I hit the ground now or do I break silence and yell out? If I hit the ground, John Boy will shoot for sure. If I yell out, the NVA would know that we were there and that would be suicide."

"John Boy! It's me—Doc!" I said, in almost a full voice. I think I must have been pleading.

"Come forth and show yourself"—or was it "thyself?" Who cares. Either John Boy was very dumb or he was very smart. I choose to think that he was very smart, since he maintained total control of a situation where others would've panicked and pulled the trigger. I started talking a mile a minute.

"Hey man, it's me, Doc." I drew closer to him so we could both fully make out each other.

"John Boy. I thought you were going to shoot me. The CP just radioed in a report of NVA heading this way. They said that some friendlies had made the spot (had been identified), so who knows what's gonna happen. Man, I thought you were going to shoot me! Thanks for keeping a cool head, amigo."

"It's all right, Doc. Something just wasn't right in your approach. I think it was 'cause you was movin' too slow for

Charlie. I don't really know. We'll keep our eyes open. Hey, thanks for letting us know. Okay, Doc?"

"Yeah, no sweat, man. See you later." I felt light as a feather with that load taken off my back.

"Oh no!" I thought. "What if Cooper opens up on me now." I decided just to *di di mau* it back *chop chop*. Surely Cooper would know I would be returning at any moment. Besides I had no energy left to walk back in the slow, strenuous, expectant pace that brought me to John Boy's spot.

I splashed through the soggy mud, double-timing it back. I was closer than I thought—I came up on Cooper quickly. He didn't shoot. Good for him. Our third man, Johnson, had moved up with Cooper by that time. We decided to all watch together.

The minutes passed by slowly. In anticipation of action, we strained our eyes and taxed our night vision. With my adrenaline up again, I was building an appetite. More time passed, and the imaginary shadows within the rain curtain never materialized into the enemy that we expected.

After more than an hour, I became very sleepy. I told Cooper to have fun without me and to wake me when the visitors appeared. I went to my "bed" and went through the ceremony of preparing the poncho liner and poncho in order to get a few minutes of precious sleep before sunrise.

Falling asleep with so much of the catecholamine hormone coursing through my body was not easy. I had mastered the technique, however; so before I knew it, the cloudy morning skies had illuminated the jungle and it was time to head back to the CP.

Nathaniel Victor had found an easier route, or perhaps he could understand English and had been monitoring our radio. Sometimes, I imagined Nathaniel as having super human instincts and abilities that far surpassed any American's.

The morning presented a good time for me to change my socks to those almost dry ones I carried next to my body. I made a point to remind myself to sleep on my other side that night as I made my sides take turns sleeping in the puddles of the water soaked ground.

I took a good look at John Boy's face that morning. No longer would I regard him as the country hick from Alabama. I asked myself, "If I had been in his shoes, would I have opened up on a potential intruder?"

I was glad that I had not been in the position to find out. With all of John Boy's unique colloquialisms and southern drawl, his IQ seemed to have bumped up at least thirty points, at least from my point of view.

The lieutenant radioed for us to run ID checks through a nearby rice paddy section on our way back. Why not? We had nothing better to do anyway. After all, we were on a Skylark mission. "What is a Skylark mission anyway?" someone asked.

We found the rice paddy, and as we came upon our first human subject, we recognized her to be a young girl. Most of the women here were about four feet to four-and-a-half feet tall.

"*Chao co - co manh gioi*?" (Good morning, young lady, how are you?) "*Can cuoc sil vous plait.*" (I had forgotten how to say 'please' in Vietnamese, but had asked for her identification.)

Surprisingly, the girl could speak some English. She said, "GI number ten. You stink!"

That was really something, coming from someone who worked in the rice paddies. How could she say that?

"I think we were insulted," Johnson remarked.

"Only because you wanted to ask her for a date. How old do you think she is, Johnson?"

That was it, we would not let up on poor Johnson for the

next hour. No matter what he did or said nothing would make it right. Johnson was a marked man.

"Look at her, she works in the rice paddies. She doesn't smell so hot herself." Johnson was on a rampage.

"So, what are you doing smelling the poor innocent thing, Johnson?" No mercy.

"I think that's called robbing the cradle, Johnson."

"Hey you guys, leave poor ol' Johnson alone. Can't you see that he's just been dumped by a baby sahn girl?"

In checking the *"Can cuocs,"* it was impossible to tell which were authentic and which were fake. At least we gave the impression that we were trying to do our job, whatever it was.

"Hey Doc! How long has it been since our last shower?" Did I sense paranoia?

"For you, about two years. Didn't they make you take one in boot camp?" I too had a hard time remembering how long it had been.

We could not help thinking and wondering whether these people were harboring the enemy. Just the night before, the NVA supposedly romped through these premises. "Where are they now?" we pondered.

"If this is Skylark, who are we saving?"

That was a good question. What was the emergency that brought us out here anyway? Nothing mattered, so why bother thinking about such things?

Once out of the rice paddies, it was silence once more. Even in the daylight, we had become conditioned to the modus operandi of stealth. Sometimes while walking in the state of combat readiness, our actions became so mechanical that hours would pass before we knew it. Yet, while engaging in a patrol, the seconds seemed like minutes and the minutes like hours.

We encountered the CP, but only eight bodies were present

since another squad had been sent out on patrol. "Home" was still a refreshing sight.

The lieutenant said we could spend one more day at that position before moving on to cover our objective. When asked what our objective was, he answered, "I think we are supposed to intercept Charlie's resupply. It's reported to be heavy in this area. They should be calling us outta here pretty soon, though, so we don't have much time to scan the area."

"The LT done got snowed," Mike quietly remarked to me.

"Hook line and sinker. He hasn't the foggiest idea what we're doing here, either. What a screw-brained idea this Skylark thing is. What's one little ol' platoon gonna do?" commented a new guy.

He was in trouble! "Who asked you, dude?"

"Is that some stateside hippie trash you're trying to feed us?"

"Just one thing and one thing only, stateside. Speak when spoken to and at no other time." That order came from me, as I was getting upset at the thought of disunity. We were not kind to the young boy because we did not appreciate his becoming familiar with us until he had been tested. The rest of us had paid our dues and we expected the same from everyone else, with no exceptions.

After our little discussion, I took a little nap on the north side of a small knoll. Life was full of little pleasures, and a nap was definitely one of them.

After waking up, I decided to heat up some water for a cup of cocoa mixed with coffee—another pleasure valued so much in the bush. Why not enjoy?—After all, I was on a roll with little pleasures! So I found an old discarded wooden crate to sit on. I really felt American; I wouldn't have to squat to make my beverage as did our Vietnamese counterparts.

As I sat on the crate and heated the water, a mortar barrage pounded the south side of the knoll. Feeling quite protected and fully *into* the "little pleasure" thing, I continued to sit on my American seat, watching my water come to a boil.

"BOOM! BOOM!" the mortars continued. Then I sat straight up and rocked forward to lift the cup from the heat tab. Suddenly, I felt a sharp whap to my hind quarters.

"Ouch! Who did that?" In a split second, I was on my feet. Something or someone had slapped my behind with a painful blow. I looked around, trying to catch suspicious looks in anyone's eyes. I noticed only puzzled looks as I carried on with my accusations.

Most of the remnant of our platoon, however, had stayed down on the ground where they had taken cover from the mortars. Perhaps that was what I should've been doing too; nevertheless, I had no answer as to what or who had just hit me. Even though the explosions occurred on the other side of another small hill, and the mortars had stopped after five rounds, they left our ears ringing. Mike made his way over to the crate on which I had been sitting.

"Doc, come here and look at this thing," he insisted.

I obeyed. There was a large hole in the top of the crate, exactly where I had been sitting. Inside the wooden box we found a piece of hot metal about the size of a golf ball. Then I placed my hand on my rear at the site of the stinging pain, and there, just as I had feared, was blood.

"Man, Doc. Do you have nine lives or what? That chunk of shrapnel must've gone straight up and then come almost directly down, just missing your head and dinging the place where you got all your brains." Mike kept me humble.

"That shrapnel fell exactly at the time I leaned forward to pick up my cup of hot water. Is that luck or divine intervention?" I commented, still in awe.

"The only way there'd be divine intervention is if God was

to take you away, making life easier for the rest of us!" As usual, I ignored Mike's sarcasm.

As I checked out my wound, I saw that it was only an abrasion. I cleansed it with peroxide, placed some antibiotic ointment on it, and fashioned a battle dressing on it as I knew that tape would never adhere with all the sweat and humidity out in the bush.

"You should get a Purple Heart for that thing, Doc?" Was the comment facetious or serious?

"I don't want to hassle with the paperwork. Besides, how would I show off the scar?"

"Yeah, I'd be embarrassed, too, if it had been me."

"Thanks for the sympathy, Greek."

"Don't mention it, Doc."

"Anybody hurt, lieutenant?"

"No, Doc. Can I get a picture of your wound?" Even the LT wouldn't let up.

"All right, you guys—all of you know where you can go and I can even help you." They finally had caused a reaction in me, which was the name of the game.

The little attack meant that we sat in full view of Charlie and would have to move quickly unless we wanted to find out whether the next round of mortars was more accurate. We did not want to be hit, so Skylark would have to move again.

We waited for the return of the squad on patrol so we could set off to "Adventure City." When the squad returned, they all were upset over not being able to rest for at least a little while.

We just told them, *"Toi xin loi."* ("I'm so sorry.")

It felt as if we were on the run. *Guerrilla* is Spanish for *little war,* and the way we fought in 'Nam certainly qualified as guerrilla. There were never large-scale battles nor were there ever rescues from the calvary. We learned to make do with what little we could carry and with the few marines we had, too.

After finding a suitable spot from which to operate for the night, I made my rounds and listened to the soldiers' complaints. Before going out on the night ambushes, a sense of loneliness came over me. If I had a problem, who could I turn to?—Actually, no one. I was the moral support for the men in my care, which included the sergeants and the lieutenant himself.

"Doc, my feet are falling apart. I don't think I can make it any more," complained Juan Gallegos.

"Take off your boots and let's see your what's wrong." His feet were indeed falling apart. They were red, swollen, blistered, and bleeding.

"You're not going anywhere, Gallegos." His boots were the problem, with hardly anything left of the top leather—it was rotten and holey. Also, the thin soles caused Juan's feet to be bruised by even the smallest pebble.

"What's wrong with you, Juan? How could you let these boots get in this condition? Man, I'm really disappointed in you. You have shoe polish to use so the leather doesn't rot. Did you forget that we have a radio? A simple call would have brought you a pair of boots on the next resupply. What am I gonna do, carry you?"

I scrubbed down his feet with antiseptic soap and poured on peroxide, followed by mercurochrome. Then I wrapped Juan's feet with a gauze dressing.

"Put your boots on," I commanded.

Like an obedient soldier Juan forced on his boots, and then I wrapped them with adhesive tape.

"Stain the tape with mud so that the white stripe won't stand out like a target. As soon as we radio in any kind of message, you're going to have a new set of boots—no excuses. Go tell Mike what size you wear, and be kind to Mike, 'cause he doesn't like you very much. You know, don't you, that you've just made it harder on the rest of us? Now we'll have to cover your spot on ambush and patrol!" I was sincerely upset.

While yelling at Juan, I realized that in the past few days, my temper had seemed to flair quite easily. After my loud criticism of Juan, I heard no more objections from anyone. But I sure did stop the complaining!

I needed to get away for awhile.

"Mike, we're going out. Get your radio. Is that all right with you Lt. Winter?"

"Sure Doc. Knock yourself out. Are you expecting trouble out there tonight?"

"Naw. Jus' wanna blow off some steam."

Sgt. Pierce led the night patrol that evening. He seemed somewhat uneasy to me; his look and mannerisms appeared much more intent and serious than normal.

"What's going on, Sarge?" Mike asked.

"Things just aren't right." Those few words as we headed out carried a cartload of concern. We needed no further explanation. Anytime a veteran made a remark like that, it was in one's best interest to listen and be more aware of everything. Those types of feelings were eighty to ninety percent correct.

The night seemed darker than usual, with a thick, overcast sky, which even the bright moon could not pierce. Our night vision did not help, either, as the foliage quickly separated us from each other. That was very dangerous.

"Halt!" came the order, with a sharp, loud whisper.

In reverse, the sarge came up from the point position saying, "It's too thick. We'll turn back 'till we find a clearer spot."

Walking through the growth caused excessive noise, and all of us were beginning to feel uneasy. The recent mortar attack and the fact that the Skylark team had even been sent here made our nerves even more tense. Charlie was out there, and he obviously knew we were out there somewhere, too.

As our little group attempted to backtrack in the pitch blackness of the night, the elephant grass, along with the never-ending vines and thorns seemed to devour us and begin its digestion. Even with a luminous compass, it was becoming useless to even guess where we were. It had been two long, tedious hours since leaving the CP. Panic mixed with frustration seeped into our subconscious. Still, we upheld the chain of command; Sgt. Pierce remained solely in charge.

"Doc, I'm going to stop right here and set up, even though there's no clearing. What do you think?" Pierce asked me. It was a hard decision.

We set up within an arm's length of each other, since any farther would have required movement of the jungle's growth. Silence should always rule in the bush, regardless of the situation. Every other man faced one direction, while his neighbor faced the opposite side. After we arranged watch with each other, the slow, quiet, fearfully dark segment of the twenty-four-hour period began.

The nocturnal sounds of beasts and insects were present, as always, but somewhat muffled by the concentrated vegetation. The ear was the only usable sense organ.

After about one and one-half hours, I heard an unnatural sound. Mike heard it too, and tapped me to get my attention. I tapped the next guy, making us all aware. The sound was too heavy to be a small, four-footed animal, too slow to be any nocturnal creature, and too numerous to be anything but a group of humans. It was the enemy on the move.

The sounds stopped. Faint grass crushing occurred at various spots. An ambush was being set up! Should we fire or not? Not being able to communicate for fear of giving away our positions, we remained silent. Sergeant Pierce would have to decide. His signal would be the first round to be fired. With light tension on our triggers, our muscles nearly spasmed.

Thoughts raced through my mind as I began plotting out my game plan to care for the wounded. How would the attack occur? Would the enemy be inclined to rush? How many of them were there? The minutes ticked away ever so slowly. My watch made loud, pounding noises, as the second hand hammered inside. Holding my position was torture—my muscles began to cramp and my joints stiffened. How much longer would I have to remain like this?

Time oozed, as our test of endurance was in its semester final. Now we battled going to sleep. All we needed was for one of us to fall asleep and begin to snore. My eyelids became quite heavy, and my head began to nod. Would it be me who would give away our position?

Who knows how many hours had elapsed. I was still awake, thank God. No shots had been fired. The mosquitoes were feasting, as we, their helpless victims could not lift a finger to swat them off.

The darkness began to give way to the early morning hours. The grass began to rustle as our adversaries rose to break their ambush.

"CRACK, CRACK, CRACK, CRACK!" We broke the silence by opening fire!

Those facing the wrong way quickly flipped over and joined the fire fight. The return fire of the AK-47s distinguished itself from our familiar M-16 fire. We were too clustered!

"Spread apart!" yelled someone, as we instinctively shifted our positions.

The characteristic crack of the Chinese AK-47 faded out as the return fire ceased. Some of our men stood to see if they could pin point the enemy. The rest of us eventually followed suit. Dawn was arriving; we had at least a little visibility. Where was Charlie?

We held our positions a little while longer to regain silence status in case Charlie would try to counter attack. The elephant grass was very dense, and sounds of movement through the greenery would indeed give us away.

The morning sun began to shine through the trees about a half hour later. We moved to where we thought the VC had been. As expected, we found no bodies, but there were some areas of blood. Then Mike called in a sit rep.

"Is anyone hungry?" I asked, as the others stared at me, probably wondering if they heard correctly.

"You know Doc—whenever there's blood, he gets hungry," Mike muttered.

"Hey man, cut me some slack. Got any peaches?"

It never took long to inhale food, so we left the area shortly after breakfast. Inhalation of food has been a legacy of my time in 'Nam until this day.

After participating in a firefight, one's sense of awareness lit up like a Las Vegas casino strip. Instead of just being aware of the surroundings, one would take note of intricate detail anticipating the next battle.

We asked questions: "Where did Charlie flee to? Would he return, now that he knew our whereabouts? Now that Charlie was here, would he be setting up more booby traps?" The questions were endless but with the adrenaline highs, our brains could temporarily handle their massive onslaught.

We arrived back at the CP without incident. Once the epinepherine wore off, fatigue set in. There was no rain that particular day which meant the hot sun pierced the steaming jungle.

Hot sun or no hot sun, we could always saw logs. The perfect sleeping arrangement was the bush hat placed over the face, with just enough room to allow the nose to ventilate. During the day, sleeping was an extra treat. We could snore all we wanted while we enjoyed sleeping flat on our backs. We'd discovered paradise again—and more of life's little pleasures.

What seemed like days was only two hours of deep sleep. I became aware of an overwhelming sensation of being watched, and I woke to a line of respectful grunts waiting for the beginning of sick call (respectful in the sense that none of them actually woke me up.) I think stares are worse than kicks in the feet. I wondered, "What's their problem this time?"

Cruger was "boil man." I've never seen anyone acquire so many boils than that boy. Coats constantly vomited blood after eating dehydrated LRP Rations. You would think he would have learned by now. Coats was a marine; what should we expect?

Jungle rot, a mixture of tropical fungal and bacterial infections, was the illness of the day. Once on the skin, the infection would cause pain and itching simultaneously. Stale swamps and rice paddies were the breeding nests for the affliction, and the usual methods of wound care seemed to be futile attempts at eradicating the scourge of Southeast Asia. The monsoons made the fungus a thriving business. If I had been in private practice, I could have paid for my kids' college educations from that infirmity alone.

My skill involved scrubbing the wounds and infections with a firm nylon brush and applying antibiotic ointment. Dressings were always plentiful, so my men looked genuinely wounded; however, no one received a Purple Heart for suffering through the affliction.

As night approached, the lieutenant graciously told me he would allow me to sit that one out and spend the night at the CP. I was thankful because my buttocks sure hurt; a minor infection had set in on the shrapnel wound. Maybe I should have received a Purple Heart for the wound, but I could have cared less at that segment of my life.

The sky was clear and the moon almost full. We hardly ever saw an open sky like that during the monsoons. This type of illuminated night was regarded as a "high threat period." High threat meant that the enemy could move much more rapidly and could also launch accurate rocket or artillery attacks since their targets were more visible in the moonlight. The ambushes we set up could also detect movement with greater ease on nights like that, which was about the only advantage we Americans had.

Mike and I shared watch together that evening. Being at the CP, we could at least whisper. On ambushes, one would have to make sure not to blink too fast as the eyelids might make too loud of a noise.

I pulled out a canteen filled with strawberry Kool Aid. Mike had saved up a few extra C-ration chocolate bars. Those weren't all that bad. We were like Indians at a pow wow, exchanging gifts before the peace talks began. No one else was involved nor would we ever let anyone else enter our little world. We both were very aware of the crime we had committed—acquiring a friend during wartime—and were willing to pay the consequences.

Who ever thought that simple friendship would become such a taboo. If one allowed it, it would have been painful to think of the other dying or being maimed, but we were no fools. Mike had mastered the art of numbing his emotions long before I had, as he was a few months my senior in this inferno.

Again, Mike began to dwell on his plans to become a millionaire after finishing college. His plan included having his wrestling scholarship renewed to aid in his college funding. Mike had a sister whom he cared for dearly, the only member of his family that Mike ever discussed. Later on in life, she became a successful singer.

That particular eventful night, an idea struck me which

actually brought me to a crossroad. For years, I had had the notion that doctors were all egghead types, bred by their parents for that profession. While growing up, the only doctors I had ever known were the ones that sewed me up or operated on me. These were all untouchable men whom I had placed up on pedestals.

One fellow corpsman had stated back in the States that his goal was to become a physician. I remembered almost immediately placing him on a pedestal like the idol that my childhood healers had occupied. From that moment on, I set apart that corpsman as in a different class from the rest of us.

Why could I not set a similar goal? What did I want to become anyway? If I ever made it out of that hell hole in at least partially fair condition, I would be a physician. This was not a promise to give myself something to live for nor was it a vow to God or to my parents. It was just a dream.

For the first time since I arrived in Vietnam, the future actually seemed like a reality. Thinking about the future was like remembering a long forgotten dream. It was uncomfortable, to say the least, but I very much liked what I was doing and did not mind the idea of being a healer for the rest of my life.

"Mike, do you realize that if I make my mind up to do something, it can become vapor in the next few minutes?"

"What are you getting at, Doc?"

"Mike, I've decided to become a doctor."

"Are you crazy? What are you doing making plans out here. When I talk, I'm only rattling off dreams. They don't mean nothin'. You're talking stateside stuff. Don't you know that making plans and thinking can get you killed out here? Come on, Doc. You're smarter than that. Imagine us out on patrol one day with your mind up in the clouds planning out your life, when a trip wire catches your leg unaware."

"You're the one who always finds those things; here you are getting yourself messed up over something that has no meaning out here in the bush. This here is reality, Doc! Snap out of it! Let's get with the program."

Mike was right. He knew that I was serious, and that scared him. "Rattling off dreams" was all he and I had ever done up until that point. Mike recognized that my attention had taken a different direction and that was dangerous to anyone.

I did drop those thoughts, but the seed was planted that ultimately changed the course of my life forever. Somehow, I seemed to experience a spark of enthusiasm in the upcoming days, but no one could tell. I think that even my voice became somewhat more authoritative. At least, that is what I thought.

We spent the rest of the moonlit night in silence, as Mike wished he had never heard me (in my thinking) take even a partial step out of bounds. I watched the ground, looking for any type of movement, with my finger loose on the trigger of my M-16.

Reality was truly there in those surroundings, with the loud noises of tropical insects, eternal mosquitoes, high humidity, and warm, if not hot, monsoon weather. I took a deep breath, squeezing what little oxygen I could from that hundred per cent humidity. As the warm, humid air entered my lungs, I realized, too, that those realistic planning sorts of thoughts were indeed out of place there in 'Nam.

It was as if I had had a brief dream that vanished as quickly as someone would wake up from a sleep. I cursed my existence there. Why did I have to be in that stinking hell hole? I yearned to be young again, and have fun on some college campus. The trouble was that I honestly could no longer remember what fun was.

The morning arrived almost unnoticed. The following two days were also just as routine as puppies chasing their own tails. Charlie called the shots in his country. He waged war on his terms and on his terms only. What that cunning enemy was up to at any given time was anybody's guess. If we had cared, never knowing what the game plan was would have probably driven all of us nuts. We didn't care, so it was not a problem.

At the end of the two days, our Skylark team was called back to the rear. The lieutenant never did mention the title Skylark again, so we assumed that a rose by any other name is still a rose. We were Marine Corps infantry, and that was that. Whenever there was trouble elsewhere, our unit was usually the one called out and sent to render assistance. What's new?

By the time had Skylark ended, most of us had grown beards and long hair, at least by military standards. Holes permeated our clothes, and our socks had worn quite thin. Jungle rot seemed to thrive on most of us, including myself. Each of us was more than ready for a little rehab in the rear.

The chopper flew in to a makeshift landing zone, and we filed aboard. No one smiled or displayed any excitement on returning to the rear, as each of us was very tired.

It needs just a little more paprika!

Chapter 13
Indian Country

As soon as the chopper landed, we all made a beeline to the chow hall, where lunch was being served. We knew we had no time for showering or shaving. Needless to say, those accustomed to the high and tight attitude of the rear ranks cast eyes of disapproval upon us. I noticed that not even the lieutenant himself seemed concerned with the rituals of the rear that time. As we approached the mess hall, we were greeted by Gunny La Fifi who wore a huge smile. In typical La Fifi fashion, he tried to look tough and mean.

"All right, you pansy sissies, fall out, off to the side! On the double!" Was the Gunny losing his marbles?

"Quick-time it up to your usual barracks." Something was just not right, but we complied, and headed in the direction La Fifi indicated.

When we arrived at our hooch, we discovered a crew of cooks barbecuing T-bone steaks. The Gunny had come through again! Drinks bobbing up and down in tubs of ice were waiting for us. In typical grunt fashion, we started eating without utensils or plates. Our stomachs had shrunk, making it difficult for any of us to consume a single whole steak. Most of us tried, however.

Mike and I sat down and leaned on the side of the hooch for a back rest. As if there had not been an interval between this moment and our last verbal encounter, we completed our previous disturbing dialogue.

"I'm okay, Mike. You don't have to worry about me."

"Promise?"

"Yeah. I promise."

That brief conversation was all it took to get ourselves straight. I had not realized what an impact a simple thought would have on me, but I guess if the tides were turned and Mike would have come out with a similar thought, I would've reacted the same. Focusing on reality meant survival.

We enjoyed every bite and every chew of our steaks. Our ice cold drinks were sent from heaven. We seemed to be wallowing in pure pleasure those few moments. Our stomachs felt as though they would burst, but we overlooked the discomfort.

After the delicious meal came the showers. The hot water did not last long, so half of us bathed in cold water. However, the cold water did not keep any of us from staying under the running water as long as possible.

I had already become accustomed to having to use scissors to trim my beard before trying to shave it off. We hardly recognized each other after getting shaved, sheared, and squeaky clean and then donning new uniforms. Some of the newly shaven grunts looked like little boys. Really though, they *were* little boys.

Back at the hooch, we sat around sharing with each other our letters and CARE packages. All of a sudden, the Gunny burst in with his clenched fists on his waist.

"Who's the baddest dude here?" Uh oh. That was a direct challenge. Most of us had already consumed too much beer to be worth anything, so nobody volunteered. Just then, good ol' John Boy decided to be the divine designator.

"Gunny, everyone here and everyone in I Corps knows that

the baddest dude we know is right here and it ain't you." That
beer sure was speaking! The gunny continued smiling from ear
to ear.

"Point him out, John Boy," commanded La Fifi.

"It's Doc, Gunny—right over there," John Boy declared,
pointing to me.

Half inebriated, I felt like an unarmed matador in a bull
pen. What was I to do? I had dodged the boxing match in
December, but there was no way out this time. Why not fight? I
was numb anyway, thanks to Uncle Schlitz.

"Come on over here, Doc. Let me tear you to pieces." I
think Goliath made the same threats to David a few thousand
years ago, using almost those exact words.

What the heck! At least the gunny wasn't angry with me.
Somehow, distant thoughts surfaced—memories of college
personal defense and karate. I walked to the middle of the
hooch and assumed a wrestling stance. "What technique do I
use?" I thought.

Gunny La Fifi walked up to me and attempted to grab me
from my waist. Wrong move. I gripped his wrist with my left
hand, pulled it backwards, lunged my hip to his under arm,
brought my right arm and hand under his left armpit, and
swung the gunny over onto the floor. The crowd exploded to a
full cheer, and the world title match was on.

In an instant, the gunny was up, holding me over his head.
I have no idea how I got there. Then he sent me the length of
the hooch, airborne, and I landed on collapsible cots. At least
they collapsed for me. I bounced up and charged at the Filipino
monster. I faked him out and slid in like a baseball player
coming into home plate.

Landing at his legs, I grabbed them with my own legs and
arms which enabled me to flip the gunny once more. That
angered him. Tossing, throwing, slamming, half Nelsons, full

Nelsons, choke holds, wrist locks, and a whole host of other illegal wrestling maneuvers followed.

Bang! Crash! Thunk! Poof! Ouch! There wasn't a cot standing after a short while. The giant wouldn't quit for anything. I was younger than him, and had run cross-country in high school; I was surely able to out-last the old man. Still, the gunny wouldn't quit! I just could not give up. The fact that I was barely holding my own was, to me, a great accomplishment, forget the winning part. Despite all the crunches, the gunny gets credit for not allowing one fisted punch to be let loose. Was my reputation at stake? If it wasn't, then perhaps I could give up. No such luck! My reputation was indeed at stake—I thought.

He had me down on the floor, ready to be pinned, and squirming like a worm. Arching my back, I was able to knock La Fifi off just enough to throw him off balance. A reversal! But since we were not really wrestling, there were no rules. Then I was able to lock the gunny's arm in a position meant for no escape unless I let go or the arm broke—in theory, that is. Again, I found myself in mid air, bewildered at how I got there.

Slam! I hit the wall, cracking the plywood. With the wind totally knocked out of me, I sat there watching those cute little birds flying in a halo around my head. Every bone and every muscle in me throbbed. I could not tell if anything was broken.

Gunny La Fifi, too, sat on the floor, huffing and puffing. As his eyes caught mine, he grinned from ear to ear. The muscle-bound marine stood up and walked over to me. "It's a draw, Doc."

To me, that meant victory. Just to stand up against that man was indeed an accomplishment. The gunny helped me up. As I stood with wobbly legs and also huffed and puffed, I speculated whether this was living or what?

"Doc, you're all right. No one's ever been able to do as

well as you just did." The gunny paused briefly, looked down, and then up, around the hooch,

"Men, take care of this man. He's already taking care of all of you. The whole world is against you, guys—the hippies back home, the politicians, the gooks, the Army, the Air Force, and even the lifers. I should know 'cause I'm one. Everyone's afraid of you and no one likes you. Stick together. You're all you've got." The gunny smiled as he spoke sentimentally.

Mike helped my abused body to the icy cold showers. No one had struck up a fire in the makeshift water heater. But the cold felt good since my body was beginning to numb and shiver in the frigid water. A few bruises appeared then and more became visible later.

My platoon was restricted to that particular hooch. We heard that too many of the grunt platoons had become involved in fights thus were not allowed to go down to the USO show. "It don't mean nothin'," we all agreed, and spent the remainder of the night enjoying electric lights, running water, being able to talk, and not having to go out on patrols. Somewhere into the evening, I collapsed from pure exhaustion.

We spent the next day at Freedom Hill—where else? There, I was introduced to steam baths—a Godsend, and in the nick of time. The fun with La Fifi had made me sore and the steam really helped the soreness.

I had ordered a suit, and it was ready, so I tried it on. What a gyp! It fit me horribly! I was so upset and raised such a stink that someone called out the MPs to avoid a major riot. I was stuck with the ill-fitting suit. What should I expect for thirty dollars? I thought it was a steal, and it sure was—they stole from me. Later, I bought one in Okinawa that fit perfectly for thirty dollars—my final appeasement.

We spent the rest of the day just enjoying ourselves. First, we bowled and made a mockery of the game. Then we went back to our old faithful Chinese restaurant and kept the wine to one bottle so we did not require being escorted out. We walked into a number of stores and acted innocent enough for the vendors to feel they could sucker us into a two-hundred-dollar Bible or a three-hundred-dollar photo album.

"Just sign here, and we'll deduct only thirty dollars each paycheck. You'll never miss it." Some of the foreign vendors became quite upset when we walked away before signing. In a way, we were suckering the vendors instead of their pulling one over on us. It was crude entertainment, but we enjoyed it. Some of the American crooks actually laughed with us and wished us luck.

After he assured the hierarchy that we would behave ourselves, the gunny had arranged for us to attend the USO show that evening. La Fifi was heavy on the threats to us if we made him a liar. Actually, no show had been scheduled for that evening, but rather an outdoor movie, *Downhill Racer*, with Robert Redford.

The movie was about an Olympic downhill snow ski racer who trained in Colorado. Watching the production brought back old memories. For a short moment, soldiers could almost forget that they were in Vietnam.

The movie was over too soon. I stayed watching the blank screen for about ten minutes after the film had ended. My mind was in one big whirlwind of a daydream as I thought of the Rocky Mountains back home. I could almost hear the wind cutting through the tall Ponderosa pines as the thin, crisp mountain air swept across my face. I thought about how, even in the summertime, the nights were cool, and how the pine and the scrub oak each had their own peculiar aromas.

"Let's go, Doc!" Leave it to Mike to burst my bubble.

"Can't you leave me alone for one second? Are you in charge of me or what?"

I did not mean to snap at Mike. It seemed that I had lost all patience. Mike understood and took no offense at my remarks. As I stood up to walk back to the barracks, I felt that someone else possessed both my mind and my body. I wondered if, perhaps my soul, too, was possessed.

I had no control over myself anymore. I said and did things that normally, in times past, I would have never even dreamed about. Within just a few minutes, those moments of deep melancholy vanished like a puff of vapor.

As we approached our hooch, I returned to my non-thinking existence—back in heaven, safe in the rear—a place where one could actually sleep and talk aloud without having paranoia.

Two days in the rear were enough to rehabilitate our weary bones. On the afternoon of the second day, we were called to an assembly. Just hours before the assembly, Red had told us the latest scuttlebutt. Red, a young, black marine from Mississippi whose hair had a tinge of red, giving him his name, had been in country about ten months and was already feeling the short-timer's syndrome.

"They gonna send us to the Que Sons. That's Indian country. That's where the 5th Marines got their butts whipped. I'm too short for this nonsense. I gotta get outta this somehow." A group of us gathered to listen to Red.

"They got tunnels down there like you wouldn't believe. There's several regimens of NVA regulars just waitin' for us. The Americal Division got overrun by a few of them already several times."

"Where you been, Red?" Gonzales asked. "Several of us came from the Fifth, and we didn't get our butts whipped. Also, we just came from the foothills of the Que Sons and there was not much going on. Just 'cause you're short doesn't mean the rest of us are going to get all paranoid. This is nothing but a clean up op, no more different than what we've been doing these last few months."

Mike decided to get in on the argument, as he and Jose were not best buddies anyway.

"Jose, you can make it sound like a picnic, but if you'll remember, I too was out there, and it was hell. This here with 3/1 has been a picnic; not up there in the Que Sons. We could send two Marine battalions and would still be outnumbered three to one. You pansies are going to learn what real fighting is, not this Mickey Mouse garbage that we've had to do down here." Mike was getting hot.

Then I decided to throw in my two bits. "Hey, Mike, let loose. Maybe you just had an upset stomach when you were up there. Don't get all bent out of shape because soon enough, all of us will find out for ourselves what's up there, and we don't need to be at each other's throats before then, either."

"Clam up, all of you, especially you, Red. Fear is contagious, and that's one thing we don't need. If you want to chicken out, I can write you a medical excuse so you can shiver in fear in the rear instead of helping out your bros. Hey man, out in the bush we're your bros. You got that straight, Red?"

We had our assembly, and sure enough, we would be off to the Que Son mountains. This time, we would be cooperating with two other companies for nearly a full-sized battalion operation. Captain Short was still trying to make the 'Nam a conventional war.

We were not too happy over having to operate with other units, as their attitudes seemed so different from ours. Not that ours was any better; but at least within our own unit, we could predict each other's actions. That meant everything during hot times, when there was no time to out guess what your comrades were doing or were about to do.

The Marines issued us food and ammo for an undetermined

amount of time. We all took a walk to the firing range, nothing more than a hillside at the edge of our base. That was something never done before. We wondered if maybe we had, for sure, experienced a picnic up to that time. We felt a certain air of expectation.

As ordered, I fired my weapons, an M-16 and my .45 pistol. "Why were we being asked to test fire our weapons?" I thought to myself.

Normally, we would have made a game of the exercise, but the whole platoon acted nervously serious. It reminded me of my first days in country, but currently, even the vets seemed uneasy.

"So tell me, what do you think, Mike?" I asked.

"What do you mean, what do I think? Think about what?"

"Get off your high horse, Greek. You're just as put out as the rest of us over this Indian Country junk. What was is like up there? Do we stand a chance?"

"Man, Doc. We're going to meet the real 'Nam. Down here, we deal with the VC most of the time. When we do meet up with Nathaniel, it's just 'cause he's on his way up to the Que Sons. They have artillery, recoilless rifles, huge mortars, underground hospitals, and tunnels like you've never seen. I even saw a Russian helicopter once that was much bigger than our own. Some of our own battalions were almost totally wiped out. There's even part of the 5th that's called, 'the walking dead,' because anyone surviving was part of the very few that lived through one huge NVA assault."

"No biggy; it don't mean nothin' anyway. All I know is that I'm going to Bangkok for my R & R. You owe it to your bod not to get too strung up on those mountains. We just gotta be just as careful up there as we are down here," he concluded.

"You're right, Mike. Why don't we go to Australia for our R & R?" Our worry and planning time came to a quick end, as it was time to eat supper. They served us as much hot food as our shrunken stomachs could hold. The food always tasted so bland—the Yankees liked it like that. If it hadn't been for Tobasco Sauce, I would have surely starved.

We spent the rest of the evening preparing our gear for the next day. Also, letter writing was in order; but it seemed so hard to do. I spent a large portion of my letter writing time figuring out what I could possibly write so as not to worry the folks back home.

With all the previous letters I had penned to my dad, I had imagined that he thought my war was a piece of cake compared to his. Perhaps it was; I don't know. All I knew was that I could not wait for the day that my time would be up in the corner of hell called *war*.

In that nook, I had carved a niche where I had exacted respect and honor. The enemy was out there and those to be trusted were right here. Of course, if anyone betrayed that trust, he was ostracized to the point of becoming almost invisible. We all knew exactly what was on each others' minds.

Your fellow marines either liked you or they didn't. If folks did not like each other, they just avoided unnecessary contact and that was it. If they did have to communicate, such as during a fire fight or something, then an automatic truce was understood, without any fear of treachery or deceit.

Come to think of it, life was really not all that bad out here. I cannot think of another time where my life had such uncomplicated questions and such simple solutions.

Tucked into my cozy little cot, I treasured the comfortable sleep indoors even though some mosquitoes still found their way through the cracks and crevices. We had no linens, blankets, or pillows. We had to use the same poncho liners as we had used out in the field. The rancid smell of the jungle permeated our hooch, even there in the rear. But we were not out in the rain, nor did we sleep on rocks and mud. Tomorrow was another time not to be dwelling on. My eyes became heavy as they tightly shut my sleeping soul.

An internal alarm sounded at morning's arrival. Most of us had developed a method of waking up at two hour intervals, and that night was no exception. I popped wide awake at every even hour. Even though we were not exactly nervous, there was still an air of apprehension.

That night was quiet—none of the usual chatter that goes along with nights in the rear. I had no particular feeling about the approaching operation, which, I presumed, was best. I no longer trusted any feeling I might have had, since so many spontaneous and unanticipated happenings in my Vietnam experience had already occurred.

Greasy eggs and bacon—although simple, still a culinary delight on that morn preceding our departure. Some of the cooks remembered us as Gunny La Fifi's pets, so they made a special effort to over-or under-cook our food. For all the good that did, I don't think any of us could tell the difference anyway. We rubbed salt into the cooks' wounds by thanking them for such a good breakfast.

Since the choppers had not yet arrived, little clicks began to form around the landing zone. The "brothers" had a small group, but not all who were eligible attended—other blacks were locked into mixed clicks.

Some of the newer guys still tried to win my favor. I guess they figured I would take special care of them if they were wounded. I reassured each marine that I took care of all my men equally. Then I added that one of these days, they too would become part of "all my men." I could not completely figure out whether or not I was joking.

When I approached him, Red was talking to some of his bros. "Hey Red, you going to be okay with this one?"

"Yeah, Doc. I'm gonna be all right. But I sure don't wanna go, man," Red said nervously. He seemed unusually insecure.

"You're one of the older men, Red. Don't go and let us down, now. You could cause these new guys to go ape on us if they see you chickening out."

"Doc, I'm just getting tired of this nonsense. We're not winning this war. They got us humping out in places where they know we're outnumbered. The 'man' just wants to thin us out. We're just peons. How many of them senators' sons you see out here? The dudes with big shot daddies never see any combat, man. What about you an' me? How come we's out here? You know just as well as I do that your daddy ain't no big shot. You're just a poh boy, like me. But don't worry none, 'cause I love you guys and I won't let none of you down. You're okay yourself, Doc."

"Hey man. There's a price to pay for freedom, you know, Red? No one ever wants to be the one that's got to go. We just got unlucky and drew the wrong straw. The fat politicians are all corrupt, but we elected them. Ours is still the best country in the world, and this small country is being overrun by communists. We can't just sit around and let them do that. Haven't you heard about the domino effect?" I speculated as to whether my words were to convince Red or myself?

"Come on, Doc. You ain't that naive. Ain't you never been discriminated against? This is a free country where man can fulfill his dream. We got apple pie, baseball, colleges, and every opportunity imaginable—so long as you're white. Are you white, Doc?"

"Do you think I am, Red?"

"Whoa there, Doc. I been wit you long enough to know when you're getting bent outta shape. You're proud to be a Chicano; everyone knows that. I only asked if you was white 'cause I know you ain't. Cut me some slack, man. I don't see why you're so patriotic when it's your rear that's getting shot at, just like mine."

"Red, you can be anything you want to be. If you won't make anything of yourself, it's not because of the 'man.' It's because you haven't even tried. The establishment is our enemy, true. We don't have to give in to the establishment. I'm going to make this country pay me back for the time I'm out here. Not with just a few bucks, either. They're going to give me respect, and they're going to have to move aside when I come barreling through. I'm not going to stay quiet and let someone else take my place at the front of the line." I paused, astonished at what I had just spewed forth.

"We're here because the U.S. made a commitment to these people. These people here have names just like you and me. You're being more prejudiced than the 'man' if you think of the Vietnamese as any less deserving of help than some other country, like Canada, let's say. Let's cut this stupid talk short. I don't want to sit with my head up in the clouds any more." That was it for me.

"You're right, Doc. We got each other to look out for. You just make sure you look out for me, you hear?"

"Sure enough, Red." Another seed of uncertainty had been added to the already-growing pile.

As I ventured back to my gear, I could hear the dreaded sounds of the helicopters descending from the tops of the nearby mountains onto the landing zone.

"The Que Sons," I announced to Mike. "I think we're finally in for it."

"Let's hope not, Doc. Let's hope not," replied Mike as we boarded for our excursion into the unknown.

The choppers flew at high altitudes to avoid sniper fire. The terrain looked so peaceful from up there. Again, I began to envy the fly boys for being able to enjoy the war from above it.

It seemed like not very many choppers were ever shot down. Of course, the only news which ever received was that which concerned us or that of another familiar unit.

Up in the air were no booby traps, ambushes, snipers, or firefights—just cool air and visible targets. As soon as their cargo had been delivered, the chopper crews headed back to the rear, to their hot food, to their nightclubs, to their soothing hot showers, and to their comfortable beds. They experienced no humping, no heavy packs, no sleeping in the rain. They could even talk out loud at night and have lights.

As we swept across the sky, I thought about how I wanted to show my disdain for helicopter crews. I wished they would have to spend a couple of weeks out in the bush with us—for them to be frightened twenty-four hours a day, not knowing what the next minute would bring. After that, I would want them to be treated like new guys, ignored and left to themselves. Yes, those were cruel thoughts, but unlike last time I flew in these choppers, it was not Christmas time. Since there was no Christmas spirit around to haunt me or to pierce any remnant of a conscience I still might possess, I permitted myself to think those evil thoughts.

As the chopper began its descent, I noticed the rich, bright green Que Sons below. The steep grade of the Que Son mountains reminded me of the Rocky Mountains back home. We were surprised that no tracers nor sniper rounds were fired at us. It was as though a monster behind a closed closet door would jump out at any moment.

When I was a little boy, the darkness of my bedroom would sometimes cause my imagination to run wild with various sorts of fears. That same feeling was edging its way into my thoughts as we landed. With a quick flick of an internal switch, I turned off the beginnings of those thoughts. What was on the other side of the helicopter ramp door would be dealt with when the time came and not before.

Someone lowered the ramp when the helicopter had not completely landed. Oh, no! Not again! "Would I have to jump again?"

The fear of jumping off the helicopter probably imprisoned me more than the enemy or anything else. It was my turn.

"Why not?" I told myself. "The worst thing that could happen to me was that I would again become a patient on the USS Sanctuary—or, I could be transferred to a hospital in Japan. What a thought! Well, here goes nothing."

I sent my two feet airborne and the rest of my body followed. Ground! My knees buckled, but I was still standing! Puff, puff, puff, puff. Now I could conquer the world! Helicopterphobia was now history—a thing of the past!

The drop off points were scattered throughout the terrain at predetermined positions known only to the officers (and probably the NVA, as well.) As usual, the choppers hastened to vacate the premises.

On that mid-January day, the sky was clear, the sun shone brightly, and the temperature climbed. Since it was only ninety-eight degrees, we enjoyed the cool winter weather.

Being spoiled, we took for granted the breathtaking scenery of the tropics, unequaled in its beauty. All that registered in our minds was the steep grade we had to march against. Yes, we were ungrateful people, but that's just the way it was.

I found great interest in watching the company radioman ahead of me. Here I was, struggling with my gear which weighed from sixty-five to seventy pounds, feeling very sorry for myself, watching this thin marine carry, with no complaining, a hundred pound radio scrambler unit plus his own gear and ammo. He seemed to walk effortlessly up the mountainside. This marine's name was Martinez.

"Man, Martinez, what are you made of? You're whizzing up these hills like nobody's business. I'm back here barely making it, dying just watching you."

"Hey Doc. My knees are killing me. If I slow down I'm afraid I couldn't get back up." Martinez smiled. He was a very strong but modest young man. Martinez never liked to be flattered.

Even though we were still in Vietnam and basically in the same region of the country that we had fought in all the past months, there was something very unfamiliar about the territory where we had landed. Perhaps it was the anticipated confrontation with a fighting unit much larger than ours and with about the same reputation. It could also be that this was the northernmost border of the well-known central highlands.

The central highlands were where the Montagnards lived. They were a feared tribal people who were very uncompromising towards the communists. Supposedly, we would not meet any of those mountain people, as we were quite far north of their dwelling places.

The uneasiness could also have been from the fact that the terrain was indeed different from that with which we had become familiar. Everywhere we witnessed the battle scars of the war. The French had fought against the Viet Minh here two decades ago.

Many battles against our own U.S. Army and U.S. Marine Corps had also taken place in these mountains. It was as if their ghosts were ever present, playing out their events in the fourth dimension of the spirit world.

We spent almost the entire first day traveling uphill. The day came to an end without incident—no sense of hostility yet. The ambushes and watches were set up and we manned them in our usual routine. We experienced no contact that evening either.

The following day, we had to walk up the steep grade again. We followed no trails on our route—it was obvious that the plan was to approach the enemy via an almost impassable path. As we struggled through steep inclines, and dense, congested vegetation, we practically scaled the cliffs. Needless to say, Nathaniel Victor would not be sending out the welcome wagon on this side of the Que Sons. That day, too, ended without incident, thank God.

On the third day, we began to encounter civilization—or at least the aftermath of civilization. We came upon an area that recently had been napalmed. It was similar to walking on another planet. There was still a layer of smoke over remains of the trees. The trees themselves were burned to black charcoal. We saw no grass or tropical growth, just ash-covered ground. We smelled the concentration of jet fuel in significant proportions in the atmosphere surrounding this devastated mountainside.

One could almost hear a ghostly wail in the distance as the wind cut through the few barren trees. The danger and fear of an ambush added to the eeriness and reality of the scene from some past Twilight Zone series.

"There's no gooks here. Let's didi outta here, like now, man." That comment came from someone towards the front, and it voiced the sentiment of us all. Without hesitation, we continued our force march through this forbidden burial ground.

Once clear of this area and well into the thick elephant grass we stopped for a break. During most breaks, I would not bother taking off my pack, but this time we all lightened our backs for a brief spell.

"What's going on with you, Crammer?" I noticed that Corporal Crammer was wiping tears from his eyes.

"Hey man, lighten up. My sister sent me this stupid book

and I just got through reading it." Crammer was on the defensive.

"Come on. Don't tell me that a book is what's making you cry? Nobody cries out here. Didn't you say that you were with the tough CAG units, man?" I truly questioned what was going on.

"All right tough guy, I'd like to see you read this thing without giving some excuse that something flew into your eye when you're done with it." Crammer always smiled. After saying that, he actually smiled wider than usual, sort of like he was a used car salesman readying to con me.

"Doc, let me read it first. I can prove anybody wrong." Mike took the challenge feet first.

While this mediocre conversation was taking place there was a commotion towards the point. I arose to investigate.

"Doc, get a load of this. Ol' Garcia almost sat on a chicom (Chinese Communist) Claymore. It was all set to make hamburger meat out of him." Garcia was from Grants, New Mexico, and pretty much stuck with his own click. Actually, Garcia was another machine gunner with John Boy.

As I scrutinized the area, they showed me the oversized booby trap. The steel corners showed no rust spots, and the wire looked fairly new. The device had been set up not too long ago—perhaps a day or two. I had never doubted that Nathaniel Victor knew of our presence here but the presence of the Claymore made the realization even more real.

"Well, Lieutenant, think our adversaries know we're here?" The lieutenant knew I was being facetious.

"We'll soon find out, Doc. We'll soon find out."

Once moving again, our pace slowed considerably—partially due to the thick grass and partially due to our awareness of booby traps. We did discover a few more anti-personnel mines that afternoon, all without detonating any of them.

Were we good or just plain lucky? Probably neither, as I'm
sure there were plenty of relatives and friends back home
praying for us. At the time, none of us were aware of it,
though.

As we neared the top of the mountain, we concluded that
the NVA were probably waiting for us. That is what intelligence had led us to believe. The heat and the constant upward
grade were beginning to overpower me.

Just below our position, a forest fire progressed. Most
likely, the napalm had ignited some dry grass and set the trees
ablaze. The smoke was already heading our direction. This
meant no retreat if we encountered heavy fighting with the
NVA regulars up ahead.

During one of our breaks, I sat down and began to read a
Stars and Stripes, the military newspaper published for GIs on
foreign soil. Our predecessors in World War II had read the
Stars and Stripes, and I guess this was a legacy that we inher-
ited. In the weather section, the weather conditions of various
cities back home were published.

It just so happened that Albuquerque, my home town, had
its weather printed on the edition I perused. It had been a
record twenty degrees below zero there! I leaned back on my
pack and gazed up at the tall trees. Here, the temp was at least
ninety-eight degrees, with a forest fire below us, the NVA
ahead of us, and I hadn't bathed in I don't know how long, and
was tired and totally numbed out. Just then, a thought crossed
my mind.

"I could not, in all good conscience, wish this circum-
stance on my worst enemy," I uttered within myself.

Then I tried to think of pleasant thoughts. The irony of the
situation was that I had no good thoughts to think of. I could
not remember what it was like to be in the cold winters of the
southern Rockies, nor could I remember what it felt like to

throw a snowball. Just as I had had a very difficult time remembering what my own family looked like during Christmas time, at this point, I could not remember what the landscape or the weather was like back home.

No, this was not a time fit for human participation. We were living in an earthly hell. I could only think of how I hated this war. I hated Vietnam. I hated the politicians who put us here. I hated the protesters that hated us for being here. I think I hated anything that moved. I felt like killing something. The smoke was starting to burn our throats and our eyes.

As we started moving again, I got word that one of the new guys had collapsed up toward the point. When I reached him, I noticed that he was burning up. His skin was hot, dry, and red. The poor boy could not even speak. This young marine had suffered a heat stroke.

There was very little time left to save his life. After not too much longer, his brain would fry and suffer irreversible damage—that is, if he survived the shock. I checked his canteens, they were empty! This stupid kid had carried empty canteens because full ones were "too heavy."

He was the reason why most marines carried only four canteens while I had to carry six. There was always some smart runt who knew better than anyone else.

Right now, he was too stuporous to drink. The only thing to do was to get his body temperature down as fast as possible.

"Gonzales. Where's the nearest stream?" Gonzales took off with only his rifle. He was back in less than thirty seconds.

"*Hay agua abajo de esta lomita muy cerquita!*" Jose was excited and had no idea what language he was speaking.

"*Bueno, pues. Dejanos llevarlo para alla.*" I didn't realize what language I spoke, either.

We picked up the heat stroke victim and carried him to the small stream at the bottom of the hill. Wasting little time, we immersed him in the cool water, trying to bring down his temperature. After a few minutes of cooling, the boy was able speak a few words.

The lieutenant set up a perimeter with a few outposts, as he had already resolved that it was impossible for a medevac to be called in. To call in choppers would blow the whole operation and place us all at risk of becoming sitting ducks.

I had the responsibility to revive the boy or lose him. Working frantically and steadily, the boy finally was able to take in a few sips of water. I forced him to swallow several salt tablets. His temperature was beginning to come down and the shock was subsiding.

"What is your name, anyway?" I asked, as I never did know who he was before this incident,

"Jones, sir. Private Sam Jones," his voice still weak.

"You know you blew it, don't you?"

"Yes sir. It won't happen again, sir," he replied weakly.

I stayed at his side the rest of the evening. After a good night's sleep and intense nurturing, Jones revived fully.

The next day, we neared our destination. The forest fire either took another direction or was quelled. Still, we had no contact with our enemy. We all wondered what kind of reception the NVA was preparing for us. Surely Nathaniel knew we were here by this time. This was his rear, his main CP. Meanwhile, we drudged on to the point of becoming almost boring—I did say *almost*.

During one of our rests, I found Mike to see how the book was coming along. Mike was always reading so I thought he should be done by now.

"Hey Mike, there's no more smoke from that fire so why's your eyes tearing?" I was practically laughing at him.

"Get lost, Doc. It's your turn next, and I'm willing to bet a month's wages that you'll cry when you read this book."

"Get outta here. It's just a stupid book. I've never seen a bunch of more pansies than you guys. Gimme that book." My curiosity had gotten the best of me. What was in that paperback that turned hardened marines to melted butter?

Crammer watched our conversation with a huge smile, all the while snickering. Some of the other marines who had read the book and had also been sucked in by the mysterious emotion that haunted the novel also looked on with a great deal of interest.

The cover had the pictures of Ali McGraw and Ryan O'Neal. Apparently, a movie had been made from the story or this book was the product of the movie; I did not know which. "Here goes nothing," I thought as I started to read. I had read a few of Mike's Agatha Christie's books and enjoyed the escape but never was so wrapped up in them that any emotion moved as of yet.

Carefully storing the book in a plastic bag in case of sudden rain or a dip in a stream or swamp, I would place it in my pack each time we saddled up. This one time, I snapped the pocket of the rucksack, swung it on my back and fit the shoulder straps on.

My mind started dwelling on the story, which I knew was dangerous. I shook my head and said to myself to straighten up or I could get myself or someone else killed. No sooner had I completed the thought than.....

"BOOM! Crack, tat, tat, tat, tat, tat, tat."

It was a booby trap followed by an ambush! We were in such a position so that it was very difficult to rush up to the point to help out. The VC either had booby traps or ambushes, not both. The NVA had both. By the time the point could be reinforced with those of us towards the back, the firefight was over. This had been well planned.

"Who's hit? Come on, tell me who's hit!" I was shouting.

"Garcia, Coats, and Smithers, Doc." John Boy was very upset, as he and Garcia were close.

Garcia was unconscious and full of blood. A quick assessment revealed that he had a sucking chest wound. I grabbed John Boy's hand and plugged the chest hole with his thumb while I triaged the other two wounded.

Coats was awake looking me straight in the eye saying, "I'm going home, Doc. You fools are gonna to hafta jus' wait y'all's turn. Going home, Doc, going home."

"Coats, you've always been the lucky one. Remember your lost rifle and when we could've shot you? Yeah, you're just plain lucky." I assessed his wounds, and they were bad enough to send him to a hospital and perhaps home. Not bad enough to really hurt him, though.

Smithers was the one who tripped the wire. His leg was torn off. There was no sign of life. "Come on heart, beat! Do something! Breathe, man, breathe! Couldn't you watch where you were going? Someone tell me what happened here. Why was Smithers walking point? He just doesn't have the experience. Who let him walk point?"

There was nothing I could do. I felt so helpless.

I thought, "I wonder what kind of family he came from?" It was time to return to patching up the other two. This was supposed to just be a triage.

John Boy still held the hole on the side of Garcia's chest in the exact same position I had placed his hand. Taking the plastic wrapper off the battle dressing and applying that wrapper as a seal over the hole would prevent the chest wound from causing further lung collapse. There were also many shrapnel holes throughout Garcia's body. After dressing all of the New Mexico lad's wounds, I patted John Boy on the back as he remained without a word at his compadre's side.

Coats, as it turned out, had a belly wound. There were no

signs of shock yet, but I could not take any chances; Coats had to remain horizontal, covered, and quiet. This was a major feat, as Coats never seemed to be quiet, even when he wasn't talking.

After applying dressings to all the visible wounds, I went ahead and started an IV to guard against shock in case the belly wound had caused internal bleeding. The thought had occurred to me that suppose there would be an even greater need for that IV bottle in the days to come? I carried only two IV bottles. The decision was already made so the consequences would be mine to bear.

Once the men had stabilized; the long wait for the choppers came next. All we needed was for one of the air ships to take in small arms fire. We had to do the best we could to cover the medevac. Often, the enemy would listen in on our conversations and throw out a smoke grenade at the same time as we did, which would confuse the pilots and sometimes succeed in luring the helicopter to the deadly trap of the NVA.

After checking on my two patients and seeing that they were all right, I found a little time to get back to the book. The couple had already fallen in love and were quite involved. I could picture the campus of Ratcliffe, with all those girls. Actually, I could picture the campus better than I could the girls. I had not gazed upon a real "round eye" from the States since the Bob Hope Show.

It seemed that I, too, was falling in love with this make-believe girl. Was this the trap that had caused my fellow-grunts to fall? Perhaps it was a subtle and powerful trap.

"All right, Doc, get ready. Here they come—a gunship and a double bladder!"

Mike coordinated the timing of the green smoke grenade for positive I.D. At exactly the specified time, the smoke grenade was thrown, and the color identified only *after* it had been thrown. The pilot radioed that he had not seen a second smoke cloud. Thankfully, the NVA were not nearby or were just not playing this time.

Our standing on a slope made loading the ramp very challenging. The chopper's tail end was the only part touching the ground. The ramp bounced as the suspended craft hovered at an angle above the ground.

Finally, Garcia, Coats and his IV, along with Smithers' body were all loaded, and the ramp shut. The blades increased their RPMs and hoisted the large airborne target back to some rear hospital. That chopper served as a big source of communication to Nathaniel since he could tell that we had suffered casualties and the size of our platoon had diminished, at least by a few.

We spent the remainder of the day pushing to a rendezvous point with the rest of the company and perhaps some of the other companies from this operation. The amount of our movement that the enemy monitored was anybody's guess. We marched steadily and cautiously, not stopping, as we had already lost substantial time. The grass cuts on our hands and arms were just deep enough to sting but not deep enough to scar. It was hot, not scorching, but hot just the same.

Finally, all thirsty and tired, we arrived at a small valley designated as the meeting place for the operation's companies. The first to arrive, we hoped that our map's orientations were correct, as none of us desired to move again this day.

I broke out that little, highly addicting, paper back novel, and was determined to finish it while we waited for the others.

This time I could dwell deeply into the subject matter of the book without having to look over my shoulder. It was true; there was safety in numbers. Mike offered to cook my gourmet dinner of Beef and Shrapnel while I completed the *Love Story*.

Again, my mind went to New England to live out this short drama. As the story continued, the hot, humid jungle disappeared. This young couple was really in love. I just knew that their love was a jab before the power punch. The story developed, and the reader had no choice but to become totally wrapped up in the lives of these two college kids.

"What! This just couldn't be! The girl died! No! Not in a story that offered a short escape from this hell hole. This had been a really good story. The death of the girl seemed so real, too. My throat developed a lump as my eyes became watery.

"This stupid book," I said angrily. Anger and hatred were the only emotions I knew what to do with. I was concerned that the book would break down the defenses that had taken so long to develop in the surviving grunt out in the bush. Still, it was a good book, and I was becoming confused over whether I should tell Crammer to quit sharing it.

"Crammer! Get over here." Crammer came, smiling as usual.

"Come on, Doc. You had tears, didn't you."

"Crammer, it's a good book. But I think you had better be careful who reads it. It could affect someone bad enough to where he'll miss a trip wire or not hit the dirt fast enough when he needs to because he's thinking about this dumb fairy tale. I think it could be quite dangerous in the wrong hands, don't you?"

"I don't know, Doc. I'll have to think about it. You're probably right though. You cried, didn't you. I wished I could've seen you. No one saw you, you know."

The "fairy tale" was bothersome and my mind dwelled on it for an extended time. Within a few hours, however, I was back to normal. Normal for a war zone, that is. My mind was clear of any rubbish that might contaminate split second decision-making.

Mike laughed as he served our C-ration supper.

"Doc, I saw those tears in your eyes. I can't believe how a

boring little paperback could have so much power over us. Man, not even someone's head getting blown off could affect me like that piece of junk."

"Mike, I think that we are all so stressed out that anything could put us over the edge. Here we have a controlled environment, but the book is something that we have no control over. The story's already in print and we have no idea where the writer has his mind. We're at his mercy."

With that behind us, we could take care of the business at hand which was, of course, the war.

The other two companies were slowly edging their way to this point. By sunset, the last of the stragglers had arrived. With appropriate security surrounding the leaders, they could hold their brainstorming session and decide the strategies of the upcoming operation. We knew that they were up to no good. Few, if any, of the leaders ever went with us to the front lines during ambushes or patrols.

What else was new? This segment was probably the biggest success of the whole operation. The NVA either did not know that we were all there or were just observing with great interest. I don't see how there would've not been an attack if they had known that we were there. Thank God for one additional night of peace.

First Sergeant Anderson had been assigned to us, along with Staff Sergeant Ramos. These two men were about as opposite as magnetic poles. Sergeant Anderson, on his third tour, loved action. He must have been a hyper-kinetic child growing up. Anderson took La Fifi's place, as La Fifi completed his six-month rotation with the grunts. Anderson, part Cherokee Indian, was a Rambo-type if I ever saw one.

Sgt. Ramos, on the other hand, was a whinny type of person who had absolutely no leadership skills. Ramos even wore a white handkerchief around his neck because of the heat.

He liked to mingle with the troops, only to talk about his girlfriend or some other distraction. When Ramos approached a small group, the group would disperse shortly thereafter. After a while, Ramos realized that he was not welcome and stopped mingling.

Corpsmen were also supposed to rotate at six-month intervals, and I had already spent more than six months out, but I saw absolutely no indication of a replacement for me anytime soon.

For a while, we did receive one other corpsman to bring our platoon up to the standard two for each platoon. Unfortunately, this fellow left for some sort of emergency leave after only about a week with us.

I didn't even bother to remember his name. The other marines had evaluated him and were not impressed. This corpsman eventually returned to our unit two months later, but when in the Que Son Mountains, I was still the only corpsman for our platoon. I believe President Nixon had cut back on the troops in his de-escalation attempt. It put additional burdens on us who remained "in country."

On a certain morning before we separated for our assigned destinations, we were supposed to be receiving replacements by chopper. The sounds of two choppers approached our mountain side. That morning, the wind was up more than usual, which meant little to the ground forces, but it was major to the air wing.

The first chopper made its approach swinging from farther down the slope and then backing its ramp to the hill to let everyone off. All the while, the ramp was the only part touching the slope, while the remainder of the chopper was suspended in air. It was a fantastic feat, causing all of us to hold our breath. Once off the chopper, the marines moved to make way for the second ship to come in.

This second chopper made an initial approach just as had the first, but either the wind blew much stronger or the pilot was much less experienced—perhaps it was a combination of the two. The pilot aborted the first attempt and progressed into a second. Again, we each held our breath, and our tension mounted with the retry.

The chopper swung below us and then upwards, trying to position itself for a backup, which began without incident. Then, out of nowhere, a gust of wind shot up from somewhere below and caught the helicopter.

"Gain control! God, gain control!" we all prayed verbally.

The wind was more than the young pilot could handle. It was as if a giant hand of the devil had grasped the helicopter from its belly and flipped it upside down, smashing it on the hillside. With a huge fireball, the magnesium-laden fuselage burst into flames!

In a matter of fifteen seconds, the aircraft converted to a crematory. We could not assist those poor boys in any way. The intense heat kept us from even getting close enough to see whether we could assist any of the possible survivors.

Five minutes passed, and then a small party of us stumbled cautiously towards the wreckage. It was a horrible sight. The fierce heat had for the most part, subsided. Some fire still burned, and the smoke coated our skin with a layer of oil-like substance.

The stench of jet fuel and burnt flesh pervaded the air. The charred bodies of nineteen young soldiers lay in disarray. I wondered how many of them were new guys, cherry to the 'Nam? They never had a chance.

I had to make a survey of everyone to make sure that we were not missing anyone who might still be alive. After the horror of the third body, my eyes numbed out as had my heart months previously. They all looked the same even though some were burned more than others.

I began cursing. I just did not know what else to do. I feared blaming God, so I cursed everyone else, including Ho Chi Minh and President Nixon. There had to be a purpose for life, for our existence, for this war. I was bound and determined to, one of those days, find out what it was. I did not know how, but I would find out; I knew I would.

Captain Short had radioed for a special team to fly in and take care of the wreckage and the dead. We all desired to not linger in this locale for longer than necessary, so we began disbursement for this operation to the preplanned quadrants on our maps. Then our platoon spent the remainder of the day force marching to another destination.

Over the radio we heard reports of scattered small skirmishes but no major clashes with the expected organized regiments of NVA. Our passage was quiet, and the day came to a welcome close as we set up for evening ambushes.

"Want some Kool Aid, Doc?" Mike whispered.

"What's the special occasion, Greek?" I whispered in return.

"Hey man! What's your problem?" Mike said, sounding annoyed.

"Gimme a swig." It was an insult not to accept a gift, so with that statement there was no apology or excuse needed.

"What do you think of your ol' stomping grounds now, Greek? Are they the same as before?"

"They know we're here in force, Doc. No telling what they're up to. They know more about what's going on at Washington than we do. I think they'll either leave us alone so that we can get pulled out of 'Nam earlier or they'll try to teach us a lesson. One thing for sure, though, they'll fight to the death if we corner them."

"Let's try and go on R & R together, Mike." We put our minds at ease best when war was not the subject. Everyone

knew what to expect in wartime. It was taxing to discuss it, so
we tried to avoid the topic.

We both took double watch again in order to stay up
together. If Mike was to die, a major portion of my humanity
would die along with him. I found myself wishing that we had
not become such good friends; but then, too, I was thankful we
trusted each other.

That night, I felt like a snobby, rich kid because I wore a
mosquito net hat that covered my head. Don't ask me how I
acquired it, as novelties came and went without much fanfare. I
didn't possess it for long, because I grew tired of its restricting
form and gave it away.

The following day, our platoon set out to comb a suspected
rear base of the NVA. We had heard that their rear bases were
usually underground and not readily visible. The slopes
remained steep, but at least they were dry.

Paydirt! We found a small cache of small arms. In it, we
discovered several SKSs, which looked like Czechoslovakian
rifles. I had never seen one up close. The stocks were wooden
with long barrels and they had some vicious-looking, hinged
aluminum bayonets attached to them.

All of the ruling class in our unit had first claim, leaving
nothing for the rest of us peons. The lieutenant took pity on me
and let me have his. Gee thanks. So I got to lug around two
rifles, with one of them probably not even working. I was not
in the souvenir mood.

In the cache, we also found a couple of empty Chicom
recoilless shell casings—AK 47s (which had to be turned in to
be recycled to the Cambodian forces) and maps and documents.

There had to be a tunnel close by—sure enough there was,
and we found it! Two smaller men braved the tunnel. Some of
us waited while others searched for an exit or vent. It was
always quite tense waiting to see what would happen to those

young heroes. Over half an hour elapsed before one of them crawled out of the opening.

"Man, you wouldn't believe it down there! There must be a whole hospital!" He was carrying some medical supplies. "Take a look at all this stuff, Doc."

Russian style thermometers, glass nebulizers, mortar and pestle, tons of gauze, some sort of medicinal powder with an acidic aroma, pills, blackened archaic surgical instruments and medical literature in French, Chinese, and Vietnamese. Those were pulled out in the first haul.

The second marine finally appeared at the opening with his loot, none of which was very valuable. I could not use any of it anyway, and it was of very little military value.

They found no sign that Nathaniel had been inside recently— very little personal equipment and no food. The two marines commented that they had dismantled a couple of booby traps; usually these tunnels were plagued with mines in every corner. We sure wondered what the enemy was up to in this case.

Captain Short had a squad lay explosives in the tunnels to destroy a home base in case the NVA had plans of returning after we left. Caboooom! It was like a mini earthquake.

Out in the distance a faint series of small arms fire sounded. After ten or fifteen minutes, Top Sergeant Anderson came strolling in from a one man patrol. He said that he had come in contact with a single NVA regular and both had exchanged fire but the NVA had fled after the brief encounter.

That scout apparently had been watching us. There must have been some sort of a plan. Perhaps Nathaniel feared our presence. Perhaps Nathaniel had set a humiliating trap for us. Off we marched to discover the plan.

The very rocky terrain, with loud streams, thick jungle, and of course, steep inclines made for slow moving. We had split into platoons to make traveling faster, which it did.

Once, we took a brief rest at an apex of a small canyon just before approaching its final hill, and I sat enjoying a treasured can of peaches in which I had crumbled some pound cake. I had waited for this desert all week and this was the day I decided to eat it. Only trouble was that I was so anxious that I could not wait for supper. "Crack."

A twig broke above me, at the top of the little hill! With one clean sweep, I grabbed my M-16, took off the safety, quietly set down my peaches, and proceeded up the hill. Along with me came the usual lot of synchronized vets, not bothering to explain to any of the new guys what was going on. We preferred that the new guys just sit and watch the show and not get in the way.

Assuming point, I crept up the hilltop, with my heart pounding and my body soaked in perspiration. Our small contingent of marines was almost completely silent when, like snakes, we edged up to hill. At the top, I stopped and slowly peeked over the edge. My piece was ready to fire instantly. "Oh God, I hope I see them before they see me," I prayed, not knowing what else to say.

There they were! Four or five uniformed regulars! They were expecting us, but from another direction, thank God. As I slowly moved my rifle up to a firing position, one of the regulars caught my movement, swung around and prepared to fire!

"POP, POP, POP, POP, POP!" I fired before he did! He fell down as the others began firing. My men were already positioned and returning fire as well. We had a full fledged firefight going! Between trying to take cover and making sure of my target, the group of NVA regulars disappeared.

They had been watching us and knew that they were outnumbered, so there was no use in engaging when the odds were against them. Thankfully, we left with no casualties.

Boy! Was I pumped full of adrenaline!

"Way to go, Doc! One confirmed for the Doc, you guys."
Crammer was building me up.

"We'd better start moving before they get reinforcements."
It was a strange feeling having knowingly killed someone. In
the past, we all fired into a group, seldom knowing whether we
hit anyone, but this time was different.

Inside of me, I could sense something trying to do or say
something but being suppressed by something else. I felt
almost sad and almost joyful, all at the same time. Perhaps if
this would have happened earlier in my tour, the sensation
would've been totally different. But I'd become nothing but a
functioning robot. I would shelve this near feeling along with
all the others until some later time in the obscure future.

My can of peaches and pound cake were still standing
upright, exactly where I had set them. With two big gulps, I
inhaled the remains of the delicacy. Theft was never tolerated,
even if it was food—just food? I should say, "especially if it
was food."

I strapped my useless SKS on my shoulder and then told
the lieutenant he could have his souvenir back but I would
finish carrying it for him until the next helicopter for shipment
back to the rear. He asked if I was sure and then thanked me. I
believe he appreciated the rifle more than I did.

We tried to follow a blood trail just as if we were deer
hunting, but the NVA had been at this war longer than any of
us, so we lost the trail very early on.

We took a break from our trek, and with the rest of the
company, compared notes and selected a rendezvous point.
Other platoons had encountered tunnels like we had, and had
not encountered much contact. Perhaps that was good. At the
time we did not care.

At that point, a news reporter from United Press International and a specially assigned rear echelon marine private

joined our platoon. We did our best to make them feel unwelcome. The news media had always portrayed the American soldier as a savage war monger who hated peace. Some of the new guys did not know the unspoken rules and they engaged in conversation with the reporter.

Our sergeants set the newsboy straight in case the greenhorns had given him misinformation or too much information. There was a hand wound movie camera in his hand—just great! All the time and effort I had spent in creating for my family the illusion that all was well and quiet was down the toilet if this clown took a picture of me.

"Doc, the UPI reporter wants to do an article on you. Go talk to him." The lieutenant told me to talk to him, but did not tell me what to say. I believe the lieutenant was just as annoyed as the rest of us.

"You want to talk to me?" I said quickly.

"Ah, yes. I understand that you're the platoon corpsman, is that correct?" I sensed obvious nervousness in his voice.

"What's it to you? I heard that you guys went wild when Jane Fonda went to Hanoi a few months ago. Is that right?" Then he became defensive.

"I didn't cover that story. Uh, what do you do as a corpsman?"

"Listen, pal, I don't want you writing a story about me or about any other corpsman, you hear? I am not going to give you any information, so just leave me alone. You got it straight?" That kind of boldness surprised even me. I truly had changed into someone else. The reporter did leave me alone, and basically kept to himself after that.

For the next two days, we continued on our routine of covering ground during the day and setting up ambushes at night. There was no contact. I guess the reporter became bored, because after these two days he departed. Before leaving, he did make some friends within our platoon. I never saw the civilian shoot any film of us. It was good that nothing happened with him around. Each of us was much more at ease after the outsider had gone.

Perhaps the war was becoming too private and personal for us. It did not seem as if the whole world witnessed our deeds. As a matter of fact, it seemed very much like the United States had misplaced us unwanted waifs in some forgotten corner of the world.

Putting up with the whining of Sgt. Ramos was like baby sitting a spoiled brat, except the brat was our superior. We also had to contend with Sgt. Vaughn. One sunny mid-morning, I took off my shirt for some "tanning while you work." Sergeant Vaughn ordered me to put my shirt back on—he said I was out of uniform. I couldn't believe the jerk would be so petty.

The lieutenant saw what was going on and told the sergeant to lighten up. The sergeant was so military and lacked so much common sense that he turned around and ordered everyone to take off their shirts. Can you imagine?

Oh well; we complied like good little soldiers. I was burning with anger on the inside. This type of behavior caused myself and others to hate the military with all its useless and senseless activity.

The lieutenant sat and talked awhile with my circle of friends. "This Sgt. Anderson is quite a Marine. He's serving his third tour over here and the guy has not the faintest idea what the word *fear* means. Anderson said that he is part Indian, which is why the guy can barely grow whiskers. Have you seen the way he's built?"

Right about that time, 1st Sgt. Anderson walked over to us. "Doc, you going out on ambush tonight?" he asked.

"Yes sir. I go out almost every night." I responded.

"Make the first three rounds in your magazine tracers. If

you see movement, fire the first round in the middle, then the second to the right, and the third to the left."

"That way, when he goes for cover he'll either dive to the right or to the left, right?" I responded.

"You got it, Doc." Sergeant Anderson then rose and departed with the lieutenant.

"Way ta go, Doc. Now you're a teacher's pet." Mike disliked the military as much as the rest of us did.

As evening neared, I placed the first three rounds as tracers in my magazine, just as the Top had instructed. So did some of the others in our ambush team. We expected something to happen that night, and I believe Sgt. Anderson did too.

We invited the Top to go out with us, but he declined, saying that he would leave the fun and games for us to enjoy. I believe he thought that we all were incompetent, much like a parent when first teaching the child.

Mentally, we were preparing for a full-fledged battle with some of Nathaniel's regulars that night, so I took along extra battle dressings. Before leaving on the excursion, a brief survey revealed that a good portion of my battle dressings had rotted and were covered with mold. I threw away most of the ruined bandages, but had to keep some for dire emergencies.

That evening, I realized that it had been days, if not weeks, since it had rained. I guess the monsoons were over; the heat was making a comeback. Was this January or February? I was confused. At least I knew which day of the week it was. I was the malaria pill man, you know.

I had always loved the mountains and 'Nam was no exception. Had we not been in wartime, I think I would've thought the Que Sons close to a paradise, save the heat of course.

After penetrating the jungle foliage for a while under the cover of dusk, the squad leader chose a spot for our ambush. It could've been a perfect picnic area or campground in other circumstances. What was happening to me? Why was I thinking such strange thoughts?

Paradise. Picnic area. Campground. To get my thoughts back in order, I shook my head until the brain within jolted. I sure did not want to get caught off guard while daydreaming about Shangrila.

We chose an L-shaped ambush because it seemed obvious that if any of the enemy would be out on patrol, they would be coming in to our area from only one direction.

I sat looking at the darkening field in front of me while rehearsing my routine with the first three rounds as tracers. Why hadn't anyone thought of this before? The idea was ingenious. I was excited and anxious to try out the scheme first hand.

The still of the night edged on, minute by minute, just as it had during the multitude of evenings preceding it. Would we see action tonight? Actually, our thoughts always anticipated action and adrenaline ran on fast idle each and every ambush night. The insects began their usual chatter.

Mike and I shared the same watch. His radio was on low so that one could only hear if he had pressed the handset against the ear. Neither of us had Kool Aid that evening. Our combined, four-hour watch seemed to be taking an unusually long time. Someone just had to come up upon our ambush. Even a mongoose would do.

In the still of the night, I heard the explosion of some artillery far away and wondered where the shell would go. I had heard that the NVA had artillery, too. Naw. This couldn't be their's.

Then we heard the air splitting jet-like sound of an artillery shell whizzing to its destination. Wait a minute! The sound did not pass over us, and it was becoming increasingly louder! The shell sheered our way, louder and louder, all in a very short time. No! This couldn't be happening!

"BOOOOOOOOM!" I had been lying in a prone position, and the intensity of the explosion thrust my body about a foot into the air. Blammm!! I hit the ground. There was shrapnel flying through the trees and the ground surrounding us. The smell of explosives also permeated the air. My ears hurt from the shock.

Without any time to recover, the screeching sound of another shell could be heard.

"WHHZRZRZRZRZRZZR....BOOOOOM!"

It was as if a huge giant was trying to swat us like flies. Again, my body was hit by the shock wave. I looked at the dirt in front of my nose; I took my thumb and made an indention in the ground. Then out of desperation, I tried to crawl into that small hole. I was so scared that I actually thought I could fit in that thumb hole.

"WHHZRZRZRZRZRZRZRZR......BOOOOOOM!" My head was pounding from the blasts. Every square inch of my body trembled.

"WHHZRZRZRZRZRZRZRZR.....BOOOOOOM!"

I heard voices over the radio handset. The radio was on the ground with Mike lying next to it.

"WHHZRZRZRZRZRZRZRZR......BOOOOOOM!" I crawled the few feet that seemed like a mile.

"Mike, Mike!" I yelled. "What's happening?"

"The Army's shelling us! They spotted movement with their night scopes and think we're NVA." Mike was yelling at the top of his lungs, too.

"WHHZRZRZRZRZRZRZRZR......BOOOOOOM!" I could hardly bear another round. I picked up the handset and began to frantically shout. "Kilo two, kilo two, tell those sorry Army jerks to cease fire! Cease fire!"

"Use proper radio procedure. We'll do the best we can. Over and out." That was it brief and simple.

"WHHZRZRZRZRZRZRZRZR......BOOOOOOM!" The shock waves were like blows from a grizzly bear. That last blast went off at tree top level sending shrapnel almost directly down upon us.

"WHHZRZRZRZRZRZRZRZR......BOOOOOOM!" "Oh God, please let me hear the blast of the next shell." In my near panic, I had no idea whether I was shouting this prayer or thinking it.

The light from the blasts was as if someone was taking flash pictures. Dirt clumps and debris flew everywhere. "WHHZRZRZRZRZRZRZRZR......BOOOOOOM!"

This last blast actually flipped me over. I turned back over immediately to cover my head with my arms. Most of the shrapnel was up higher than ground level as these 105 millimeter rounds sunk into the ground before exploding. I was still praying my simple prayer for me to be able to hear the blast. If I heard the blast that meant I was still alive and not vaporized into thin air.

"WHHZRZRZRZRZRZRZRZR......BOOOOOOM!" My face buried itself into the earth with both mouth and nostrils packed with soil. I don't know if I was even breathing. Every muscle tensed spastically.

As each explosion detonated, I became stiff like a board, and bounced up in the air. Every organ within me shivered like an electric buzzer.

"WHHZRZRZRZRZRZRZRZR......BOOOOOOM!" The idea of hot shrapnel flying over our backs and crashing into the trees and jungle growth around us caused us to have visualizations of bright red, jagged pieces of metal tearing into human flesh. We all waited, shivering with fear and anticipation for the next incoming round.

"Hit, you dirty round, hit," mumbled someone into the dirt. The foliage, branches, rocks, and dirt continued falling on us. Eventually, the fallout slowed to nothing. We anxiously prepared for the next round to come crashing down—nothing—ten or fifteen minutes passed and still nothing.

I turned my head to the side and exhaled to rid my airways of the impacted clay, allowing me to breathe. My pulse rate was faster than that of a crying newborn baby. It was hard to tell if the agony of my groanings was from pain or from hysteria. Still, thankfully, I perceived no more rounds.

I established some voluntary motion, as my arms began to move. In a partial push-up position, I grabbed a quick glimpse of the surroundings. There was no sign of life. My arms collapsed, and I lay there lifeless for another fifteen minutes. The shelling indeed had ceased.

The jungle was ghostly quiet. My ears rang loudly. Forcing myself to get partially up, I began to crawl at a snail's pace. I managed no leg strength or function, but did maintain arm movement. Mike was the first person in my path, and I truly expected him to be dead.

Mike was alive, although not talking or moving. I generated a slow, strenuous effort to evaluate the rest of the squad. As I crawled up to each of them, I had a very difficult time remembering their names. To my surprise and relief, they all lacked any external injuries. They each, however, were just as stunned as Mike and I.

After surveying the troops, I lay back, staring at the black sky. An hour or two passed without any movement or communication. Finally, we all congregated in a circle. Mike was trying to report to the CP, but only garble would emanate from his mouth. No one else made any attempt to speak, as we each experienced the same situation.

"We were almost done in by the stupid Army. I can't believe it," Crammer said, staring at the ground.

We heard the radio sending out messages from the captain requesting a sit rep. Finally, Mike was able to speak, "Situation contained. All present and accounted for. Over and out." That was it. Nothing more need be added.

I dozed off out of sheer exhaustion. I don't know if anyone took his turn at watch for the remainder of the night. It just did not matter.

The sun rose a few hours later, and automatically, we arose. If there ever had been opportunity to sleep in, none of us would have known how to do it. The smell of the artillery shelling still hung in the air. With light available, the scene was actually worse than we had imagined. Smoldering craters had been blasted everywhere—105 mm artillery do not make impressive craters, but they make craters just the same. How any of us survived unscathed is either a mystery or a miracle.

Still experiencing the aftershock of the bombardment, we all kept very quiet, with headaches and ringing ears. However, anger bred in our hearts against the Americal Division for being so ignorant about their target. We might have had civil war if the fire base had been within walking distance.

When we arrived at the CP, the look in our eyes shut out the inquisitions of everyone, including our superior officer. However, it was good to be back home with our platoon. We had a few rounds of C-rations for breakfast and saddled up for travel that same morning. The fact that we all made it back consoled us somewhat after the Army's blunder of the previous night. No one ever mentioned the incident, at least not to us.

Rumor had it that a royal chewing out of the illustrious Americal Division by our officers was performed in typical Marine Corps tradition—the Marines were very protective of their own.

We continued in our state of stupor, and several days passed before any of us became fully aware of our surroundings. To this day, I do not know whether we even went out on patrol during that time. I think that we were led around like simpletons during that recovery period. In a matter of days, however, we returned to "close to normal" (whatever that meant.)

A little later, someone at the rear scheduled another rendezvous for resupply and school—yes, school. Ever so often, some well-trained individual was sent out to the bush to teach us about some special device or technique.

This time, our government salesman came to show us a PSID, a Personnel Seismetic Intrusion Device. The little electronic wonder was a probe in the form of a stake that was pressed into the ground. Lead wires ran from the stake in the ground instrument to a control box. Then from the control box ran a set of earphones from which we could detect any movement in the vicinity.

The "specialist" also demonstrated a bullet-proof flak jacket to us. The standard issue flak jacket had been designed only for some, not all, types of shrapnel. This new protective gear had a ceramic-like breast plate inside a nylon camouflage vest. The young marine detailing the equipment said that it could stop a bullet from penetrating. The only trouble was that only one bullet could be stopped as the ceramic would shatter and would thus require replacement.

"What about machine gun fire?" someone asked.

The breastplate attached itself on the side with Velcro. Velcro was new back then and awfully noisy. We joked about opening the vest at night during an ambush to keep ourselves awake and to signal back to the CP that all was well. The jacket also had a built-in back pack. Woopie doo! We did not accept that piece of equipment. Another platoon, we heard later, had been coerced by their lieutenant into using the vest. Those poor souls had nothing good to say about their experimental gear.

We enjoyed the comedy of the first night we used the PSID. Every single bit of movement in the area was picked up by this little stick in the ground. Listening to it was like listening to a pass and review at boot camp. In a pass and review, all the new graduates marched in parade formation in front of the base commanders and some family members.

Just the normal movements out in the bush sounded as though a whole regimen was passing right in front of our noses and we never caught a glimpse of them. It seemed that every little animal in the jungle had heard about this new sensor and tried it out to see if it worked. I was a nervous wreck by the time my watch was over. Needless to say, it only took a few nights before we returned the gadget for a refund.

Still in somewhat of a dazed condition from the friendly fire incident, I began to realize that we had not yet engaged in any heavy fighting in Indian Country. For whatever the reason, we were all grateful, but stayed prepared just the same. The jungle itself made up for the lull. We realized that we had to defend ourselves not only from the human enemy, but also from the environment. Different elements of nature could be quite hostile at times.

One night, we had set up an ambush overlooking a valley up on a hill. As dawn approached, I took my turn at the last watch of the evening. As with every morning, there is a certain stillness right before sunrise. This particular morning, as my eyes were doing their best to fight drowsiness, a peculiar stench permeated the air. It smelled of dead flesh. The weird thing was that I had not smelled that foul odor all night. "Perhaps," I thought, "a small wind had just blown over a dead body nearby." Whew! At least the stink brought me wide awake.

The skies were lit as the sun made its debut. I stood up to

Quit yer gripin' ! You git to sit on my shoulders in the next swamp!

wake the others when it caught my eye—walking down the hill, towards the valley just below us was a full-sized, humongous tiger! I was not about to shoot it. Our experience with that wild boar had been enough to convince anyone that usually large animals are merely annoyed with an M-16's initial fire. Cautiously walking backwards to the rest of the squad, my eyes stayed fixed on the beast.

As I looked down to awaken my comrades, there they were! Gigantic paw prints completely surrounded our place! The tiger had been prowling about our area without making a sound. For some reason, the tiger decided that we were not his particular desire for breakfast.

It was a miracle as far as I was concerned, that none of us had been touched. Actually, no one had been aware of the man-eating cat's presence. As a few of the squad rose for the morning, they too, saw the tiger as it was strutting along making its way to whatever was down in the valley. The looks that men gave me said, "What were you doing on watch?"

Another "natural environment" incident occurred while we were wading through a swamp in the Que Son Mountains. That particular swamp was deeper than usual. Most swamps were around waist deep and filled with murky water, but the water level of that swamp was at our chests. My wax-coated pack helped with buoyancy. Mike, however, being a smaller size, needed some help, since the water was at mouth level to him.

Lifting him by his pack, we both slowly and quietly waded across the body of water. In front of us, Spencer looked off to the side and then towards us with eyes as round as saucers. Obviously very frantic, and with his rifle over his head, he pointed off to the side. Mike looked in response to Spencer's gesture.

"Doc! An alligator!" Mike exclaimed.

Quickly, I too looked off to the side. Sure enough, the tail of an alligator slid into the water. It was heading straight for us, thinking someone had fed him his afternoon feeding. Like a nightmare of someone chasing you and your feet will not move was just how it was trying to run from an alligator with a full load on back in fifty inches of water and a muddy, soft bottom.

I imagined the alligator right on my heels readying to take a chunk off my buttocks. Actually, I figured that I would be a sure meal for the overgrown lizard. Still, with tremendous effort all four of my extremities moved as fast as they could.

After about a five-second period, a horrible thought crossed my mind. "I had let go of Mike! Oh no! Was this the reason the alligator had not attacked me yet?"

Finally, after seconds that seemed like hours, I saw the bank right in front of me. A hand reached down and grabbed hold of my wrist, pulling me out as fast as it could. Looking up, I saw that the hand was Mike's!

"How did you...?" I was dumbfounded.

"I don't know, Doc. I think that I must've run on top of the water. All I know is that I got here before you did, and I thought you were a goner, Doc."

We both broke out laughing and laughed until our bellies hurt. The few troops behind us decided to walk around the swamp, so we waited for them. I could still feel that 'gator right behind me. We all broke out in laughter again.

The tour through the Que Sons was coming to a close, since we had swept through most of the suspected NVA hideouts. We never did encounter the big numbers we had anticipated, but that was of no consequence.

Concerning the absence of Nathaniel, we grunts had come to the conclusion that he just did not want to jeopardize President Nixon's plans of U.S. troop withdrawal from Vietnam. If fighting picked up, Nixon would probably hold us in 'Nam a little longer. We were tired of this war anyway, so we did not at all mind the lack of fighting. The only problem was that we could not let down our guard for one second.

On the day before we were to be airlifted out, we had convened in a partial clearing to regroup. Someone had to make a water run, so John Boy and I collected all of the canteens that needed to be refilled, strung them through a strap, and made way to a nearby stream downhill from our position.

At the stream, we encountered very tall trees and huge rocks. Also, the vegetation, as expected, was thick. While John Boy filled his strand of canteens, I stood guard over him like a good sentry. Definitely, we sensed danger among the trees. Of course, I think I felt a sense of danger everywhere we were located, anyway. John Boy filled his string of canteens, and then came my turn.

As I filled the canteens one by one, my eyes scanned the trees thoroughly, readying for an attack as we did consistently. While capping one of the canteens, I took my eyes off the trees, and, "BANG!" The water splashed on my face, momentarily blinding me. As I ducked for cover, John Boy began returning fire.

"Where's it coming from?" I shouted.

"I dunno, Doc," That was not the answer we needed.

"PING! SPLAT! ZING!" Rounds were impacting the rocks and the water. Straining my eyes, I could not tell, for the world, the position of the sniper. "He's got to be right over there, Doc," John Boy yelled, pointing at three o'clock from where we sat.

"Let's do it, kid!" Then we both opened fire.

"Crack Crack Crack, Pop, Pop, Pop!"

We found no sign of a hit. We both waited momentarily, and then, like good marines, we chased after the ghost sniper. The shooting stopped, and after twenty minutes of searching, we ceased our pursuit and went back to pick up our water.

Those snipers sure could make a person feel extremely vulnerable when that one was the target. Even while we walked back to the canteens, the sense of being watched felt like a piercing laser on the backs of our heads. With each second at the stream, John Boy and I were filled with an ever-increasing amount of anxiety.

Once we had filled all the water containers, we scrambled back to our CP and reported the minor assault on the water team. Then we returned to our little plots of *tierra sagrada* claimed for the moment. Whatever the location, the small sections of soil that we occupied became private property. Perhaps we would even fight to the death if our space was violated. It could be that man's instinct and drive for the possession of land was the impelling force behind most wars. I don't know.

Waiting until the choppers arrived to transport us back was as unnerving as waiting for them to fly us out.

I heard the comment, "I wonder what's in store for us when we go back?" It must have been a new guy questioning aloud. The ones of us who had been in country awhile took what came next; that way, there were never any disappointments.

The Que Sons had been much less dangerous than any of us had expected, which was a pleasant surprise, so to speak. Most of us survived, and we were thankful. That last evening, the meal and the night watch were almost lax enough to allow our guards to be dropped.

The night fell, and the morning brought another day. The choppers coming to take us out of the Que Sons could be heard in the valley to the east of us. This meant the operation was over.

"Your ears still ringing, Doc?" Mike asked.

"Yeah, but who cares?" I did not want to be reminded of

the artillery barrage. Mike felt the same; he merely had a slip of the tongue. We said no more. The choppers arrived.

"Bon voyage, Nathaniel. Try and be better hosts next time. We won't bite. We'll just eat you alive."

Chapter 14
OP Revisited

"All right, you slimy maggots, we couldn't think of a worse job for you losers than manning the observation posts— don't blow this one," the lieutenant ordered with humor that seemed out of place. However, we could forgive him this one time, since a reward like being sent to an observation post was like being sent to the garden of Eden.

"How long, lieutenant?" If we were supposed to stay for three days, we wouldn't mind. Less than three days; however, would be grounds for divorce.

"About two weeks. Squad leaders meet me here in ten minutes for assignments. You're dismissed."

The LT assigned me to Alpha and Bravo squad on top of the mountain just northwest of the 3rd Battalion headquarters. Mike stayed with the lieutenant at a post on the other side of the mountain from us. The climb up to our post took about forty-five minutes with no rest stops. It was a hefty climb, but the months of humping the jungles and their highlands had turned our legs into leather work machines. Climbing the mountain seemed easy to most of us by then.

At the top of the mountain sat a sandbag bunker with plywood walls and a sandbag roof—we'd be indoors again— what a life! Right next to the hooch a radio relay station had been built. It was manned by a lone marine radioman with blonde hair and very fair skin. The young lad had a slight pot belly and wore blue jeans. At first I could not take my eyes off of his blue jeans. I must have looked like some hick from the backwoods staring at his Levis.

"Why are you wearing those jeans?" I asked in pure amazement.

"Hey man, there ain't no inspections or no officers up here. Any of you guys got any new jams—you know, tapes?... music?"

"What do you think we are, pogues? Are you a pogue?" said Crammer after being hit by the radioman's sour note.

"I spent my first six months humping just like you guys. Cut me some slack. I've been out here for six weeks nonstop. The last squad was pretty much space cadets, and I was hoping you guys would be different." He knew how to handle himself.

"What you got in that hooch of yours, radioman? You could listen to all the jams you want if you was a real radioman. Or is it that all you do in there is blow weed?" I felt just as sarcastic as Crammer, but I had no fight left in me today.

This radioman turned out to be compatible, but he did smoke his share of marijuana. Our squad, being human, had its own potheads, so our radioman made friends easily. There was nothing to this post so we had plenty of free time on our hands. It seemed the only way one could be productive was for that one to actually be busy. If there was too much time on our hands, then that was usually nonproductive.

I was able to catch up on some Agatha Christie reading and a little target practice. Before long, I was able to shoot as well as Doc Potter with his .45 semi-automatic pistol. At fifty yards, I could hit a grouping of approximately four inches in diameter; and one handed at that.

Down the trail lived Bravo squad. We had split up our two squads between the two outposts. I made medical rounds every two days or so, just to make sure there were no sick individuals—

and, of course on Sundays, to make sure each marine took his malaria pill.

No matter where we subsisted, the Vietnamese were also there, being like most enterprising Asians, always selling their goods. Those "goods" included Coca Cola, French beer, various types of clothing, marijuana, and an occasional "sick little girl." These girls were prostitutes. No one had access to prophylactics out in the bush, so whenever we were not out in the real bush and had too much time on our hands, I was usually very busy trying to convince the troops that the VD out there could affect them for life, causing sterility.

Seldom did any of my scare tactics have any affect on these young bucks, but at least I tried. I did carry antibiotics with me, but usually sent a clap-infested marine back to the rear to get specific treatment for a specific diagnosis. To our platoon, it was like having a wounded soldier, since while he was getting his body cured, the platoon was without that body.

During my time at the OP, I was able to authorize myself a trip or two to the rear for resupply or some other made-up reason. Since I lived within walking distance from the rear, I took advantage of it.

On one of my visits to the battalion rear, I decided to visit the Battalion Aid Station (BAS). I did not recognize anyone, so I introduced myself to the group of pale, anemic-looking, rear echelon corpsmen. At first, I felt somewhat content with the idea of not being able to talk shop with fellow corpsmen, but now I wasn't too sure.

"How long were you out in the bush?" I asked one corpsman as he banged away at a typewriter.

"I uh, er, ah didn't have to go out to the bush. There were no slots for me when I arrived." He went on banging at his machine.

As the situation would have it, fewer than half of the group of corpsmen had ever been assigned to a bush unit before being assigned to a job in the rear. We were supposed to spend six months out in the bush and six months in the rear. Most of those boys had spent fewer than four months total "in country." I had already been out in the toolies over seven months. I was infuriated, and my whole personality had become savage.

"Do you have an assignment roster?" I asked another pale, neat and clean, secretary boy. He recognized potential trouble, so he called out to the NCO in charge.

"What seems to be the trouble, son?" The NCO was in his mid-thirties who was the apologetic type and wanted peace at all costs.

"None of you rear people have any idea who I am, do you?" I clenched and gritted my teeth.

"What do you mean, son?"

"Over on the wall, I notice that you have a roster of which corpsmen are assigned to the various specific companies and platoons. I am looking at my platoon, and I don't see my name anywhere. Now I am going to walk out of here without telling you my name or which company and platoon I'm attached to. And then I just might drop my senator a note, and again, I might not. Good day, gentlemen."

During the brief moment of silence, I stole away. I was in no mood to engage in any type of discussion. Well, at least I knew where I stood. I was a grunt and those at BAS were rear echelon pogues. We were in two different worlds, and in a way, it was better that way.

Back at the OP, I talked to Mike over the radio, asking him to come on over and take a look at the relay setup we had here. Actually, we had to speak in code, since we could not just come right out and say, "We have this relay station here, and it is so vital to all our operations. Golly."

Mike did come over for a couple of days, as he was in

charge of changing out code books to the squad radiomen for our platoon. The first night, we decided to have a party. I had smuggled some Schlitz from the rear, and it was nice and warm (no ice). Not having partaken in the vices for a long time, our circulatory system had remained fairly pure, so it took very little to totally bomb us out.

Being quite inebriated, we decided to produce some fantastic entertainment at Uncle Sam's expense. Over the radio, Mike staged a sighting of a regimen of sappers out in the valley which our outpost overlooked.

In stormed the artillery. They always seemed to miss their targets, putting us in at least some risk of being hit, but we took the chance anyway. Then the jets dispersed their napalm— fantastic light show! Last came the Broncos with their basket-ball illums. That production was ten times more brilliant than any Fourth of July display I had ever seen.

Mike and I jumped up and bestowed a standing ovation upon the fly boys, "Bravo, bravo, bravo." We estimated that about a quarter of a million dollars had been spent to entertain us that night.

The rest of the night, we stuffed our faces with C-rations. Thumping on my belly after the feast reminded me of Paul Newman in *Cool Hand Luke* after he had devoured fifty hard boiled eggs. We had put on a good party for the occasion and for the time.

The following morning, my head pounded severely as the beer chalked up another casualty on its list of victories. As I lay on the ground trying to study my eyelids, one of the new guys was frantically whispering to me.

"Doc, Doc! Wake up! Wake up!"

I was already awake. "What do you want? It'd better be good."

"Don't move, Doc! You got a bright green snake getting

ready to attack you. What do I do?" The poor kid was desperate.

"Hand me that shovel over there, now!" I said without moving. What the newcomer had just described was a bamboo viper, or as we called it, a two stepper.

The small military folding shovel was slipped into my hand. Then with no waste of time I crushed the head of the bamboo viper, killing it on the spot. After glancing over to make sure the viper was dead, I laid my head back down to resume my hangover nap.

I had become the classic mirror image of that corpsman I had met the first day I set foot in this country—the one sleeping in the dirt. Just as had the corpsman on that day months earlier, I displayed no panic, no emotion, no unnecessary chatter—I had become a stone clothed in military garments. No one except the new guy made any fuss about the viper, either.

The two week vacation came to an end all too quickly. I had spent a lot of time humping up and down the mountain, tending to the troops. Actually, during the two weeks, I became bored, and made the rounds just to keep myself occupied. We were anxious to get back to the life and death situations faced everyday in the bush.

The epinephrine rush of combat can probably be equated to a type of amphetamine drug. The addiction and the thrill of both the natural occurrence and the artificial drugs do change individuals. What else could drive someone to actively seek a dangerous environment in exchange for a comfortable, safe base. It just doesn't make sense. When one is out in the bush, all he does is wish he was out of there and curse every step he makes. When he is back in the rear, or in a safe place, all he does is wish he was back out in the bush engaging in combat.

Later, as we exchanged the guarding of the mountaintop observation post, I noticed the new platoon taking our place

was not a traditional grunt unit. They were part of the 106 mm
Recoilless Rifle team. I noticed one of their members carried
on his back a full, feather-stuffed mattress. Now that was
totally ridiculous. As I approached the panting soldier, I was
preparing to render him a hard time. Wait a minute! I knew that
guy!

That mattress-bearing slug had been my roommate back at
Long Beach, California. Gordon Hays—I couldn't believe it. I
had been in the military eighteen months before arriving to
"the 'Nam." I had known a large number of corpsmen and
sailors, but I had yet to meet anyone I knew other than Lucero.

It felt strange to meet someone from the past. I was being
exposed to a part of life I had tried to forget. Hays brought me
up-to-date on all the other corpsmen who had come over after
Lucero and I had landed in that war-torn piece of earth. Only a
small portion of those men actually had been stationed with
combat troops. Of those stationed with grunts, I was the only
one still out in the bush, even though I had been "in country"
the longest.

I had become indifferent to those types of stories and was
even regarding all corpsmen in the same light as any rear
echelon pogue. Hays had been part of a very close knit group
of friends back in California, but I felt no camaraderie towards
him now. I left Hays, returning to my squads and wishing that I
had never seen him. My attitude towards Hays was just another
reminder of the very thing I had become.

At Battalion headquarters, the platoon regrouped for a
briefing of an upcoming mission. The company was to begin to
assist the ARVNs in South Vietnam's push into Laos. Supposedly, we could offer them only air support since Congress had
just forbidden American troops in Vietnam's neighboring
country. So, under the pretense of rescuing downed pilots and

liberating POW camps, we were to spearhead and soften the invasion for the ARVN troops.

No one thought much of the South Vietnamese soldiers. They were thought of like someone on welfare when the everyday Joe worked like a dog to have the fruits of his efforts shared by those who did absolutely nothing. Nonetheless, this was just another operation under our belts. The superiors warned us not to write any of this in our letters, as it would jeopardize the entire Marine Corps effort. We were compliant, as usual.

With only one afternoon to collect our new supplies and to have the various strategies reviewed by our officers and NCOs, we did not have any time for rehab. This was acceptable, as our short tour on the OPs more than made up for this inconvenience. The next morning before sunrise, we were herded like cattle down to the helicopter pad. No time for even a cup of coffee.

"What do you think, Mike?"

"I'd like to see those pea-brained ARVNs help us out for a change. That would be a laugh." Mike voiced a common opinion.

Then I spewed forth my thoughts, "These stupid colonels and generals sit in their air conditioned hooches planning the whole war for us, never once stepping even one foot in the bush. They have no idea how to fight this war. We had no-fire zones. What place does a no-fire zone have in a war?"

"Then there's the pacification teams. What a contradiction in terms! We never fight the war on our terms; it's always on the terms of the VC and the NVA. Those gooks know that they can fight anyway they want, while we honor borders and some dumb paper signed in 1954."

"If the enemy wants to wage a conventional campaign, it's just fine. If they want to keep it at the guerrilla level, that's perfectly fine with us because we got plenty of boys. If we run out of troops over here, we just send for more from the mainland. After all, we don't want to offend anyone. We've been here since 1962. The North knows that we have no intention of ending this war. Who knows how many senators and manufacturing companies have gotten rich from our little stay here."

"We haven't helped this country any. Only the corrupt Vietnamese politicians benefit from our being here—it's like working for the Mafia. These corrupt leaders swim in their wealth, with their money in Swiss banks, ready for the moment they have to escape. The poor people out in the villes are torn between the oppression of the communists and the indifference and corruption of their own government."

"Who are we helping here? We're supposed to be stopping the spread of communism—sure—meanwhile, we're lining the pockets of everyone else. As soon as we leave, Mike, I give this place a little over a year to fall completely. If you or me die, it'll be for nothing. No one cares that we're even here. Our own leaders just think of us as numbers. The people back home actually hate us. So what do we do, Mike?"

If I couldn't talk to Mike who could I talk to?

"Doc, you've got a soft spot for the people here. That's okay, but I don't care what happens to them. It's because they've allowed their own leaders to take power that this country is in the shape it's in. They themselves are to blame."

"I don't even know if I'm patriotic or not. I used to be patriotic before I came here. Now I just hate all governments, ours included. You and I should be back in college enjoying life. Instead of worrying about semester finals, we're wondering whether we're going to survive the next few hours."

"Look at me, Doc. Have you ever seen me happy? Of course not. Everyone knows that I'm filled with hate and anger. This'll probably mess me up for the rest of my life too, I don't

know. All I know is that we don't want to be in this hell hole
but we're here and there's nothing we can do about it."

"You and I aren't cowards, so we do what our country asks
us to. When I get out, I guarantee that I'll never work for
anyone. The slave days are over. I may even move out of the
country. No, I'll just become rich and thumb everyone in the
nose."

Mike and I both felt very confused about our roles there in
'Nam. The frustration we felt could not be directed towards
anyone. I think we were experiencing a hatred towards the evil
that causes every war. Protesting only hurt those fulfilling their
duty and resulted in dividing the country. The protesters
themselves caused more bloodshed than the armies they
taunted. Premature withdrawal, demoralization, and the
abandonment of a helpless nation resulted in more thousands
dead than if a McArthur attitude of resolving the war had been
hastily adopted.

The choppers arrived. It was still dark, but the sun had
begun to lighten the skies before it ascended. I had already
forgotten where we were going. I didn't care. The war had
become routine. I was experiencing an abundance of anger at
this moment. I remember imagining how welcome a firefight
would have been at that moment—at least I could have destroyed something.

Chapter 15
Vietnamization

High up in the clouds, we could not tell where they were taking us. It was all too familiar, this chopper scene. While the new guys were scared to death, the short timers seemed apprehensive about surviving until their return to the states, and the rest of us didn't care one way or the other. We never had to worry whether we forgot anything, as almost everything we owned rode on our backs. You can rest assured that none of us owned very much either.

We were landing. "How long had this trip taken?" I thought, "It had seemed awfully long." The chopper landed on solid ground and did not bounce. As the ramp door opened, I was hoping that my old fears of jumping off a chopper had truly disappeared. They had.

It was cloudy and cool by jungle standards. Perhaps the monsoons were not completely over like we had thought. Fog, this morning, added to the eerie scene. We were not told on which side of the Laotian border we stood, but where else does one find the Ho Chi Minh Trail?

"Next stop, men—the Ho Chi Minh Trail." Then the lieutenant disclosed our objective. We were to set up ambushes and disrupt any flow of Northern support that would counter the South's efforts. Our whole company was involved, but what about other Americans? Were they elsewhere?

The entire company, including officers, mortar maggots,

sergeants, and ancillary personnel comprised just a few more than ninety men. Just once, I'd like to feel that Kilo Company, 2nd Platoon wasn't fighting this war alone.

The Ho Chi Minh Trail was not a single path, but rather a conglomeration of roads for trucks and foot trails for troops and rice humpers. Blocking one road or setting a booby trap on one trail wouldn't make a dent in the enemy movement.

Many times, the numerous big bombers of the United States had dumped hundreds of pounds of explosives over miles of suspected roads, but the NVA continued their flow into South Vietnam, just the same. There we were, one company, split into three platoons on the Ho Chi Minh Trail, and of course, we were going to stop the North Vietnamese Army.

In the usual single file, staggered position, we ventured into swamps like the ones seen in horror movies.

The water was the average waist-to-chest depth as we waded across the first few swamps. However, the leeches seemed more abundant.

Our minds were beginning to deceive us as we imagined things being different there—first it was the leeches—who knew what next? After a day of humping, we had detected no sign of a trail or a road. Were we off course or were the choppers just being cautious in not letting us off too close to the "trail?"

We set up for the night, each of us wondering, "Were the jungle sounds louder here? What would happen if we became trapped on this illegal side of the border? What if we needed to be extracted? What kind of cover up would that take?" Fortunately, we encountered no enemy that first day.

The following day, we came upon more bodies of water. Once we had to cross a river, and the depth began like most—average. The water was safe only close to the bank. About fifteen feet out, the bottom dropped out. We almost lost our point man as he attempted to reach the other side.

We were always supposed to carry an inflatable air mattress called a "rubber lady." No one ever did, of course; it was just unnecessary weight. On that clandestine operation, however, we had no idea what we were getting into; therefore, we selected one out of every three individuals to carry one of the formally useless pieces of equipment.

That day, we used the "rubber ladies" as floating devices to get ourselves across the river. I don't know whose idea it was, but we mentally thanked him just the same. It took quite a little time to get all of the mattresses blown up, and we felt like sitting ducks out on the bank. In reality, we were exactly that, with no shots fired.

Once aboard the rafts, we experienced one of the most insecure moments of the tour. Three men boarded each mattress—each carrying a full pack and weaponry. One slip would send the soldier straight to the bottom. It was a major feat just trying to hold on to a flimsy, inflated piece of rubber with two others also struggling to keep afloat.

Most of our effort was in keeping the direction of our leg kicks coordinated in order to cross the river and not be carried downstream by it. We found it frightfully hilarious to see some other trio spinning in circles as they kicked out of control.

My little group took its turn spinning like a ballerina, too. Due to the frantic kicking, my legs began to cramp. All could see the anguish on each other's faces as we all grimaced while crossing. After what seemed like hours, our raft reached the opposite bank. Someone timed the trip at an average of thirty minutes for each member; a long time.

Recovery involved deflating the "rubber ladies" and saddling up again. Our packs had to be emptied of their water and our poncho liners rung out to lighten the weight somewhat. Even after that, we were still weighed down by excess water.

No sooner had we begun moving again than we encountered another body of water. When I saw that swamp, I wanted to quit right then and there.

The point man waded across, probably in hopes that he could make it all the way without turning back. He wanted to show us that we wouldn't have to use those mattresses again. Thank God, the point man did make it to the other side.

The cloudy sky darkened. It was the end of the day, and we were still in the swamps. We would have to set up our hooches in the mud and slime, again. However, exhaustion allowed us to be content with the situation. We set up in our usual fashion, but were much more attentive since we knew we would "sleep" in very unfamiliar territory.

We had long since discarded our PSIDs, so we relied on the natural ear, which had become quite well tuned. Even though fatigue was working itself into our minds and bodies, the imagined sounds of motorized convoys kept our attention in overdrive.

When the next morning arrived without contact, we again began wondering if the chopper pilot who delivered us had miscalculated the drop-off spot. The enlisted ranks began showing restlessness. With the dawn of that new day, the clouds had cleared away, and we started moving afoot down a valley-like area.

We hadn't walked far when we discerned a vaguely familiar sound coming up the valley just north of our platoon. The sound resembled that of a helicopter but it was different.

"Look up ahead, Lieutenant." The point man knelt on one knee and pointed out something to our platoon leader.

There it was—as if straight out of a Godzilla movie—a giant grasshopper! That giant grasshopper—a Russian helicopter—had a jet engine and a huge rotary blade.

The tides had turned this time. We were the ones hiding and fearing the big whirlybird. Had we been discovered? Were we the hunted game? As we hid under the brush, we formed a small recon team. I wanted to go, but I followed orders, just like everyone else. I was still the only corpsman for our platoon as the other corpsman had managed to arrange some sort of emergency leave.

The helicopter had landed some distance off so it took a while for our recon unit to reach their destination. Several hours passed while we nervously waited. Since it was daylight, our every move could be easily seen by the NVA's own designated reconnaissance people.

Our wait was approaching the point when the bones become stiff. Finally, we detected the sound of movement in the brush ahead. One of the men, limping on an injured right leg or foot, was being held up by two others. Joe Lizzio's face revealed the anguish of an obvious injury. The other two brought him immediately to me, laid him down at my feet, and then began their report—no sighting of anyone—plenty of tracks, however.

"Where does it hurt, pretty boy?" I asked.

"Oh, Doc. I'm so stupid. My ankle is sprained or broken, I dunno which. I can't walk on it. What are we gonna do?"

Lizzio's question was legitimate. What would we do? If we medevaced him out, our whole cover would be published. If we kept him with us, he would slow us to a dangerous pace. We could leave him with a small group for protection until we returned. We were under radio silence unless we had an emergency. Would this constitute an emergency? The decision was the lieutenant's.

Feeling Lizzio's ankle without taking his boot off revealed only a sprained ankle, although a fracture could be ruled out only with an X-ray. I took a cloth cravat and tied it around the ankle, outside of the boot. We made a makeshift crutch for Joe and he attempted to walk on it. The best thing for the ankle, of course, would have been to rest it with the leg elevated. Sure.

"Can you walk on it, Lizzio?" Lt. Winter asked.

Lieutenant Winter would soon be replaced, as his six months in the bush were long overdue. The new platoon leader, a stateside named Robert Mandrel was from Silver City, New Mexico. Mandrel looked younger than most of the nineteen year-olds with us, but he was our leader just the same. It seemed like Lt. Winter was showing off to Mandrel by trying to prove that Lizzio was tough and would walk.

Lizzio, on the other hand, would try to walk so that our position would not be exposed. Joe was not really that tough, but team spirit ran thick in his veins. Joe stood up and hobbled, saying, "Let's go Lieutenant." That was all the lieutenant needed to feed his ego.

We all pitched in and carried Joe's pack and supplies. Joe was a machine gunner so he hauled some heavy equipment. As Joe attempted to keep up with us, he found that it was more difficult than he had imagined. The narrow foot of the crutch did not move quickly over the soft, muddy ground.

After about an hour of frustration, I told the lieutenant that we just would be asking for trouble if we continued to force Lizzio to try to keep up with us. If we kept his pace, we would be useless, and worse yet, probably just targets. Winter agreed.

Lieutenant Winter appointed Lizzio's whole machine gun team to stay behind and guard each other. There were four of them, including Joe. The LT gave them a radio in case of trouble, which was like giving a boy a safety pin for protection after placing him in a den of lions.

None of us liked that decision, but the only other alternative was to scrub the whole mission and call in the choppers. Calling the choppers might pull the curtains on the rest of us,

too. It would be like throwing a friend overboard to save a
sinking ship. The lieutenant understood how we felt about each
other, but thought his decision was the only one that could be
made.

Dead silence prevailed among the platoon, even during our
rest periods . Two days slowly passed as we made our way to
the Ho Chi Minh Trail. We actually had crossed several of the
smaller trails, but ventured on so we could set up ambushes.
We detected no sign of anybody. It just did not make sense.
This was the enemy's road, and he should, by all rights, be
traveling it. Nothing ever made sense in this stupid war.

Suddenly, our point man came to an abrupt halt, and knelt
on one knee while the rest of us froze. The two lieutenants
crawled up to the forwardmost position to see what the point
man had discovered. There it was—the first time any of us had
seen such a sight—an NVA prison camp. Just the thought that
Americans might be held captive down in that POW camp
produced lumps in our throats.

By this time, all of us were staring at the camp. After some
time of visual exploration from our unwavering positions,
Winter signaled for Alpha squad to venture down towards the
camp. We all knew the purpose of the command was to draw
fire. We all shared the wish to keep that squad safe.

No fire had been drawn. The squad made its way into the
compound. Still no fire. One member then signaled for the rest
of us to come down. Winter agreed, giving the platoon the go
ahead to descend. The threat of booby traps was probably
worse around the POW compound than in any other place we
had ever walked.

The camp had been built entirely of wood and bamboo. We
discovered and disengaged a few booby traps, but found no one
in the compound. It looked as though there had not been
anyone in the camp for several weeks at least.

A few baskets of rice and some cooking artifacts were all that remained—no evidence of American POWs. The bamboo cells were small, not allowing the occupant to stand erect. The floors had also been made of bamboo poles, which made any position uncomfortable for a prisoner.

As we climbed back to the top of the hill from where we first spotted the camp, radio silence was broken! I drew close to Mike to find out if it was Lizzio. The message was quick and to the point. Captain Short briefly ordered us to lay our mines and depart. As we stood in silence, the reason for the order became obvious.

From up the valley, we heard motorized vehicles. Why should we retreat? There was no guess work. If we did not retreat, we would be greatly outnumbered. To stay would be suicide.

Quickly finding those trails again, we buried land mines as inconspicuously as possible. We did not have enough shovels, so with hands, branches, and whatever we could find, everyone participated in a near-panic attempt to cause some destruction to the enemy.

With the mines all in place and with sweat-producing caution, we exited, careful not to step on the freshly-placed booby traps. Once away from the trails, a few marines lagged behind to erase foot prints and to try to make the landscape look as natural as possible. After they rejoined us, we quick-timed it out of the area. It seemed like a burst of energy penetrated our tired bodies as we zipped through the jungle, backtracking to where we had left Lizzio and his team.

After about two hours on the move, we began to distinguish a few explosions. The urge to go back to intimidate, snipe, and ambush the NVA crept into our thoughts. However, we knew we had our orders. The victory did not fulfill. At the end of the day, we stopped and hastily set up a perimeter for the night.

Expecting the NVA to heavily patrol the area, we sat still, not moving a muscle. We experienced no movement that night. Quickly, after a rushed, one-can breakfast, we continued to make way to the machine gun team. Radio silence continued, since we had received no directive to do otherwise.

A thought entered my mind as we neared the four marines, "What if they don't recognize us and start firing? I don't want to go through that again."

The same thought hit Sgt. Pierce about the same time, so he told the lieutenant, "Winter, we gotta break radio silence unless you want some casualties."

On the same wave length, the lieutenant understood Sgt. Pierce immediately and okayed the order for a brief message to the stranded team. Soon after confirmation of our message, we found the four, just as fat and sassy as when we left them. What a relief!

Being corpsman from the core, I made rounds on my patient. "How's the ankle, pretty boy?"

"It's pretty swollen, Doc. What did you guys find up there anyway? What's that Ho Chi Minh Trail like?" As I told him of the brief encounter with the infamous trail, a look of envy entered Joe's eyes. It was always difficult to be left behind during excitement.

Since all was well with the machine gun team, and we need not hurry, we gradually made our way back to the banks of that deep, long river.

Someone came up with an idea of how to get our platoon across the river without using air mattresses. We would have one person with a rope tied around his waist paddle across on his "rubber lady." Once on the other side, that soldier would tie his end to a sturdy tree or stump. Then, we would tie our end likewise, and each would pull ourselves across the river on the rope, not needing to inflate our own mattresses.

Johnson, a quiet, black, new guy, volunteered for the job without hesitation. He had already been accepted much sooner than the average new guy; everyone liked Johnson. Always wearing black leather gloves, Johnson readied himself for his swim.

After removing those gloves and then his boots, Johnson climbed into the water, hanging onto his inflated mattress. Slowly, he swam across with the current carrying him down stream a distance.

We had to tie two ropes together in order to reach across the river's width. It seemed like Johnson would never cross, but eventually he did. Walking back up the bank, he found a suitable tree, and tied his end of the rope around it and we tied ours.

It turned out to be an excellent idea, as the whole platoon crossed in a fraction of the time it had on the way over. Gonzales, being the last, untied his end of the rope, and shouted for us to pull him in. It was customary to never leave anything behind that might aid Charlie or Nathaniel. A rope was a valuable tool to enemy and friend alike. Six of us decided to give Gonzales the ride of his life, and we hauled him in like a speed boat. The water spraying on his face made us pull even faster. I don't know who had more fun, Gonzales or us.

Once we were on the other side, Lt. Winter decided that we had had enough fun, so he designated a landing zone about half a click away and called in the choppers.

We could not decide whether this had been a successful mission or not. By military standards, the mission was probably a failure, but by corpsman standards, we experienced success.

As history would have it, the ARVN push into Laos ultimately ended in failure, as did everything else they ever tried. Back at the rear, we bid *bon voyage* to our platoon leader, Lt. Winter, and tried to break in the new LT.

Mike and I knew that we were becoming short timers, which placed us on the endangered list. Most short timers became overly cautious as their thoughts began to reopen the visions of home. That hadn't happened to us, and we were determined not to let it happen. Of course, like everything else in the 'Nam, all soldiers conformed to the war on schedule. It wouldn't hurt to try to be the exception, though.

We had earned some rehab time, a short time of convalescence, so Freedom Hill once more would be unsafe. We marines were about to invade its premises. Probably, we looked forward more to that little excursion than we had to any other, since it had been too long since we had been able to let our hair down.

On the road to Freedom Hill, over to the left, I saw First Med. From the back of the truck, I yelled to the truck driver to stop and as he slowed down, I dismounted. Amarante Lucero was still stationed at First Med. "It will be good to see Art," I thought.

I walked into the main office of First Med to inquire about my long-lost friend. At the desk appeared a very familiar face. It was Steve McCarty, who had been another of my three former roommates in the apartment we shared back at Long Beach, California. Steve, a decent and trustworthy individual, would give you the shirt off his back any time.

"Bob! You sorry excuse for a human, what are you doing here?" Steve was genuinely surprised.

"I dropped in to see ol' Art and who do I find getting fat? Are there any more of the old gang here?"

"Besides Art and me, there's Garza and Forester, plus some others from the Naval Hospital at Long Beach. Art says you've been out in the bush all this time. I thought you were supposed to be out for six months or less. What are you doing, serving time for striking an officer or something?" Steve, with his style of humor, could always make a person laugh.

"Who knows, Steve? Maybe they're just prejudiced or something. All I know is that we've been short of corpsmen for a long time and here I find all you guys idle, doing nothing. This government never ceases to amaze me."

"Come on, Bob. Let me show you around. How long can you stay? Maybe we can knock off early and go to the club after we eat." Steve was acting as though he was talking to his closest relative. It was comforting to be treated in this manner.

"I got until curfew tonight so let's have at it!"

Steve was able to get together about four men from the old crew, including Art, for our big reunion. The only ones missing were Gordon Hays from the 106 mm Recoilless Rifles Team and Joe Uridel, the would-be doctor who had his future all planned from the beginning. Duker, from Santa Fe never made it out to Long Beach, but word had it that he was out in the bush somewhere. Duker, however, never really was a close part of our little clique of characters.

Before catching malaria, Art had been out in the bush for only a month. Uridel also had been out in the bush, but he, too, caught malaria and was shipped to Okinawa after his hospital stay in Japan. I felt like Little Orphan Annie, being the only one still misplaced out in the bush.

Art, Steve, and the rest made every effort to make this impromptu party a success. First, I was taken on a tour of the compound. Although when spread out, it really wasn't as big as it had seemed.

The barracks were air conditioned, and each enlisted man had real bedding. There were even indoor toilets and showers. The *mama sahns* cleaned up after the messy boys and even ironed their uniforms. Art pointed out a picture hanging in his locker. It was one of my drawings of a grunt that I had sent in a letter sometime in the past. For some reason, my natural disdain for rear echelon pogues was not experienced there at First Med. Perhaps I was too biased and just plain ol' glad to see my old friends.

We all ate at First Med's mess hall which served superb food. I had not eaten that well since the USS Sanctuary. After supper, we hit the club for awhile and later took the party to one of their hooches.

By the time we realized when curfew was, it was already midnight. None of us had any regard for time. The old times had resurfaced, even if for only a short while. Days in California, hospital experiences, old friends, and lots of joking around made the night complete.

Art talked of his wife and all the things she had sent him. Most had to do with trends in modern thinking as she was an intellectual hippie type. Of course, Art gloated over how good a lover he was and went into detail with bedroom escapades with his wife.

Garza whined in jealousy, while the rest of us took turns making fun of him. Forester was the single lover boy who told us stories that made even Art blush. None of us really believed Forester, but played along just the same.

Steve, on the other hand, was totally different from the rest. It made no difference whether anyone made fun of Steve, as he could role with any punch and end up with the upper hand. In fact, anyone puffing himself up with pride could rest assured that Steve would burst his balloon. No one was sacred to Steve. There was an art to the way Steve executed his comebacks so that in all honesty, no one ever was ever insulted. Torn apart, yes, but in a manner that had everyone in stitches until his sides hurt. Even the victim would laugh 'til he cried.

When it came my turn to describe things that I had done and seen or escapades I had experienced, the laughter died down. Normally, a bull session among the grunts telling funny war stories would cause the roof to cave in. This evening, I was in a group of corpsmen who saw the war from another perspective. They had to receive all the casualties, and later the fatalities, on their front steps.

Most of my friends wondered what was really going on out there to cause such misery and grief. As it turned out, each one of my old friends admitted that they feared the day that one of them would be receiving me off of a medevac chopper with an ID label tied to my wrist. So my jokes and adventures went over like a lead balloon.

We still cared about each other, but Art told me that I had changed and not for the better. He and I stayed up talking after the others had gone. Art shared that he feared what I had become and feared that the metamorphosis would continue to distort his friend from New Mexico.

I did not know what to say, since I knew deep inside that what he said was exactly true. There had been so much I had originally wanted to say to Art and the rest but could not think of it when I had the opportunity.

"It don't mean nothin'," I thought to myself as I prepared to get a good night's sleep.

That night was the most soundly I had slept since arriving to the 'Nam. Perhaps it was due to being surrounded by the security of old friends or perhaps it was just forgetting where I was for a small increment of time. In any event, I was thankful for that one, peaceful evening.

Morning appeared, and I had to rush back to the battalion rear for roll call which took place right after breakfast. The goodbyes had been said the night before, so I stole out of the First Med compound without a word. There was not very much traffic in the early morning, so my effort to hitch a ride was touch and go for awhile.

I did finally hitch a ride on a truck. I signaled the driver when I wanted off, and he came to an incomplete stop. I jumped off and waved him on, arriving at the battalion rear in plenty of time. But I felt like I was sneaking in after being out too late. My platoon family was waiting, with arms folded and feet tapping. Mike spoke, "Well, what have you got to say for yourself? We didn't even realize you jumped off before Freedom Hill."

I could see why Mike was concerned about where I had been, since I never did tell anyone of my plans. But that was because I had no plans; the First Med visit had been as spontaneous as a hiccup.

"Where you been, Doc? We almost gave up on you, you know."

"Hey man, lighten up. I was just paying a visit to some old buddies at First Med. What did you guys do, anyway?"

Sitting there with my platoon, I felt as though I had just come back home from a visit with distant relatives. It was nice to have seen the old gang of corpsmen, but my real home was here with these poor misfits. Mike and the others said they did not have a very good time with a missing link in their chain. I didn't tell them that I had a great time.

Immediately after roll call, we were given a briefing of our next assignment. The ARVN push into Laos was just beginning, so we would act as road security for the convoys. There were not many highways in all of Vietnam, so we could feasibly secure all the routes to be used in this major operation. It sounded good, but we were sure that the communists had plans of their own

"Men, we are assigned a segment to secure on the Hai Van Pass. We will secure the areas that surround it first and then we'll set up a watch station on the road itself. Who knows what we'll encounter there? Lieutenant Mandrel will be in charge; I'm passing the torch to him now. It has been a pleasure to serve such a high caliber of marines. Go easy on Mandrel or I'll sic Gunny La Fifi on the whole lot of you. Good luck."

Lieutenant Winter was never clever with words, and had great difficulty saying goodbye. However, Lt. Mandrel had some breaking-in to do. The novice in him was all too evident; a quivering tone appeared in his simplest orders.

Rather than ridicule the lieutenant, we just helped him along with appropriate and timely suggestions. Warfare taught at Camp Pendleton was orchestrated by generals who had no idea what took place at the front in Vietnam.

Lt. Mandrel was honest enough to admit that as a short-coming and welcomed any suggestions. On the other hand, Lt. Winter had the arrogance of a lifer, and often ignored wise counsel from his subordinates. Lt. Mandrel was in the Marine Corps as an ROTC obligation, unlike his counterpart, a career officer.

The company corpsman also rotated for a second or a third time since I had joined the group. The new corpsman was a scared young lad, still very white and clean—the red clay of the mountains had a way of changing one's skin color, regardless of race—the unspoiled corpsman seemed so very lily white.

Carver was his last name; I never knew his first. On being introduced to him, I ignored him. This was not out of malice, rather, it was just the conditioned response we had for all new guys, whether they were our superiors or not.

Some kind of post-monsoon front had moved in—the sky was overcast and the temperature dropped. Gunny La Fifi gave Sgt. Pierce one field jacket for the entire platoon—just in case. With the thick condensation, the choppers could not safely fly, so we had to be trucked in. Our main objective would be to secure the highway. Somehow, our being trucked in just did not make any sense.

The highway could not be secure already; that was obvious. The Gunny realized that and protested very verbally. Finally, there was a compromise. They trucked us only part of the distance to the Pass, then we humped the remainder of the way parallel to Highway One, off a hundred meters or so. Highway One would lead us to Hai Van Pass. This little excursion should take three to five days. There was thick jungle up ahead, which made perfect ambush and getaway coverage for Nathaniel.

Mike and I both were long overdue for R & R, and we both were becoming fidgety.

"Doc, why don't you put in for Bangkok with me. I put in for around three weeks from now."

"Mike, you put in for R & R two months ago and they told you to wait a few more weeks 'cause they really needed you. What makes you think things are different now? I've been asking for R & R since my seventh week. That's what we're all supposed to get. Eligibility for R & R begins after seven weeks, man. You've been out here over ten months and haven't gone even once. The pogues in the rear go every seven weeks."

"Does that mean that you're not going to put in with me or what?" Mike had been totally oblivious to my words.

"No, I'll put in and see what we come up with. You know I hate dealing with those useless morons in the rear. Did I tell you that my name isn't even on their roster? They don't even know I'm out here. When I went to First Med, I did not meet a single corpsman who had been out in the bush as long as I have."

"Before you came, we had a corpsman named Doc Potter. All this time, I thought he had been with the platoon a long time before I joined, but come to find out, he's still in the

'Nam. Potter had been with this platoon only three months when I arrived! The replacement they sent has turned out to be a joke—nothing but a goof off. He has spent maybe two weeks with us. The rest of the time he's out on some kind of fabricated emergency leave."

"Mike, it's nothing but a battle between the people in the rear and us, and they hold all the cards. The only one back there who cares for us even half way is the Gunny. The rest of them get their laughs by messing with us. They hate us."

"You should hear all the war stories they have. Those stories make the real thing look like a Sunday school, and yet none of their stories are true. We live in two different worlds out here in the 'Nam, Mike. Ours is a living hell and there's is all fun and games— at our expense. You'll never get a fair deal from the rear. I hope we can get our R & R, but I'm not going to hold my breath." I sighed as I completed my oratory.

"Don't get all bent outta shape, Doc. There's nobody that hates the green machine more than me. I don't expect anything from them, but I'm still gonna try. Look at us. We've become animals. You used to be all optimistic and happy. Now you complain more than I do, and that's bad. In a few months, we'll both be outta here, so we have to start getting our act together. If we go back like this, they'll kick us out of the States."

"Quit thinking about going home, Mike. You know what happens to grunts who are getting short and start thinking about the green grass back home. We will both be all right when we leave this place. We've adjusted out here so we can adjust anywhere. All we need is a little time."

"We have to complain, Mike. If we don't, then we'll end up becoming like the very thing we hate. Complaining is a form of resisting. The only way to avoid conforming is to resist. The second you stop resisting, then they've got you."

"Man, I'm so confused about what's going on and what

we've become. I think we're resisting, then I listen to the way we talk and it sounds like everyone else. I look at what we do, and that, too, is just like what everyone else does."

"I don't want to talk about this anymore. When we go home, we'll deal with the problems then and there. Right now, we need to keep on getting on each other's nerves and that's the way we're gonna make it out of here."

"Doc, you're full of hot air!"

"Mike, you'll do everyone a favor if you'll put your face in that mud puddle for about an hour straight."

"Go show me how, Doc."

We had both quit our daydreaming for a while, which was good. The trucks arrived, and we began loading up.

Chapter 16
Hai Van Pass

For our truck ride to the drop off point, the weather remained cloudy with intermittent rain—cool, by our standards. It must have been in the low eighties or high seventies, which was cool enough to cause a shiver in that dampness.

The four marine-hauling trucks travelled as fast as possible, since the drivers did not like the idea of being ambushed any more than the soldiers did. That loud roar of the diesel engines and the peculiar exhaust hitting our faces seem as real to me today as then. I think I liked the choppers better, which, of course, is an understatement. For lengthy travel over the muddy, uneven roads, those wooden benches in the backs of the trucks tested our endurance, as had almost everything in this little country.

About an hour or so passed before we reached our destination. I had no trouble jumping off of the truck, even though the bed sat five feet above the ground. My phobia for disembarking was only from helicopters.

Highway One ran about a hundred meters to our east as we headed north. We had to wait a while until the rest of the company disembarked; it seemed to be another company operation. Actually, just one other platoon showed up. The 3rd Platoon had been sent out somewhere else.

It seemed like new guys made up at least two-thirds of the

whole group, and our lieutenant acted very uneasy when he was the lone leader. He would learn. To top it off, our new company corpsman appeared to be as scared as they come.

As usual, most of the new guys carried an excessive amount of gear, so we told the truck drivers to wait while we shook down the new guys to lighten their loads. We loaded up the bed of one truck with all their useless equipment. Those poor kids had trash in their packs that even Boy Scouts wouldn't carry on a campout. After the load lightening exercise, we knew we were in for trouble. Never had I seen such inexperience within our ranks.

All of us were giving the newcomers tips on how to survive—Lizzio explained how to carry the weight of the machine gun; Pierce told them how to take cover immediately; Mike stressed the importance of staying quiet; and others gave very pertinent pointers on how to avoid getting someone else or themselves killed.

Gonzales had rotated out of the bush, and it was at times like this that we needed him the most. We knew that Juan was alive, well, and getting fat in some posh, rear position. Soon Gonzales would be home. We were glad for him, but we missed him all the same.

With everyone ready and the trucks gone, we began our patrol. As usual, the jungle was extremely thick, so we were moving only about seventy-five to one-hundred meters an hour. With the weather still uncommonly cool and it raining steadily, my glasses steamed up and became splattered with water and mud. After adjusting to it, I could actually see around the water spots without cleaning the lenses on my spectacles.

I began to shiver after walking in the rain for fifteen minutes or so. None of us who had been in country for any length of time were used to that cool weather. The ponchos and rain suits did help keep some of the warmth next to our bodies.

I knew why the gunny had sent a field jacket with the platoon, but who had it now? One field jacket—probably the only one in all of Vietnam!

That muddy, slippery trek up the mountain was par for the course. I could not help but recollect a story I had read some time earlier in the *Stars and Stripes*.

It was about a Marine who wore a North Vietnamese poncho during a downpour. For some reason, the Marine had become misplaced from his unit and found himself in the middle of an NVA squad of regulars. Because of the rain, he was not recognized as an American, but was taken as one of their own, solely because of the poncho. After realizing the mess he was in, the soldier decided to play along just until he could make a break, but on his way out he opened fire.

The young man escaped unharmed and claimed three verifieds in his attack. I wondered whether an NVA wearing an American poncho could become mixed in with our unit, just as that young marine had done. No one would know the difference with all the new guys and the rainshowers.

The company passed hours in that robot-like activity—one foot in front of the other—over and over—again and again. Some of the new guys began to fizzle out. We wished we had brought some cattle prods. We could not offer any words of encouragement, just a cold, "Get moving!" The new lieutenant watched for the sergeants to indicate the proper time for a rest period.

By the time we reached the top of one mountain, the rains had let up. The lieutenants of both platoons took that rest time to plan our strategy. I did not recognize the other platoon's leader, so I assumed that he, like our LT, was green. Just thinking about the predicament made me shake my head and roll back my eyes. I saw Mike talking with some of the people from the other platoon; he signaled for me to go up to where he stood.

"Hey Doc! Have you met your new boss, Doc Carver?"

"Yeah. How you doing?" Was I even interested? I couldn't tell if Mike was trying to irritate me or if he had had a nervous breakdown and had become neighborly. I doubted the latter.

"So you're Doc Bob! I've been wanting to meet you. I started hearing about you as soon as I arrived in Kilo Company. Back in the rear, no one knew who exactly was out here. Hey, what do I need to look out for and what did the other company corpsmen do?" Carver's voice trembled a bit.

I took a step back and sized up Carver. His uniform, besides being wet, looked new and clean and his boots were not yet broken in. Carver stood about five-ten, with pale skin and a boyish face. He wore horn-rimmed glasses and kept his dark brown hair trimmed very short. That dark hair made his face look even whiter than it already was.

His lapel carried the insignia of a Second Class Corpsman. Also, Carver toted an M-16 and the same amount of ammo as a regular grunt. We must have been about the same age, but even the nineteen-year-old vets looked much older than that new guy.

"So tell me, Carver. Why do you have an M-16? Why not just carry your .45 pistol and let the marines do the shooting? If any of them are down, you're going to have to crawl up to them to patch up the wounds. If you've got the hots to shoot back at Charlie, then just use a wounded marine's rifle. You're going to be at the CP anyway; you guys seldom see any action."

"I don't know what to tell you about your job, because the corpsmen before you never did anything that I could tell. In fact, I saw one of them only a couple times the whole time he was out in the bush. The other chief came and went without my even seeing him once."

"Bob, I'd like to be different. I'm really going to try and help out you platoon docs as much as I can."

"Carver, just make sure we're well supplied. It takes about a month for any supplies to come in after I've asked for them. By the time they arrive, I can't remember what it was I asked for in the first place. If it wasn't for a nurse friend I have back in Long Beach, I would never have anything. I can write her and get the shipment in eight days. I've lost touch with the rear, but I really don't care about it, either. The troops here call me Doc."

"Ah...er...uh Doc, is it true that you were once shot out of a helicopter and your helmet sliced your nose on a crash land and that's why you always wear a paratrooper's chin strap?"

"Yup, that's true. Nice meeting you, Carver. Mike, we've got to get back to the platoon. Let's go."

On our way down the hill, Mike was laughing at me. He knew how I would react to the new corpsman. Mike had a good laugh which meant that I would have my turn later at my own discretion.

The inexperienced platoon leaders decided that it was best for the two platoons to split up until we reached our destination. That wasn't a bad idea, as larger crowds draw larger fire. They designated our platoon as point; 1st Platoon was told to trail behind. Good—with our platoon working alone, the situation became more manageable. We would not have to worry about the blundering of some other unit. If we in 2nd Platoon erred, we could deal with it directly and feel confident that it would not happen again.

We spent the next two days trudging along through the dense foliage, mud, and rain. We set up the usual peripheral ambushes during the nights, and heated our C-rations under ponchos.

"Don't you just wish we would get in a firefight and be over and done with it, Doc?" Mike had contracted short timer's fever, even though it was mild case. His tone carried with it an air of uneasiness and a bit of over-caution. Those thoughts could be lethal if dwelt on too long.

On the third day, as we continued patrolling towards Hai Van Pass, Mike received a radio message about a skirmish up ahead. An ARVN unit which also patrolled along Highway One had been hit by the VC. We radioed the response that we would be there ASAP to assist.

Mike looked at me and asked, "ARVNs?"

I shook my head in acknowledgment. Often when hit, the ARVNs responded by shooting blindly behind their cover or even at times, up in the air. What kind of mess were we getting ourselves into?

After an hour or so, we arrived at the ARVN position. They had not been hit bad—only one casualty—a leg wound. Gonzales had interpreted for us before he went home, but now no one knew Vietnamese. One of the ARVNs could speak very broken English which helped a little. Apparently only a couple of VC had ambushed the unit of eight ARVNs. They suspected no VC casualties.

I tended to the wounded Vietnamese soldier while the lieutenant and Sergeant Pierce tried to figure out which way the VC went and what their next move might be. Sergeant Pierce tried to politely tell the young lieutenant that there was no use in trying to out-think Charlie, as this worthy enemy had majored in warfare chess.

While most of us were busy doing odds and ends, some of the new guys decided that they would be ambassadors and befriend the ARVNs. I glanced up and saw two of them huddled together with three of the ARVNs. To group as they did was an obviously foolish maneuver.

Just as I was preparing to break up the cluster......

"BOOOOOOOM!" In a conditioned response to the

explosion, I immediately hit the ground. The blast had come from the clustered boys. My heart froze as thoughts flashed through my mind—thoughts of what might have happened.

"Was that incoming?" I thought as I lifted my head to make a survey of the damage. There were no more explosions. "What happened? What happened? Who can tell me what went on?" I needed to know so I would know what to do next.

I ran up to the explosion site. Stunned soldiers gazed at themselves and at each other. Three lifeless bodies lay on the ground. I triaged the wounded: one American had a few superficial shrapnel wounds and four ARVNs displayed an array of different types of wounds. One of the three bodies was the other American; the other two were Vietnamese.

"I knew these ARVNs would be nothing but trouble!" I shouted. "Who knows what happened?"

The wounded marine spoke, "The ARVNs were showing us a Chicom Claymore mine they found, and it went off. Where's Freeman, Doc?"

"Who's Freeman?" I asked.

"He's the other new guy, Doc." Lizzio answered.

"What's your name, son?" I asked the wounded marine.

"Sanford, Doc, sir. It's Albert Sanford."

"Well, Albert, your friend is dead. I'm sorry. Don't ever cluster yourself again. And stay away from those ARVNs; they're trouble." The young, green kid began to cry. It was strange seeing someone cry. I envied the boy for being able to have some emotion. I felt nothing for his deceased comrade.

The choppers still could not fly because of the rains, so we would have to have to carry the three KIAs to Highway One to be picked up by ground transport. The wounded would ride back to the CP, too. As I filled out the ID tags for the American, I tried to reflect on his family and what they would be going through when they received the news of their son and how he died in that God-forsaken hole in the ground. God, I hated it there.

We wrapped the bodies in ponchos, forming makeshift stretchers. The wounded could walk by themselves, but they needed help carrying their gear. The ones not helping with the gear took turns struggling with the flimsy stretchers.

Carrying the bodies was extremely exhausting. My arms felt as if they would tear off at the shoulder from the burning weight. We stopped every fifty feet to trade off, but the interval seemed far too short until our rotation arrived again. I don't know the actual distance to the highway, but it took us more than three hours to get there.

All of us were huffing, puffing, and ready to collapse with painful hands and fingers, burning shoulders and elbows, aching backs, and very tired legs. My hands stayed in a gripped position for half an hour after we finally completed the trip. Every muscle throbbed and with each throb, hurt.

"Those were heavy dudes," Mike joked.

He radioed a truck with some sort of security and it was on its way. I checked over the wounded to see how they had weathered the trip. All of them seemed stable. The ARVNs knew that we blamed them for the mishap so they remained silent and out of our way, which was just fine.

The highway wound its way along the outer edges of the mountainside, passing by the area where we had chosen to stop. After about an hour or so, through the drizzling rain, the truck arrived with two armed marines standing on its bed. Those poor souls knew that they were moving targets while they rode in the open bed like that.

Onto the truck, we hoisted the poncho-covered, lifeless shells that had recently been young men. The wounded climbed up with their dead comrades and were off on their journey back to a rear hospital. I often wondered who decided who would go where. I was glad my experience was limited on that issue.

As the truck made its way back down the winding path, I was beginning the wish that I had been one of those lucky stiffs on his voyage back to the rear. Not only was I physically tired at that point; I was also exhausted mentally.

I was expressing the first symptoms of a defeated spirit. I had always bucked the system while maintaining a degree of integrity and individuality; but at that point, I realized I was being soaked by the very machine I had fought so hard to defy.

Just then Mike relayed a radio message he had just received. It stated that we were to maintain proper uniform attire at all times, since a group of dignitaries might be touring the front any time.

"Sure" someone commented. "Their idea of the front is a staged combat unit and throwing a few smoke grenades—no live ammunition, of course!" Everyone's rolling back their eyes gave mutual ownership to that statement.

When the truck was out of our sight and hearing, we headed back to the side roads that paralleled the highway on our trek towards Hai Van Pass. One could see the China Sea from up there. It would almost look scenic if it had not been wartime.

Feeling hungry, I tried to remember the taste of a McDonald's hamburger. It was useless—like having amnesia. There probably had been a memory of such an object in the past but it was impossible to recollect.

The mist was unusually cold, even though we walked in full gear up the steep grades. I shook my head angrily as if waking up from a doze while driving solo on a trip.

"I've got to stay sharp and not let down my guard," I chanted to myself. The short timer's syndrome was already infecting me. However, the realization of carrying those two bodies sobered me into the reality of the present moment.

The pitter patter of the rain drops hitting the plastic hood of my rain parka stole my sense of hearing as a functioning tool of detection. Glancing from side to side was as automatic for me at that moment as is blinking now. My thumb was positioned, ready to flip the safety off my M-16 at a moment's notice. The adrenaline started to flow again. I thought, "Maybe there is hope for me yet in this stage of the game." I wondered how Mike was doing. He was even shorter than I.

As the day neared its end; the sky began to darken above the low-lying clouds. The lieutenant wanted to stop dead in our tracks and set up for the night. He had not yet learned the lesson of not clustering. Mike gently suggested that we not do that. Mike seemed to have a way with the new lieutenant—most of the suggestions he offered were taken quite well.

Even though my poncho liner was soaking wet, the synthetic material seemed to maintain its ability to keep me warm, considering the cool, damp conditions. For about two hours, I felt as cozy as a teddy bear in front of an open fire place on a winter's night; however, my hips ached from being submersed in the cold puddle wherein I slept.

During my watch that evening, it seemed as though the night creatures were especially loud. My friends the mosquitoes never ceased teasing me. My thoughts tried to wander, but I said to them under my breath, "Not so fast there, you ornery critter—you still got a ways to go yet before you go home." That took the cake! My thoughts were speaking like John Wayne talked!

For some reason, I paid closer attention to the surroundings that night than on most evenings. A keen sense prevailed that the enemy was close at hand. If there ever was such a thing as extrasensory perception, it sure was evident that night. The night was pitch black, with the clouds still very low and heavy, thick with condensation. No light shone from the stars or the moon. Only my imagination illuminated the night.

"Come on, Nat or Chuck, whichever you are. Show your faces so this night can come to an end. I'm dead dog tired of waiting for you." As usual, no one showed up, even after I had waited for hours.

The next day, we humped especially fast so we would reach our assigned post in one day. It seemed like we walked uphill all the way—probably because *it was* uphill all the way. We encountered no booby traps, no sniper fire, and no ambushes. We had free passage to our imagined vacation spot.

By midday, we arrived at what looked like an abandoned outpost. On the east side of the road stood a sandbagged bunker with a pitched roof tower on top, which was also encircled with sandbags. To the north, we saw a makeshift mortar pit.

Concertina wire bordered the small encampment, with one opening to the adjacent highway. The highway was nothing more than a two lane, paved road. The fact that it was paved made it an item of pride for this country. On the west side of the road an old, concrete French bunker was situated. After twenty years, it still stood—and in fairly good shape, at that! On its roof was positioned a type of turret for a machine gun.

Mandrel appointed two squads for the east side and two for the west. He assigned the machine gunners to the French bunker, while the command post took the sandbagged hooch. The mortar maggots, of course, took the pit. The sandbagged hooch had two closet-sized rooms to it, so Mike and I chose the smaller of the two.

Before occupying any of the quarters, some of the marines made a sweep to ensure that there were no mines. We found none, which was a relief. We spent the first day cleaning out our new home, making it at least a little livable.

"Can you imagine, Doc, we must really be living right to deserve being indoors for once. Right?"

"Sure, Mike, sure. When did you say you're going on your R & R? This hooch just makes it easier for Charlie to know where we are at night. I guess there's a price to pay for luxury. Right, Mike?"

"You're sick, Doc. Real sick."

"This is luxury, I tell you, Mike; it is! Look over there, down the mountain. What do you see?"

Mike's face looked blank. "I don't see anything, Doc."

"Come on, man, that's the South China Sea! This is like a million dollar home in Malibu or Carmel—up high on the mountains overlooking the ocean. This is great!"

"You *are* sick Doc. Hare you been smoking those funny cigarettes? I bet you have. This is the 'Nam, man. There ain't nothing beautiful out here."

"You know? Come to think of it, you're right. It is kind of nice out here." Mike and I both showed more signs of the short timer's syndrome.

The mortar maggots cleaned their area and renovated their pit. It looked nice, but they had no protection, as the sandbags were only about ten inches high. When asked why the skimpy wall, the maggots just offered the diagrams in their manual—their pit *was* identical to the manual!

Most of the young men with us were new to the 'Nam, but they did have one fellow with them who had been with us during my first operation. His name was Mitchell. At the time Dino was killed, Mitchell had been wounded and had spent several months in a hospital somewhere. He was also wounded a second time, but I cannot remember when or where.

In any event, Mitchell was very cynical about Vietnam, and

was always referring to the war as a *joke*. It was a joke for him, as he never spent any real time fighting in the war. Here was Mitchell again, back with his old unit, having to hump the jungles just like everyone else. Of course, nothing but complaints ever bubbled out of the poor, miserable lad. Having been attached to the 1st Marine Division for so long did not make him any wiser. He was just as stupid and foolish as any new guy.

For all practical purposes, this assignment was easy. There were no long range patrols or lengthy ambushes. We needed only to guard the road for the upcoming, lengthy Laotian drive.

Once everyone was settled, I made my traditional rounds to assess the health status of the troops. I think the day was Sunday, so that meant I would distribute the weekly malaria tablets. Half the time, no one really knew what day it was, so being off a day or two didn't matter to anyone. Two of Alpha squad's men had minor cases of jungle rot. They gritted their teeth when I applied the Phisohex soap with a scrub brush. It didn't hurt me a bit.

One soldier in Bravo squad had profound diarrhea. Lomotil resolved the problem. A couple of others had simple upper respiratory infections. Most of the other corpsmen could not carry antibiotics, but my connection in Long Beach had kept me supplied, at least until this operation.

It had been many months since a fresh shipment had arrived, so I assumed that the novelty of sending CARE packages to the boys overseas had died down. Nonetheless, the antibiotics I had may have been a little stale since they had been carried on my back for all those months, but they accomplished their duty anyway.

While with the machine gunners, I became fascinated with the French bunker. One could hear the echoes of past battles vibrating within its walls. The French soldiers finally called it quits in 1954, after being defeated by the Viet Minh in the battle at Dien Bien Phu. They had occupied French Indochina since 1848, and had passed on a distinct culture to the small land.

Some people called Saigon the "Paris of the Orient." The Vietnamese language was infested with French words as evidence of the French domination. Much of the architecture was undoubtedly French, too. Even the cemeteries, with their oversized tombstones, were of French design.

American influence was *Johnny-come-lately* in that land of many faces. The northern part of Vietnam had closer ties with China, and the southern portion was more independent and had frequented many wars with the North over the centuries. The communist stronghold on the North was the result of Ho Chi Minh finally asking China for help in his bid for freedom from France. Some have said that Ho Chi Minh had actually asked President Eisenhower for assistance before approaching Mao Tsi Tung. Such are the turn of events.

Lizzio had rigged up a machine gun nest on his new turret. Old French graffiti was written inside. The floor of the bunker was concrete, just as were the walls and the roof—a mini fortress. Lissio's location, by far, had the advantage of superior surveillance over the American sandbag bunker.

The other two squad sites were merely a gathering of marines with a couple of hastily erected poncho hooches.

During my rounds, I had a chance to meet and speak with some of the new guys, who were all very scared. I joked with them until they found themselves laughing at fear and at things like getting wounded. The only way to really break them in, of course, would be with a few firefights, lots of anticipation, and waiting.

The CP hooch had two helmet pots of a stew mixture ready by the time I returned. It bothered me that the lieutenant seemed to be becoming too friendly with us. He really needed to keep a measure of distance so he could maintain authority rather than the familiarity I saw being established, especially for those crucial times. The stew tasted good.

The seasoned vets were on edge which is the way it was supposed to be. This kept the new guys wondering, and made them careful not to become too comfortable themselves.

Darkness fell all too soon. Mike and I took watch together again. Both reluctant to sit in the sandbagged tower, we sat on our bunker's side, facing the road and upper slope of the mountain. The backdrop of the hooch wall would serve as some camouflage during the night, maybe protecting us from a would-be sniper. It was Kool Aid time also. Mike and I celebrated just *being* at this passive vacation spot.

During our time off of watch, we entered our bunker room, which incidentally, was about four feet high, to try to get some sleep. During that time, I felt what seemed like a small dog running across my feet.

"Mike! Fire up your Zippo (lighter)! There's something at my feet!" I whispered loudly.

"Yeah, sure, Doc." Mike pulled out his Zippo and struck it up.

"Oh my God! What is it?" Mike spoke in a full loud voice, probably the first time during a night that he had done so since being in the 'Nam.

"It's a big mamma rat! Don't move that light. I'm gonna shoot it." Then I pulled back the hammer of the .45 that I always kept next to me.

"Shoot him between the eyes, Doc. I hear they charge when they're wounded." That very same scene, except with Willie and Joe, was the subject of a cartoon by Bill Mauldin in *Up Front* .

"BLAAAAAMMMM!" The shot was so intense that it

blew out Mike's Zippo. The rat was nothing more than a splattering on the wall.

"Ouch, ouch, ouch! My ears!" That blast caused tremendous pain and ringing to my ears, since we were in such a small, confined enclosure. What a dumb move! That rat hadn't hurt anyone—but my ears hurt. Luckily the pain was short-lived; within fifteen minutes, there was only ringing.

Needless to say, we both had plenty of explaining to do when everyone in the small compound came out, fully armed and ready for a big confrontation. Shooting that rat was a pretty stupid thing to do, any way we looked at it. And then we had to clean up the pieces of flesh so that we would not have the putrefied stench of rotting meat driving us out of our quarters.

As we tried to go back to sleep, Mike and I broke out in almost uncontrolled laughter. That poor rat didn't have a sliver of a chance.

The next morning, still cold and damp since the clouds seemed to hang unusually low, found that jacket that Gunny La Fifi had given us taking a long time to make its rounds to keep us warm. The ponchos substituted okay as coats for a while, anyway.

The highway gradually became congested, as the convoys began their ascent to the Laotian border. The ARVNs, almost as if caged up, looked like little reluctant kids sitting in their transport trucks. A large number were sitting with their legs hanging out, holding onto the side rails which resembled bars on a jail or a crib. The steel helmets were too big for their heads, and each of their weapons looked oversized in their hands.

It was as if we were witnessing sheep on their way to their slaughter. There did not seem to be any strategy to this war. Corruption in the hierarchy sure was evident, with a blundering operation like the "Vietnamization" project.

Some of our troops were yelling, "Dinky dao ARVNs.

Number ten." Literally this meant, "Crazy ARVN's, the worst ever." The ARVNs smiled back and waved. Of course they yelled something back at us, which I'm sure was not very nice either.

The convoys of ARVNs were not all grouped together. Their random dispersions was probably the idea of a front-line sergeant. Its strategy and practicality were obviously not that of a rear command officer. We were glad to see at least one smart move.

Several days passed as intermittent groups of military trucks made their way to some strange invasion. It was becoming boring. We knew that we were sitting ducks—easy targets for any small group of VC or NVA. Guarding the observation posts was different, since the rear battalion was within spitting distance from them. Here, no other Americans were near. We could easily become pinned down, without any hope of reinforcements. Choppers could not help us, with the skies being the way they were. The scenario looked bleak.

One day, a jeep arrived from the rear, bringing us mail and supplies. With the roads guarded, the rear command felt safe in sending just one jeep with no escort. I guess most other people felt the same way; the traffic seemed to pick up.

Busloads of civilians paraded past our check point with cargo packed to the hilt. We were not supposed to stop anyone; our orders were just to guard the road. Undoubtedly Charlie rode among those "civilians" reviewing the security of Highway One. We waved at him just like we did everyone else. I don't know why we were not told to stop and check vehicles.

Word from the rear came that a replacement for me was in the process.

"A replacement? I don't want to go back to the rear!" I was actually appalled at the idea of becoming a rear pogue.

"Doc, you owe it to your bod to get out of this hell hole.

Besides, don't count your chickens before they hatch. Anything can happen between now and then." Leave it to Mike.

"Any word on my R & R?" Mike asked.

"Yeah, sure Pulos. You're going to Bangkok in about a week." The rear officer's words brought about a big yahoo from Mike's normally stoic manner.

"What about my R & R?" I asked, dejected.

"Sorry, Doc. There was no mention about you and an R & R. Did you know that none of the corpsmen in the rear even knew you were out here?" The lieutenant looked puzzled.

"Yeah, I knew. What else is new? I put in for an R & R with Mike—the same time he did. What happened to the request? Are you guys prejudiced against corpsmen or chicanos? Did you know that I have been here almost ten months, and I've never been granted even one single R & R?" I was starting to lash out.

"I'll see what I can do, Doc." The lieutenant was a former platoon leader, so I was not intimidating him at all. He understood.

To make the day complete, after mail call, I was left empty-handed. I got not even a single letter. I might as well have taken up permanent residence there in the bush, for all life was worth. I did not continue to let it bother me, however. We had been through a whole lot worse than that. As a matter of fact, I found that little incident to be like water rolling off a duck's back. I truly had become calloused. I did not even count on the replacement that had just been promised. Anything could happen between now and then, anyway.

Lieutenant Mandrel started to console me, but he saw the look in my eye that asked, "What are you talking about, man?" And he promptly stopped. It seemed that the LT was learning quickly.

The jeep sped away to take news and mail to the other

platoon. The thought of being in an open vehicle puttering along the mountainous highway made me nervous. Those poor saps were like shooting gallery ducks.

"It don't mean nothin', Doc. Before you know it, you'll be back stateside. Can you imagine? Here I am in the middle of the jungle, among a world full of orientals. I want a vacation and guess what? I got a vacation in the jungles among a world full of Orientals. We should've put in for Australia.

"What do you want to eat for supper? I don't have anything good. Let's just make a stew or something." Mike seemed somewhat relaxed as he sat on the ground and began meal preparations.

As the days progressed with no enemy contact, it became evident that our honeymoon would soon be over. After all, we were guarding a major highway being used to transport the ARVNs into Laos. It was the biggest military and political maneuver thus far engaged in by the South Vietnamese government. The unusual mixture of traffic continued—civilian buses, an occasional Mercedez with some rich Vietnamese passengers, and the ARVN convoys.

The day after Mike and I talked about R & R found everyone nervously rearranging and reinforcing their particular areas so as not to be caught off guard. We also filled more sandbags to thicken the armor surrounding our abode.

We were required to wear full uniform, which included helmets and flak jackets, to impress any dignitary that might be browsing in the neighborhood. Mitchell, our cynical mortar maggot, decided to take the flak plates off his flak jacket to "make it lighter." Some people never learn.

Early one afternoon, a jeep from the northern part of Highway One made a mad dash to our post. The driver and passenger, members of the 101st Airborne (known as the

Screaming Eagles), looked nearly panic stricken. They, too, had been guarding the road, about two kilometers north.

"Where's your platoon leader?" asked the sergeant.

"Here I am," Mandrel was already present when the jeep arrived. "What's going on?" he continued.

"We're being hit hard just up ahead. There seems to be quite a few NVA. Can you spare any men?"

"Alpha squad. Load up, pronto!" The lieutenant gave his first wartime command.

"I'm going with them, LT, just in case." Actually I'd become bored just watching traffic.

We crowded like sardines into that jeep, and the driver floored the accelerator. With our combined weight, traveling uphill slowed the speed to only forty miles per hour.

We identified small arms fire, mortar explosions, enemy RPGs and B-40 rockets. Just like us, only one platoon had been stationed at the location. The fighting was intense, and the smell of explosives thick. I actually looked forward to partaking in some action. Was I crazy or what?

The jeep stopped short of the position so we would not be in the direct line of fire. We all jumped out before the jeep came to a complete halt.

As we made our way up the hill to help the Screaming Eagles, we heard the pulsating sound of a helicopter behind us. Turning around, I witnessed a lone Huey flying low as it began to fire its automatic blooper.

"This has got to be a 101 Airborne chopper. Who else would fly in this weather?" I said to Lizzio.

"They're just looking out for their own," answered Joe.

We had to lay low since the rounds from the chopper's automatic blooper flew over our heads trying to hit Nathaniel's hiding spot. "Thump, thump, thump, thump, thump," the explosions from the M-79 rapidly exploded; Nathaniel seemed to be taking a pounding. The chopper made just two passes before it retreated. Probably the cloud cover was making it impossible for more sorties.

We scurried to the CP and found several wounded. They had two medics so I was not needed there.

"What do you marines do at times like this?" asked one of their NCOs.

We were taken back by that remark. It seemed inconceivable that supposedly seasoned soldiers would have to ask a question with such an obvious answer.

"We counter," advised one of our squad's privates. He was right on the money, too. When being hit, we had been taught to counter with a rush towards the enemy. However, it seldom worked and we seldom practiced it in a real situation. Most of the time, given the present terrain, a counter would mean suicide. Today, it was the only option.

"All right! Get your men saddled up, and I'll round up a couple of my squads. We'll head out in one minute flat." Their platoon leader spoke with reluctance as any leader would in the same situation.

The small arms fire seemed to die down once we began our assault up the muddy mountain—and no casualties, yet. Amidst the cool, damp weather, we sweated profusely. My adrenaline was really pumped up. We all expected to be hit by a barrage of fire any time.

"SWOOOOOOSH.......BOOOOOOM!" Nathaniel fired an RPG at us. An army grunt slouched down and grabbed his lower leg in excruciating pain. I signaled the Marines to keep on with the assault. I stayed behind with a few of the wounded grunt's comrades to assist their "P." The soldier had a gaping wound on his shin caused by shrapnel from that RPG. After I bandaged the wound, two of the wounded man's buddies helped the Purple Heart recipient down the slope. As the trio began to make their descent, "BOOO BOOO BOOO BOOOOOMM!!"

I couldn't believe the bad luck those people were having. They had tripped a "daisy chain"—a series of booby traps set to go off in close sequence with the intent of taking out a whole squad, which it nearly did!

I looked down at my body, almost afraid to learn whether I had been hit—thankfully, no apparent wounds. My heart was beating so fast that if I had been hit, I doubt I would have felt anything. The wounded soldier and his two buddies, along with the extra man accompanying them had all been hit. I was the only one left standing. What a disaster!

As I dressed the wounds of the four, the cooperative assault team came back down to assist. Actually, they were just curious. The rest of the platoon down below also made their way up to the disaster scene. Their medics promptly took over while the lieutenant beckoned me to himself.

"Tell your squad leader to get your men back down to your position. Your unit's being hit pretty hard right at this moment. Your lieutenant just radioed us. We'll make it; thanks for helping."

That was just great! What a day! We all hurried to the road, at first trying to figure out how we would return to our platoon. The army driver came down to us in a full run, and told us to jump back into the jeep. In one sweep, we were all in. Descending the road took much less time as we were going downhill.

We, in helping a neighboring military unit for the sake of action, had left our own unit vulnerable. I guess we really had no choice, since they'd asked for our help. Actually, I was the only one who volunteered—bad decision.

The driver stopped within a hundred meters of our position. There was a traffic jam, since several civilian buses had pulled over with their passengers taking cover among the boulders on the side of the road.

The sounds of weapons exchange could be heard as we neared our position. Explosions sounded off intermittently. American M-60 machine gun fire returned greetings to Nathaniel.

As we arrived, we also took cover between the rocks. Most of the squad ran between the boulders to return to their French bunker, while I stayed in a neutral position near the road to help whoever needed me. One of the new guys of Alpha squad stayed with me. He had found himself too frightened to follow the rest of his squad to their fortress. I did not say anything, since I knew well the feeling.

"Crack, crack, crack, crack. Zing. Ptewww. Boom!" That firefight was no ordinary firefight. The NVA—not Charlie was our enemy in the firefight. The VC fought for short periods and then would leave after a very brief encounter. I tried to position myself to see where all the fire was coming from. I don't think Nathaniel knew that I was behind the rock, as no bullets ricocheted off of it. Ah ha! Paydirt! I spotted a rifleman.

I had only a pistol, so I grabbed the new guy's M-16 and took aim. I found the NVA rifleman in my sights. Up the mountain close to a cliff-like dropoff, where the road had cut through the mountain, was an NVA regular, squatting, taking aim, and popping off his weapon. Two large-leafed bushes next to him almost camouflaged his silhouette. My finger began to squeeze the trigger as if on its own accord.

"Pop!" Then once more, "Pop!" The silhouette slumped over. In one second, another NVA regular came to his assistance. My eyes were still behind the sights so, "Pop, pop, pop," I fired again.

That time, I could not tell whether I had a direct hit, or not. The young newcomer next to me sat there, staring at me with huge eyes that depicted disbelief. He was the only witness to a small victory. I later learned that the poor boy never even saw the two NVA, so I guess I had no true witnesses to attest to my deed.

Bullets continued to shower down on us, and then an occasional B-40 or RPG. Even though we returned fire, we could not see the enemy. If there were any hits, it was merely a coincidence. Mine was the only hit actually seen, even if it was seen only by my eyes. Our entire platoon was pinned down.

I was situated directly across the pavement from the sandbagged command post. Mike exposed his head and began to call out to me, "Doc! Doc! Mitchell and Samuels got hit with a B-40 in their mortar pit. I've got them in the bunker with us. Whenever there's a break, you need to take a look at them. They're holding their own now, so don't rush it."

Right. Don't rush it.

I yelled in return, "Mike, I'm too short to take any chances. They'll just have to wait until everything is quiet before I show my face. I've got a replacement on the way sometime soon, you know."

I don't know what got into Mike at that moment. As a matter of fact, I don't know what got into me either. The same specter of insanity overtook two inseparable comrades simultaneously. What transpired next should go down in the *Guiness Book of World Record Foolish Deeds.*

Mike waved an MPC twenty dollar bill high in the air. "Doc, I'll bet you twenty bucks you can't make it across in one piece."

"You're on, Greek."

I handed the new guy his M-16, cocked my .45, strapped my chin strap on tight, fastened my flak jacket, and grabbed hold of the two boulders on each side of me, resembling a downhill ski racer as he comes out of the shoot. I was loaded down with my medical bag, flak jacket, webbed belt with its canteens, helmet, and the pistol with ammo.

With one big thrust, I lunged forward into a black hole of the mysterious unknown. I had to run directly into the line of fire, since the only opening to the CP bunker was down the road, towards the core of the enemy. Time seemed to slow to a snail's pace, as my legs, although fully flexed, seemed to move in very slow motion. With the pistol in one hand, and the other hand fisted to try to force my legs to move faster, I sprinted down the road, facing the hidden enemy. I'm sure I was yelling the whole time.

I imagined or actually saw flashes coming from the brush as I uttered to myself, "Oh man, what do you think you are doing? Too late to turn back. Just finish this thing—quick!"

"Crack!" Right next to my left ear, the sound barrier had been broken with an ultra sonic projectile.

"Crack, crack!" Next to my right ear, the sound barrier again was broken by the bullet's jetting in close proximity. Those mini-shockwaves actually hurt as they jolted my tympanic membranes.

"Ping!" Directly between my legs, a round hit the pavement sending stinging fragments of asphalt to my inner thighs and even to my face.

"Crack, crack, crack, crack, crack!" The rounds continued over my head, off to the sides, and, seemingly, between my arms. What had I gotten myself into? "This is really it," I thought.

The opening into the compound still seemed so far away; my legs were in a state of tetany; they moved as fast as they could. The medical bag, strapped over my right shoulder, hung off my left side, and bounced around, preventing a coordinated run. I had to grab the bag with my free hand, thus slowing my speed.

There were those flashes again, without sound. Of course, who could hear anything at a time like that? I began shooting wildly at the flashes to send some kind of message to my assailants. I wanted them to stop shooting.

"Pop, pop, pop, pop, pop, pop, pop, pop!" Those stacattoed sounds came from behind me. I was sure those shots were from my marines, attempting to cover me. Besides, M-16 shots could be recognized anywhere.

"Crack, crack! Pop, pop, pop!" The firefight went on, with me right in the middle, literally.

The distance I darted could not have been more than fifty feet, but for all I was concerned, it was two miles. Huffing and puffing, my lungs burned as air was forced in and out, faster than a steam locomotive. Also, my legs were starting to cramp. Oh no! I came to an opening in the concertina wire!

"Thank you, dear God!" I tried turning into the compound, but the inertia acquired in the speed of the sprint caused me to keep going past the opening! I slid into a full brody.

There I was, face down, sliding on the dirt at the side of the road. Bullets hit the surrounding ground and rocks. My eyes were partially blinded from the sprayed dirt of the rico-cheting missiles. Even before coming to a complete halt, my hands and legs moved frantically in the fastest four legged crawl in history.

One big rock ahead, and swoosh, I dove behind the rock for brief cover. The firefight had not slowed down one bit. It seemed that all of Nathaniel's sights were aimed at me.

I wondered, "Is this just sport for them, or have they figured that I was the one who shot one of theirs? Naw, surely they couldn't suspect me for doing that."

"Ping, ping, ping, ping, ping!" The rounds continued to pound my rock.

"There's another rock ahead—might as well finish off this little escapade," I said to myself.

Again, making a mad dash for the rock, I dove behind it. I could now see that my platoon was indeed covering me as everyone was out behind a rock or a sandbag, shooting. It had become a high stakes game for everyone on both sides.

"There's Doc!" yelled Mike. The lieutenant waved me on as he said the coast was clear. I really did not believe him, but I made the final run to the bunker anyway. That time, I ran in soft sand.

"Zip, zip!" The rounds from Nathaniel were muffled by the sandy ground and sand bags.

Puffing, I was out of breath. Finally, I was at the bunker!

"Zip, zip, zip" again the enemy rounds spoke their deadly words ever so close to me!

"Splat!" I threw myself on the ground behind the line of fire which was the only way I could stop without running past the fortress.

"Puff, puff, puff, puff, puff," I stared up and they stared down.

"Where's my twenty bucks, Greek?" If looks could kill, I'd be dead. Mike chose to remain quiet for the next few minutes. I just lay on the ground looking up, saying nothing for a few minutes.

"Man, Doc!" Mike said nothing else.

"Where's those hurt people?" I was still breathing at fast rate.

"They're inside the bunker. We did what we could. I don't think either one is hurt all that bad. What do you think, Doc?" Mike was obviously in charge, the lieutenant was just standing in the sidelines keeping quiet.

Mitchell was lying on the ground in the bunker, carrying on about the whole thing being stupid or something similar. Others no longer found him amusing. Mitchell's flak jacket had offered no protection from shrapnel. Most of his wounds resembled deep-skin ulcers. A few wounds were bleeding, but otherwise he was okay.

Then Mike began to rattle on, "These guys stayed out in their pit when the fire broke out. Said they were trying to get some bearings. They tried to return mortar fire, but took too much time. They never got off one single round. I miss the old guys. None of them were ever this slow or this stupid. Anyway, a B-40 rocket hit right in the center, blowing these two dudes entirely out of the pit."

"Mitchell over here, went berserk when he saw his chest. He had a hole right over his heart area with what he thought was blood coming out! The color of the dude's face was as white as a sheet."

"When I looked at the so-called blood, I wiped my finger over it and licked it to see what flavor it was. It was peach. Mitchell had a can of peaches inside his left breast pocket! That tin can could've easily saved the jerk's life! Who knows? The shrapnel may not have had the velocity it needed."

"Anyway, Mitchell gets all grossed out 'cause I say that his 'blood' tastes good—I tell you, Doc, it was hilarious! Sanders, over there, has no idea what went on. He's got some shrapnel, but not bad."

"The lieutenant takes the cake though. We were both on top of the bunker on watch when we got hit. I made a beeline to the ground, but the lieutenant sits up there wondering why the sand bags are making funny popping noises. I saw that he wasn't moving, so I got up there and grabbed him by the collar to pull him down to where it was safe. He's okay now, but I don't think he's ever going to live this day down. You should've been here."

"By the way, what kept you guys so long getting back? I thought we were going to get overrun. There's a bunch of

Nathaniels out there, and it doesn't look like they're going to leave anytime soon. We tried to counter twice but only got pounded. We can't even tell exactly where he is."

While Mike was talking, I was busy patching up Mitchell and Sanders. The third time was a charm. I knew that Mitchell needed to get out of this place, because the next time, his luck would run out for sure. For the time being, however, these two would have to stay with us, as there was no way to evacuate either of them.

I talked with Lt. Mandrel to see how he was handling everything. Surprisingly, the lieutenant was doing quite well. He was openly joking about the sand bags popping. With his attitude, Mandrel would adjust very quickly without becoming a *prima donna*.

What Mike and I had just done had allowed everyone to see the insanity of the whole situation in a world with no rule book. The new guys realized that probably, they would some-day become like us. The older vets saw themselves in my mad dash across the bullet-ridden highway. Mike and I saw our-selves as two beings who survived by letting go and allowing friendship to form. Actually, it was not a victory for us; rather, an open sign of accepting defeat—defeat in realizing how mortal and insignificant we were.

Truly, our personal wars had their origin that day. We both had no idea what would face us in the near future. There could be years, perhaps decades ahead, of endless, unresolved battles caused by our tours in Vietnam. At that moment, however, we felt a small victory in just being alive.

After that, the NVA slowed down the intensity of their aggression, thus allowing some traffic to move. Every time *we* tried to cross the road; however, Nathaniel was not so tolerant. It became more of a nuisance than anything else, as we were not sustaining any further casualties. I felt like I was a soldier in the trenches during W.W. I, like I had read in *All is Quiet on the Western Front.*

"Lieutenant, we gotta go put those poor dudes outta their misery. Let's get a counter-assault going," said Sergeant Pierce, who was fidgety, and did not like being pinned down like we were.

After darting across the road once, I was not too anxious to travel it again. A spirit of reluctance entered me, but I mechanically readied myself and followed the rest. And there was no barrage upon us. Actually, not a single shot was fired as we scurried across the highway that just a few minutes earlier, had been impassable. We made it to the French bunker across the highway without incident. Had Nathaniel already left?

We picked up more marines at the cement bunker and began exiting to make our assault. No sooner had the point man shown his face outside the door than a hailstorm of bullets began again. Several RPGs hit the outside wall of the antique fortress, but there was no penetration. This time, we were really pinned down. Nathaniel, once again, had made his presence known. There was no use in even trying to leave, as the bunker's only doorway allowed just one man at a time to slip out. It was at least twenty five meters before any cover could be reached, so we were sitting ducks.

"Might as well make the best of it. Anybody got any peaches?" Pierce sounded very frustrated, as we all were.

"Forget about those peaches. Let's get the job done. Saddle up! If Doc can do it, so can we. We're goin' to attack that hill an' give it all we've got."

"Johnson, take point. Move it, men!" The lieutenant gave his second wartime command and did a good job of it.

"Lock and load!"

Before we knew it, we were outside scrambling for the southernmost brush. Nathaniel, probably being astonished by the sudden charge, slowed down a little in firing, but continued just the same. One helmet took a round, but deflected the missile without causing any harm to the wearer—what a fortunate individual! That was the only near casualty for the first twenty five meters.

When we all made it to the brush, we began fast-pacing it up the mountainside. We could not be seen by the NVA, and of course, they could not be seen by us either, under the cover of the jungle. Our jungle tactics once again employed, we spoke not a word.

"I'm just about to be replaced, and here I am, not knowing if I'm going to make the next fifteen minutes or not. What else is new here in the 'Nam?" my thoughts ran away again.

Our eyes scanned everything, as we knew that the group of NVA regulars we'd encountered liked Daisy chains. The point man had his hands full, and was still somewhat green, so we all pitched in to help.

Johnson made a sudden, very quiet halt, as he raised his gloved left hand. We halted likewise. He was frozen. This meant that Johnson sensed something, but was not actually seeing what the danger was. His wartime sixth sense made its debut.

At about forehead level, I saw it, just inches away from Johnson's head. I was two men in back of him.

"Don't move! There's a wire in front of your head," I whispered loudly.

With Johnson in place and not moving a hair, Pierce and I walked slowly to the wire. A close inspection revealed that it was indeed a Daisy chain. Chicom grenades were used in it, which meant that it was new and had been laid by our present foes. The VC almost always used American-made grenades for their booby traps. They would capture the grenades from the ARVNs or sometimes, from the Americans.

After carefully tying a length of twine to the wire, we all found cover a good distance away, and set off the mine. We would be in the area for some time to come, perhaps, so we could not chance another patrol's not being so fortunate in finding the trap the way we did.

"BOOO, BOOO, BOOO, BOOO, BOOOMMM!!!" Shrapnel flew overhead, making noise as it penetrated the thick jungle. Hopefully, Nathaniel would think we were hit, and perhaps out of curiosity, they would stay a little while longer to see what had happened. We moved quickly to where we thought the enemy was.

Nobody was there—relief and disappointment rolled into one. We searched thoroughly. Satisfied, the lieutenant gave the order to return to the bunkers. I could not help but feel that we were being watched as we headed down the hill.

The afternoon graduated into night, and the night dragged on. Sniper fire was sporadic throughout the evening, with some of our rambunctious, younger marines returning the fire to where they thought the flashes had originated. We told them that it was useless and wasteful to fire back, as that only gave away our position.

We took our standard, two-hour increments of sleep before the sun began to rise. Yes, the sun! There were few clouds that next morning, and with the sun, came heat, and I think the heat was welcomed by most of us. The sniper fire had stopped. I made the rounds again and found that no one else had been injured during the night.

We were not attacked any more from that group of marauders. They did create skirmishes with the other platoon a day or so later; however, which resulted in a few casualties.

Approximately ten additional days passed without further incident. The convoys trickled on, which meant that we had to stay put. Mike was making plans for his R & R. I was a little jealous, but was also glad that at least one of us would be given a fair deal. Mike gave me his address back home, and I gave him mine. Perhaps we would see each other a few more times, but not at the front. I would be sent back to the rear, and once Mike returned from his trip, he would probably be shipped stateside. The grunts were usually given their last two months back in the rear, but somehow Mike was overlooked just as I had been.

I dreaded the thought of serving the rest of my tour in the rear, but on the other hand, I was tired of the bush. It didn't mean nothing. I was determined to adjust, no matter where they put me.

One morning, a truck and a jeep arrived at our compound with supplies. Among the supplies was a scrawny-looking pogue with eyes as big as saucers. This underweight reject carried a medical pouch that resembled the unit one I had discarded when I first arrived. That small soldier was my replacement.

"Hey Mike! This is it. Take it easy, buddy. Write when you get stateside." At first, I did not talk to the new guy.

"See you around, Doc. I'll see you before I leave this God-forsaken dirthole," was the Greek's last comment to me.

"What's your name?" I finally asked the new corpsman.

"Gandy, sir," he mumbled.

"Don't call me 'sir.' Here's your morphine. Take care of it. You will be responsible for much. Don't go screw up with these men here. Listen to the ones who've been here awhile, and you just might get out in one piece. That's no guarantee, though," I expressed with no emotion.

I grabbed my pack and climbed into the truck. This was it. The days of the bush were over. It just did not seem possible. All during the ride back, I tried but had a hard time imagining life in the rear.

Chapter 17
Homeward Bound

My days in the rear deserve only a brief mention. Most of the other corpsmen there at the 3/1 Battalion Aid Station had served in the bush six months or less prior to their rear assignments. Many of them had never even set foot on the battlefront. Working with them made me miserable at first. I did grow somewhat used to it towards the end of my time, but I never really fit in. Most of those boys found me too aggressive.

Perhaps I did have a chip on my shoulder and never gave them a chance, but I had no desire to associate with any of the rear pogues. Although corpsmen, most reminded me of typical pogues in that they had no concept of what the bush was like nor did they care what happened to grunts out there getting shot at. Their attitude was to pass their time doing as little as possible. At least that's what my impression was.

On my first full day, they assigned me to a desk with a typewriter. I objected profoundly and actually picked up the typewriter and threw it out the window. As I walked out, I told the chief that I wanted to be transferred—either back to the bush or to First Med. The chief ran after me and offered me a position in the lab where I would be my own boss. One of the other outgoing corpsmen would teach me lab procedures, and when he left, I would man the lab alone. I finally agreed.

Each time my unit came back to the rear, I would take a leave of absence and spend time with them. Once, when partying with my old Ps, I got into a little trouble and some MPs clubbed me for disorderly conduct, but they spared sending me to the brig.

Later, instead of the promised R & R, the top brass sent me back to the United States. In all truthfulness, that was the worst thing they could've done for me. Only confusion resulted, as the whole time I was in the States, I knew I would have to return to the 'Nam. I sure wished I could have taken an R & R in a foreign country.

Mike came and visited me once before they shipped him back home. It was a fine visit. We must have turned the place upside down with our celebrating—and we didn't even get into trouble! What could they do to us? Send us to Vietnam?

For the past year, Mike had helped me maintain my sanity, and I appreciated him for it. We pulled each other out of that place in one piece, and I've never forgotten it. Friendship mattered and it was worth gold—no matter what anyone said.

President Nixon pulled the Marines out of Vietnam but did so too late for Mike and me; we ended up serving full tours. My unit left by ship back to Camp Pendleton without me. I had fulfilled the required sea duty and had accepted orders to attend school at Pensacola, Florida.

To bide my time, I was stuck with an Air Force unit in Da Nang for three additional weeks. I attended roll call at seven each morning and spent the rest of the day body surfing at China Beach. By the end of the three weeks, my skin became very dark and leathery.

My orders came in, stating that I was to extend my time in the service another two years and needless to say, I refused them. Finally a compromise came which asked that I extend for six months. I agreed, and was eventually sent home.

On the last evening there with the Air Force, an air raid siren sounded, as it always did with any sort of imagined threat. I did not escape to the bunkers like the rest of the pogues. I stood at the top balcony of my barracks jeering at all the cowards below.

That final night, as the others were running to their sand-bagged protections, I saw a bright red streak make its way towards my building. "Thud!" A six-foot rocket, as they were called, had landed about seventy-five meters in front of me. It was a dudd. I laughed.

"So long, Vietnam. I give you less than two years to fall to the communists. Both of our corrupt governments just couldn't save you."

The next morning, I was shipped to Okinawa, where I had to take part in a four-day stage-down to become re-indoctrinated, whatever that means. Then came the long-awaited flight home.

Steve McCarty, my corpsman friend from Long Beach, was with me at Okinawa and during our flight back home. He was from California so he would arrive at his home sooner than I would to mine.

This trip home was quite different from the first. During the first voyage (for my two-week leave), I was in a daze the whole time, not really grasping the fact that I was actually stateside. This time, I knew I would be home for good. No more war! No more intense heat and humidity! Sanity! Feelings! Hamburgers!

The plane landed. A resounding hurrah burst from the troops within. Customs check was completed, and I proceeded through the terminal of Los Angeles International Airport.

There, a good-looking, young girl with big, round, green eyes approached me. I anticipated a big welcome-home hug or kiss.

"How does it feel to kill babies, you war monger?" she sneered.

Taken back by the unexpected remark, I did not know just how to respond. Then my survival instinct took over.

"It feels good," I replied, as I walked off, fortunately still numb.

Epilogue

It has been more than twenty years since that one year in my life. In a twenty-year period of any person's life, many extraordinary events occur. In my case, what could have been a disaster, turned out favorably. Today I sit here, able to write with ease about events which, to this day, many of my country-men still cannot discuss freely.

After arriving in the States, I spent a short time in Florida. Then they transferred me to my hometown recruiting station. I still had two years to serve in the Navy. I had become so disillusioned with the military and the war that I fervently searched for a way out of the armed forces. After studying the Manual of the Bureau of Naval Personnel, it became evident that the only way I could receive an early discharge was to become a conscientious objector. What could they do to me; send me back to 'Nam? Within six months of returning to my homeland, I received a full and honorable discharge. Then I returned to undergraduate school to earn pre-med requirements, after which medical school became a realistic goal. Within three semesters after my discharge from the service, I had completed all the prerequisites for medical school by overlap-ping many of the classes and was ultimately accepted to two schools.

Substantial unrest still occupied my soul, though. I had not yet personally resolved the war. Before beginning medical school, I took off more than a month and ventured into Mexico. I was very tired of this country, with its anti-war protests and the way many Americans were treating Vietnam veterans. The purpose of my trip to Mexico was to decide whether to go to medical school or to Angola, Africa, as a mercenary. Covertly, lots of young veterans were being recruited to fight Cubans.

The turmoil I felt had its first, small glimpse of resolution when I encountered a family of Christians in Mexico. That particular family exhibited a joy and a peace that I had never experienced or witnessed. Their lifestyle was different than any I had ever known. That family had no need for the props and devices used by others in the world to procure enjoyment. Liquor, profanity, coarse jesting, and bickering were seemingly foreign to this family. They took pleasure in talking about God, in being kind, and in being totally different than the generally accepted norm of the society I knew.

Needless to say, I did not choose Angola, but rather took the other option and attended medical school. Gradually, I began to see the futility of life as most see it. The only real purpose for life, it seemed, was to serve God. How does an imperfect human serve a perfect God? Just wanting to serve Him and make my life count for something did not completely answer my questions. It did not bring me the peace I knew was possible. I determined that I was about as wretched as any person on this earth. Before the time I spent in Mexico, I thought that there were good people and there were bad people. After spending time with the family of "Christ's Ones," I realized that we are all bad people. Our nature is to become so thoroughly addicted to the evils and dangers of this world, that eventually, anyone would crave to return to a war situation. There was no such thing as innocence anymore, and I discovered that the Bible teaches that very tenet. How does a depraved man please an almighty, perfect God? I could not please Him with my works, as some of my works would forever carry the stench of blood, while others would carry the stench of jealousy, cheating, lying, and the whole gamut of wrong doings.

One Sunday, when out of disappointment and emptiness, I was leaving a church early, a lone man stood outside. He invited me to his house to study the Bible, attracting me with this question, "If you were to die today, where would you spend eternity?"

I told him that *no one* knew the answer to that question—and that no one *could* know.

Holding his Bible up in the air, he countered, "No! You can be *absolutely* certain! God gave us the directions right here."

After visiting that man weekly for about two years, I finally decided that I had to make a decision to either accept or reject everything the Bible had to say. I knew that I could not ride the fence any longer. The war had buried scars deep in my heart. I could not ever fully forgive myself for all I had done in 'Nam and thought no one else could, either. However, I finally realized several things. First, that sin requires a payment of eternal death in a place called hell. Secondly, that God had supplied an alternative to the debt of death that had to be paid—His provision was the death of His own Son, Jesus Christ. Third, if I would accept God's Son's death as payment in full for my debt, I would be fully forgiven and accepted by God.

I did accept God's plan, and from that moment forward, my life changed, and it continues to change. I am forgiven and no longer dream the nightmares of war. I am His property—His slave—yet I never have felt any freer than I felt after accepting Christ on His terms.

My desire is for everyone—especially those who feel unforgiven—to accept God on God's terms. I beg them to consider the great things He has done—to look to God above for forgiveness and cleansing. To my comrades in arms, I dedicate this request.